PENNSYLVANIA DUTCH

❋ COUNTRY COOKING ❋

PENNSYLVANIA DUTCH
❧ COUNTRY COOKING ❧

WILLIAM WOYS WEAVER

PHOTOGRAPHS BY JERRY ORABONA

ABBEVILLE PRESS PUBLISHERS
NEW YORK   LONDON   PARIS

FOR IVAN GLICK, A GENTLE DUTCHMAN
WHO OPENED THE DOORS TO MY PAST

Front cover: The Mahantongo Valley, Schuylkill County, Pennsylvania.
Center picture: Chickweed Pie.
Back Cover: Peach and Tomato Slump with Sage and sausages.
Page 1: March snow lingers by a duck pond near Ronks, Lancaster County.
Frontispiece: Pennsylvania Dutch farm stand with Smokehouse apples, Green Gage plums (center), Moon-and-Stars watermelons (yellow-spotted melon), groundcherries, herbs, flowers, and home-made canned goods often compete with quilts, baskets, and other local craftwares.
Page 4: Brothers Johannes and Christian begin fall plowing with Star and Bright, oxen at Christiansbrunn Cloister.
Page 8: Symbols of Pennsylvania Dutch culture: the mythical Elbedritsch (top left), morels, chow-chow, bird-trees, Ringelros flowers, Schwartemawe (center), and spelt (grain lower left).

Pennsylvania Dutch Country Cooking has been selected by the Pennsylvania German Society as its 1993 Annual Publication, Volume XXVII

EDITOR: Sarah Key
DESIGNER: Patricia Fabricant
COPYEDITOR: Virginia Croft
PRODUCTION EDITOR: Paul Macirowski
PRODUCTION SUPERVISOR: Simone René

Library of Congress Cataloging-in-Publication Data

Weaver, William Woys, 1947-
    Pennsylvania Dutch country cooking / William Woys Weaver ; photographs by Jerry Orabona.
        p.   cm.
    Includes index.
    ISBN 1-55859-568-6
    1. Cookery—Pennsylvania. 2. Cookery, German. I. Title.
TX721.W37   1993
641.59748—dc20   93-1558
                                                            CIP

PREFACE

In Pennsylvania we know William Woys Weaver simply as one of our most talented and experimental regional cooks. Elsewhere he has been described as a national treasure and a blend of James Beard and M.F.K. Fisher. *The New York Times* has called him a pioneering figure in American food history. Internationally acclaimed, self-effacing to the letter, he has been exploring the foods and foodways of the Pennsylvania German people for nearly twenty-five years.

A direct descendent of seventeenth-century Swiss Anabaptist martyr Georg Weber, a thirteenth-generation Pennsylvanian, scion of one of the oldest and most influential Mennonite families in the state, William Woys Weaver brings to his subject a unique perspective. His work reflects not only a scholarly interest in historical roots but also the real enthusiasm of a native son who has grown up in a family well known regionally for its culinary accomplishments. A long view of history has given him special insight into our traditional culinary ingredients like spelt and sunflower oil, and such nutritionally rich heirloom foods as chickweed, lazy wife beans, chinquapins, bladder campion, and Catawissa onions.

Trained by the same gardeners and country cooks he has interviewed, embracing this rare knowledge with keen respect for disappearing foodways, William Woys Weaver has filled this book with his unique sense of connectedness, fresh scholarship, and his innate cooking sensibilities. He has divided Pennsylvania German cookery into several families of dishes, and he has provided the proper *Pennsylfaanisch* names for them. None of this has ever been attempted before in any of the books about Pennsylvania Dutch cookery. No other American regional cookbook is as thorough in its treatment.

For these reasons, and for the first time in its 100-year history, the Pennsylvania German Society has chosen cookery as the theme of its 1993 annual book selection. We hope that our endorsement of *Pennsylvania Dutch Country Cooking* will spur renewed interest in our rich food traditions and provide an authoritative guide to America's most complex regional cuisine, a cuisine that spread to Ontario, Ohio and the Midwest, and the Upland South with the Pennsylvania barn, the Lancaster rifle, and the Conestoga wagon.

The Pennsylvania Dutch are a relaxed people, and our cookery reflects this. Let us dispense here with the usual formal salutations and *bon appetits,* and rally our readers with the *luschtich* dinner blessing that ends with *Amen-un-schlag nei –* joyously dig in!

– Editors for the Pennsylvania German Society:
Rev. Willard W. Wetzel, Pastor, Zion's Stone Church, Kreidersville, Pennsylvania
Dr. Don Yoder, Professor Emeritus, University of Pennsylvania

CONTENTS

FOREWORD

This is a book about the cookery of the Pennsylvania Dutch and the nurturing earth that sustains it. Ours is a land of the thistle finch and saffron, of the mythical *Elbedritsch* and the *Belschnickel,* of the hex sign and powwow magic. It is a land of rolling hills, lush green in summer, powder blue in autumn haze, of snug valleys filled in winter with the muffled sound of Amish sleigh bells and the crackle of poprobin soup.

The Pennsylvania Dutch are a people of many beliefs, of many lifestyles, but we share one thing in common: our cookery is the product of our land. We are America's "farmers next door," kitchen gardeners to New York and Philadelphia, and to a great many places farther away. Our down-to-earth style of cooking, robust, rich in flavor, captures the essence of ingredients that come out of our own backyards. Indeed, our soil is so rich, even our weeds taste good.

When we are working in our backyard gardens—whether they are in Kutztown, Pennsylvania; Lancaster, Ohio; or Harrisonburg, Virginia—we discuss our foods in a language called Pennsylfaanisch. This is the language of the Pennsylvania Dutch hearthside, the language of our farmers and of our cooks.

Like our cookery, Pennsylfaanisch is a product of the American soil. In some parts of the United States, it has been spoken longer than the English language. This is the first cookbook in which Pennsylfaanisch names are provided for *all* the recipes, in addition to a pronunciation guide and brief glossary of additional Pennsylfaanisch food terms (p. 179).

Ours is largely a cuisine of one-pot meals, fare that is designed around ancient dish concepts, to provide convenience and to strengthen the act of eating together at table. Our best cookery is also our most private cookery, for it is family-centered, a style of cooking that has evolved out of sharing from a common pot. It is a formula that has stood the test of time, not just three centuries of New World evolution but, in the case of dishes like *Gumbis* and *Schales, Ritscher,* and *Dummes,* more than a thousand years of continuing adaptation.

Happily, many of the old peasant dishes from the past, especially the vegetarian ones and those we share with Pennsylvania-German Jews, have opened a whole new area of dietary possibilities, pushing tradition over the edge into the twenty-first century. Peasant food, food from the land, food in tune with the natural cycle of things, not only is growing in popularity because of the way it tastes but is also good for us, plain and simple.

The guiding inspiration for this book is a return to culinary roots, to a sensible "preventive cookery," with ingredients like rapeseed oil, spelt (a relative of wheat), cabbage, root vegetables, and whole grains. Yet this is not a collection of historical recipes or a call for a retreat into the past. This is a book geared to the here and now, with a preponderance of material coming from living cooks.

Hex signs on the 1880 DeTurk barn in Oley Valley, Berks County.

Our best cooks still cook at home. Food writer Anna del Conte has said the same thing about the cookery of Italy. But unlike Italians, we never developed a vibrant restaurant culture in tandem with good home cookery, certainly nothing that would encourage professional chefs to dabble in our culinary style. Our cookery is grossly misrepresented, even though many of our dishes resemble the same sort of foods found on menus in upscale bistros.

The one factor that makes Pennsylvania Dutch cookery so vastly different from Cajun or Mexican-American cookery is that the Pennsylvania Dutch are Protestants of many disagreeing strands. Protestantism has never encouraged the kind of food culture that gives rise to lively public eating and feasting. Good eating is something done in private.

Yet, if there is one cookery that reflects the crossroads of American culture, it is surely that of the Pennsylvania Dutch. I have attempted to choose a range of recipes from this culinary crossroads for every level of cooking ability and every type of taste. Beyond this, I hope that my book will encourage sustainable agriculture. Ours is a cookery that retains both a sense of garden freshness and a focus on the family farm. With that in mind, I have used organically grown products from local farms or my own garden in most of my recipes. I encourage readers to use high-quality local products for two essentially Pennsylvania Dutch reasons.

First, some Dutch have always preoccupied themselves with health. When it comes to cures, they are particularly tight-fisted: better to invest the money in decent food than squander it later in life on doctors. A body fed well is worth more gold than medicine. The survival of farmers' markets in our part of the country—more than in any other region of the United States—is one proof of this way of thinking.

The other reason is spiritual, a relationship many Dutch see between the cook and the soil that sustains them. Here we enter the deep and murky well of the Pennsylvania

German soul, where mysticism and pietism flow like mineral springs. It is said, in the old folktales of my people, that when God held up the earth to behold this extraordinary creation, it transformed itself into a mirror in which He saw a woman's face. To the Pennsylvania Dutch mystics of old, this was the face of the Virgin Sophia, a feminine image of God, who created our homeland of Pennsylvania, a land of peace and plenty. Sophia's folklore is amazingly rich; she embodies the attitudes prevalent in our culture, for her image crops up everywhere.

The Virgin Sophia as she appears on the 1809 Frederick Bentle House, Old Economy, Pennsylvania.

Sophia is often depicted in the form of an angel on gravestones or carved over windows and doors, as in the case of the Harmonite buildings in Beaver County, Pennsylvania. In folklore she can appear in the form of Three Sisters or as the extremely complex Triplet Mother: Mother the Virgin Daughter, Mother the Wife Who Bears, Mother the Wise Widow. She is the mother who is at once the Silver Snake of Bucks County legend, guardian of buried treasures, or the lightning bolts of an angry Nature.

Pennsylvania Dutch folktales about the young Genoveva lost in the woods—still popular among the Amish incidentally—deal with the theme of the Virgin Daughter. Aldi, the Old One who lives in wells and spring houses and is shaped like a mermaid, is our Baby Bringer, our form of the stork. She is the aspect of Sophia that is a bearing wife and is often depicted as a mermaid on painted dower chests and in Fraktur art. A living personification of the Wise Widow was Mountain Mary, an herb granny who lived in the hills of Berks County, a revered figure in Pennsylvania Dutch folk culture even to this day. Her grave, at Oley Hills Church, is the site of a commemorative ceremony every year.

There is an old hymn or folksong among the Pennsylvania Germans that my grandfather used to sing when we would drive his racing pigeons into the country for practice runs. He used to sing it in Pennsylfaanisch, and now I can only remember parts. It extolled the Virgin Sophia as a personification of the ties between the Pennsylvania Dutch people and their land. It is an image I will never forget because we always let the pigeons go from hilltops, from where I gazed down on the vast stretches of fertile farmland, the corn, the wheat, the smell of cut hay. That song made it all very clear.

In a mystical sense, it has to do with Sophia herself as a component of the earth. She may be that faint cinnamon taste that flows up out of the rocks and imparts to our produce and our wines their lush intensity and characteristic robustness, an elemental force long ago recognized by the hymn writers of Snow Hill and Ephrata Cloister. I do not know how my grandfather came to learn the words, but the final lines in his Sophia song speak of this extraordinary sense of connectedness, that the food we eat is more than material sustenance. It is truly a cuisine of the soul.

Honor the Mother
who carried you
near to her Heart;
Honor the Soil
from which she
has molded the Land;
Honor the Bread
that she brings forth
from the Womb of the Earth.

WILLIAM WOYS WEAVER
Lichtmess, 1993

COOKING PENNSYLVANIA DUTCH STYLE

A regional cookery as complex as that of the Pennsylvania Dutch is a language of many changing textures, flavors, and smells. Yet above all else it is a cookery with a sense of place, a cuisine that recognizes the unchanging essence of *Bodegeschmack,* meaning that our food has in it the taste of the land. *Bodegeschmack* is what gives great wines their character. It is what gives cheese a nuance of the grass and meadows on which the animals grazed. It comes from the natural soil, soil derived from the rocky earth below it, a product of the intimate connectedness between plant and mineral.

There are many components to our cookery other than *Bodegeschmack,* for it is only one interlinking element in the larger unity we call the "taste" of our culture. It is a taste created not by one or two famous chefs, or by a handful of certain "ethnic" ingredients, but by a vast orchestra of hands in kitchens down through the past three hundred years that pounded, shaped, rolled, kneaded, and molded the fruits of our landscape into a child of our own genius.

The Pennsylvania Dutch style was created by thousands upon thousands of cooks who quickly honed their European experience to American conditions. However, after interviewing Pennsylvania Dutch cooks in many parts of the United States, not to mention their Old World counterparts in Germany, France, and Switzerland, I discovered that our "classic" cookery is most like that of Alsace. Few of our country cooks would find the contents of Marguerite Doerflinger's and Georges Klein's *Toute la cuisine alsacienne* odd or, for that matter, foreign. Even the dialect names in Alsatian German have a familiar ring. Yet, unlike nineteenth-century German immigrants who were influenced by concepts of nationality, the Pennsylvania Dutch had no loyalty to the Old World or its institutions. There was no reason to establish Bavarian beer fests or Donauschwaben dancing clubs, no reason to cling to *Wiener Schnitzel* or Black Forest Cake as emblems of Old World identity. Regardless of their European antecedents, most of the core dishes in our cookery have become thoroughly Americanized, reflecting all the culinary influences that have affected North American cookery over the past three hundred years. The Pennsylvania Dutch do not consider themselves an ethnic group; they consider themselves Americans.

While it is safe to say that our food is thoroughly American, it is also distinctively Dutch. One of the primary purposes of this book is to explore those Dutch distinctions.

To the Pennsylvania Dutch, our name presents a perennial dilemma because most of us no longer live in Pennsylvania and very few of us come from Holland. While we argue continually among ourselves whether we are the Pennsylvania Dutch or the Pennsylvania Germans, the rest

Fall plowing near Bird-in-Hand, Pennsylvania.

of the world assumes we are Amish. In fact, we represent roughly forty percent of the population of Pennsylvania, and several hundred thousand people still use Pennsylfaanisch as their first language. Although the Amish also speak Pennsylfaanisch, they represent only about eight percent of the total Pennsylvania German community.[1]

Our culture, like our cookery, took shape in the eighteenth century in an accelerated evolution that mimicked in one hundred years what Europeans took centuries to develop. One of the reasons for this was that Pennsylvania was similar in soil and climate to many of the places in Europe where we came from.

The Pennsylvania German people are a composite of immigrants originating from four major regions of Central Europe: Swabia in the present German state of Baden-Württemberg; Alsace in France (formerly a German-speaking area); the Pfalz in the present German state of Rheinland-Pfalz (next door to Alsace), and Switzerland. Smaller groups of settlers came from Hesse in Germany; from Westphalia in the north of Germany near the Dutch border; from other parts of the Rhineland; and from Saxony in southeastern Germany, in what was recently the German Democratic Republic. A tiny religious sect called the Schwenkfelders came to Pennsylvania in the 1730s from Silesia, which is now chiefly a part of Poland. All of these groups retained distinctive regional foods and foodways, certain dialect terms, and manners of speech that reflected their diversity.

Yet given this enormous variety, the culture quickly developed a common language and common characteristics in its cookery, in spite of the fact that the original settlement area is spread out over a thirty-county section of Pennsylvania roughly the same size as Switzerland. This little country, which defies political boundaries, is what we refer to as the Pennsylvania Dutch Homeland.

From its cultural diversity, Pennsylvania has been described as a microcosm of the United States. But we are different from other states in one major respect: Pennsylvania has four historical culinary regions aside from that of the Pennsylvania Dutch. Across the northern counties we find a broad band of New England cookery. In southwestern Pennsylvania we find a large area devoted to Cohee cookery, the Scotch-Irish cookery of the Appalachian South. In a small ring of counties surrounding Philadelphia, there is a definite Anglo-Welsh cookery deriving from the Quakers who settled and farmed in that region. Then there is Philadelphia itself, with its distinctive French and Caribbean cuisine dating from the eighteenth century, when it was the most important port in colonial America, as well as its culinary capital. In fact, there is even a sixth culinary zone, a small pocket of pre-Columbian cookery surviving among the Cornplanter Indians who reside in northwestern Pennsylvania along the Allegheny River. Pennsylvania is the only state in the country where so many major regional cookeries ebb and flow side by side.

If Pennsylvania is a microcosm of the country at large, then the Pennsylvania Dutch part of it is certainly a microcosm of the state. Our cookery may be subdivided into smaller regions within the Dutch Homeland, areas, for example, where maple sugar is a primary sweetening ingredient or where saffron plays a large role in the cookery. The map is dotted with local specialties and cooking nuances.

Pennsylvania Dutch cookery may be divided into two broad categories: the food of the Dutch Country—that thirty-county area— and the food of the diaspora, the vast settlements of Pennsylvania Dutch who live beyond Pennsylvania's borders. Those areas consist of Maryland, the valley of Virginia, parts of West Virginia, a broad belt across the middle of Ohio extending west into Indiana, Illinois, Iowa, and

Keystone cake cutter, nineteenth century.

even Wisconsin, and north of the Great Lakes a large settlement around Kitchener, Ontario.

Outside Pennsylvania, the regions that have developed the most distinctive Pennsylvania Dutch cookeries are Ohio, Maryland, and Ontario, all of which have produced a lively cookbook literature. In fact, the first cookbook to use the term Pennsylvania German in its title was printed in Ohio. Furthermore, the demographic center of the Pennsylvania Dutch population is probably somewhere in Indiana. In spite of this, it is the Dutch Homeland that continues to influence and define the cuisine.

THE PENNSYLVANIA DUTCH SCHOOL

I have used the phrase "classic Pennsylvania Dutch cookery" as though at one time there existed a school or style of cookery with a definable character. While the boundaries of this style are somewhat nebulous and like cookery itself ever-shifting, the core themes may be said to center on a group of cookbooks that have served as guides and inspiration.

It is true that cookbooks have taken back seat to oral tradition, especially to the "historical" dishes at the heart of our cookery and to the vast culinary lore buried in Pennsylvania Dutch newspapers and almanacs—the real mass literature of the culture. But for professionals and the social elite who, by their example, have furnished the rest of the Pennsylvania Germans with culinary models, cookbooks have certainly been important and avidly collected.

The most popular cookbook among Pennsylvania Dutch housewives following the American Revolution was the *Oekonomisches Handbuch für Frauenzimmer* (*Economical Manual of Domestic*

Arts) by Swabian-born Friederike Löffler (1744–1805). Löffler's book especially appealed to the large Swabian faction within the Pennsylvania German world. But the recipes were also highly representative of foods found throughout southwestern Germany, Switzerland, and even Alsace.

The book contains hundreds of dishes that would be familiar to Pennsylvania Dutch cooks even today. Among them are *Dampfnudeln* (steamed dumplings), known as *Dampgnepp* in Pennsylfaanisch; *Gebrennte Suppe* (roux, or fried flour, soup), called *G'reeschte Mehlsupp* by the Dutch; *Bubenschenkel*, a type of stuffed noodle; *Brezeln von Hefetaig*, the soft pretzels of Philadelphia fame; and many popular holiday recipes from *Gansleber Pastete* (Goose Liver Pie) to *Fastnachts*. The fact that multitudes of Löffler's recipes surface in Pennsylvania German almanacs of the period should alone speak for her popularity.

Of the other foreign cookbooks that belong to the library of "classical" Pennsylvania Dutch cookery, there are only Anna Fürst's *Vollständiges Kochbuch für alle Stände* (*Complete Cookbook for all Social Classes*) and Anna Bergner's *Pfälzer Kochbuch* (*Palatine Cookbook*). Fürst's cookbook, issued under her pen name, Marianne Strüf, in 1838, was another southern German cookbook that had wide appeal because of the kind of everyday, working-class dishes it included.

Anna Bergner, owner of the Four Seasons Inn at Dürkheim, a famous wine town in the Pfalz, was far more popular with the Pennsylvania Dutch intelligentsia. This was primarily because of the influential writings of Ludwig Wollenweber (1807–1888), which were widely circulated in Pennsylvania German newspapers. Wollenweber had been born in the Pfalz and had known Anna Bergner personally. Having arrived in Pennsylvania after the failed revolution of 1832 in Germany, he became editor of the influential German newspaper *Philadelphia Demokrat*. In addition, he wrote many books about the Pennsylvania Dutch. Several recipes that I found in the course of my fieldwork can be traced directly to Bergner's cookbook, among them the recipe for Pheasant Sausage from the Haldeman family (p. 139) and the recipe for Snippled Beans (p. 125).

Anna Bergner's cookbook first appeared in 1858, just

Left: This 1933 cookbook was one of the first to commercialize the Amish image. To the right are Whoopie Cakes, a popular Amish snack.

before Pennsylvania German culture underwent its first tenuous revival in the 1860s. Bergner was connected to this revival through Wollenweber, primarily because he was a great lover of good food and wine and saw many obvious connections between the food of Pennsylvania and that of his homeland. In his 1869 *Gemälde aus dem Pennsylvanischen Volksleben* (*Pictures of Pennsylvania Dutch Folk Life*), Wollenweber described a visit to Womelsdorf in Berks County. At the time Womelsdorf was a well-known party town, with summer boarding houses devoted to feasting and late-night frolics. It was the old summer capital of classic Pennsylvania Dutch cookery.

With Anna Bergner obviously in mind, even punning her last name, Wollenweber described one of the popular hotels in the village, operated by a famous local doyenne known irreverently as *Barrick Lehne* (Mountain Lena), who maintained a delightful inn on the *Adlersbarrick*, or Eagle Hill, near the town.[2] Wollenweber claimed at the time that Lena was better known in the Dutch country than the Pope was to Romans. In any case, she held forth in her establishment with comparable grandeur, and her saloons were packed summer and winter for the weekly Saturday night concerts and balls that created a pretext for heavy trysting.

Most of all, *die Lehne* took great precautions with her food. Visitors were offered nothing less than the best imported mineral waters; the freshest milk and butter, "just as in Switzerland," commented Wollenweber; first-rate rye breads; *Handkees* (hand cheese); Swiss cheese, what we now call farmer's cheese in Pennsylvania; Lebanon and Reading bolognas; sugar pretzels; Lauer's lager beer from Reading; American catawba and German Rhine wines; and a popular semi-frozen drink called *Schlury-Cadury*.

Despite the popularity of the books just mentioned, two other cookbooks appeared in the 1840s and 1850s that may be considered the basic texts of classical Pennsylvania Dutch cookery, both written by professional chefs.

Philadelphia-trained George Girardey published his *Höchst nützliches Handbuch über Kochkunst* (*Manual of Domestic Cookery*) in Cincinnati in 1841 and a partial adaptation in English in Dayton, Ohio, that same year. Written for caterers and hoteliers like *Barrick Lehne*, it is a mixture of fashionable recipes and down-to-earth country fare. Girardey published a recipe for *Gumbis*—and even used that term—

and a number of other peculiarly Pennsylvania Dutch preparations, including an apple butter and mustard mixture used for basting grilled meats. The honey mustard rage of the present is a revival of this very old-fashioned idea.

Many of Girardey's recipes are French, which gives the entire book an Alsatian cast in its blend of things German and Gallic. Yet it would be a mistake to assume that even his French recipes appeared at table literally as written. After all, it was an easy matter for Pennsylvania German cooks to take a duck stewed with white wine and turnips and subtly alter it into something unmistakably Pennsylfaanisch.

Even more influential than Girardey, whose books have always been difficult to obtain, was Swiss-trained William Vollmer of Philadelphia. Vollmer's *Vollständiges deutsches Vereinigten Staaten Kochbuch* (Philadelphia, 1856), which was sold in English under the title *The United States Cook Book*, was the virtual bible of classical Pennsylvania Dutch cookery and a regional bestseller. Anyone curious about the foods eaten by well-to-do Pennsylvania Germans in the nineteenth century need only to consult Vollmer.

Vollmer's only real competitor was another cookbook, much smaller in size and far less pretentious in content, compiled by a Harrisburg printer in 1847. Its author was Gustav Sigismund Peters, an enthusiastic gourmand who knew little about the mechanics of cookery. Titled *Die Geschickte Hausfrau* (*The Handy Housewife*), Peters's book was a compilation of recipes purloined from other American cookbooks and translated, sometimes incorrectly, into German.

THE SWISS COMPONENT

The Swiss element in Pennsylvania Dutch culture has always exerted an influence much larger in proportion to its size than the other groups. The Hersheys have put their chocolate bars on the world map; the Smuckers have done likewise with their jams and jellies; and the Guldens have done the same with their mustard. Certainly the Amish, who originate almost exclusively from Switzerland, stand out as a highly visible reminder of the Swiss connection. But beyond the Amish, many families in the Pennsylvania Dutch world claim Swiss ancestry and preserve certain Swiss foods and foodways, sometimes without even realizing it.

One of these dishes is a white cassoulet known as *Schweizer Ritscher*. The *Ritscher* (pronounced "RICH-er") is a one-pot dish usually made with pearl barley and white beans or more rarely with peas and brown barley or even lentils. *Schweizer Ritscher* acquired its name from the fact that it was eaten primarily by the Swiss Mennonites who settled in Pennsylvania in the early eighteenth century. Because the dish contained barley, it was viewed as a peculiarly Swiss food by other Pennsylvania Germans. Among the Swiss Mennonites the *Ritscher* was a popular spring dish for Sunday dinner. It survives today in the form of the white bean dishes served by the Amish after *G'mee* (religious meeting for worship).

Weissebrei ("VICE-eh-brigh"), or White Mush, is another barley dish associated with Swiss origins. It is made with pearl barley grits and is called white to distinguish it from other forms of mush, like the brown or yellow mush made with plain or roasted cornmeal, and from *Schwatzebrei* (Black Mush, p. 30) made with buckwheat. To the colonial settler, the whiteness of *Weissebrei* also suggested its superiority to other foods. In dairying cultures like those of Alpine Switzerland and early Pennsylvania, white foods were valued as good, healthful, and particularly clean. An appreciation of cleanliness becomes obvious to anyone who tries to prepare white food on an open hearth.

Perhaps it was for such cleanliness that Pennsylvania-German Jews included *Weissebrei* among their dishes for the Sabbath. The dish is also meatless and therefore can fit into a kosher diet. Instead of using milk and cheese, Jewish cooks boiled the barley grits in chicken stock until thick, then mixed it with *Gribben* (chicken cracklings).

What makes White Mush most interesting to food ethnologists is the fact that barley grits cooked until thick is the original polenta of ancient Switzerland and northern Italy, polenta as it was made before the introduction of maize to Europe.[3]

Another Swiss contribution is *Eepieskuche* ("A-peas-KOO-keh"), a small loaf cake originally baked for Epiphany but now eaten by the Pennsylvania Dutch as a breakfast or coffee cake. It derives its name directly from Switzerland, where it is called *Äpieskuchen*, *Äpies* being Swiss dialect for Epiphany, or Twelfth Night. The original *Eepieskuche* made among the Pennsylvania Dutch was introduced by Swiss

Catholics who settled at Bally in Berks County during the early part of the eighteenth century. The Bally *Eepiskuche* was leavened with yeast or beaten eggs and contained two beans, one for the "king" and one for the "queen," as the lucky individuals who found them were called. The recipe from Sumneytown (p. 160) retains more of an older, traditional character than most of the *Eepiskuche* that are sold in farm markets today.

Cup cheese, another food of Swiss origin, has suffered from the same blurring of identity as *Eepiskuche*. Years ago, when egg cheese was described in Pennsylfaanisch, it went by two names: *Eierkees* (egg cheese) and *Ziegerkees* (goat cheese).[4] *Ziegerkees* ("ZEEG-er-CASE") was the preferred term, and I suspect that originally, in the eighteenth century, only goat milk was used, as is still the custom in some parts of rural Switzerland.

Egg cheese today, at least the species sold in most of our farm markets, is generally called cup cheese (it is packaged in cups) and resembles custard, sugar being the only "spice," and no goat milk is present. The true egg cheese of classic Pennsylvania Dutch cookery was not a custard but a rich cheese spread made with eggs and goat milk, as in the recipe from the Grube family of Kissel Hill in Lancaster County (p. 42).

Not only does the written record confirm the existence of this older type of cheese, but material evidence abounds in the form of old glazed redware pots that once served as market containers for the goat cheese spread. Christian Link (d. 1910), a potter who lived in Exeter Township, Berks County, produced thousands of black glazed pots specifically for the *Ziegerkees* vendors of Reading and Philadelphia. He was one of the last country potters to cater to that specialized trade.

Aside from the Swiss component, there are several families of dishes that trace their origins ultimately to the regional cookery of southern Germany and Switzerland. It is this extremely old body of dishes that forms the most distinctive part of Pennsylvania Dutch cookery. In Pennsylfaanisch they are called *Gumbis*, *Schales*, *Schaumkuche*, and *Dummes*, terms that I have retrieved from historical sources.

GUMBIS: *A DISH OF MANY LAYERS*

Gumbis ("GOOM-biss") is a dialect corruption of the Latin word *compositum*, the past participle of the verb *componere*, which has several root meanings.[5] One of these is "to put together," as in the act of creating something out of small parts. Thus, in culinary terms, *composita* are "compositions" assembled from layered ingredients. This is the meaning of *Gumbis* as it is understood in most Swiss dialects and is also the meaning in Pennsylfaanisch.[6] Any baked deep-dish casserole made with layered ingredients fits the definition of a Pennsylvania Dutch *Gumbis*.

Another species of *Gumbis* is the type made by layering noodles. These are generally referred to by the Pennsylvania Dutch as potpies. The true potpie of colonial America actually belongs to a separate tribe of recipes based on the cauldron cookery of the British Isles, whereby an iron cookpot is lined with a disposable crust.

That was doubtless the type of potpie prepared for Henrich Freitag, a well digger by trade, who settled in Stark County, Ohio, about 1805.[7] Until his first planting of crops matured, Henrich and his family were forced to live off game and wild berries. Then, when locusts appeared to ravage his new fields, Henrich, with a practical turn of mind, had his wife make potpie out of them. After eating the pie, Freitag remarked, *"Ess iss der bescht poy ass mer mache kann"* ("It's the best pie you can make!"). His descendants have not preserved the recipe.

Today the Pennsylfaanisch term *Botboi* (potpie) is the name for the dish and the flat noodles that go into it. The idea of connecting a term for pie to a noodle is consistent with medieval German and may trace back to the root meaning of *pie* itself. Modern English dictionaries certainly give *pie* the wrong etymological explanation in assuming that it meant simply "a medley."

The term *pie* probably derives from the Celtic *bih* or *bei*, a word for something small, as in the Gaulish *beic*. The French words *petit* and *pièce* both derive from *beic*. Thus, in its root culinary meaning, a pie was probably either a form of stuffed pasta, as in Italian ravioli, or a similarly shaped finger food such as a pasty. The core concept of ravioli is that pockets of dough contain a variety of fillings served together on the same dish, for *ravioli* derives from the Latin *farrago* (a medley) plus *-iolum*, a diminutive. This linkage of pies with noodle dough was carried forward into German Renaissance cookery; the dough for both pasties and stuffed pastas is consistently called *Tortenteig* in period sources.

In a 1553 manuscript cookbook compiled by Augsburg housewife Sabina Welser, there is a recipe for noodle dough called *Tortentaig*.[8] *Torte* is a word familiar to most Americans in the name of a famous Austrian dessert called Linzer Torte and in Pennsylfaanisch as the name of sandtarts, a sugar cookie. *Torte* did not come into widespread use in German until the 1500s, but its root meaning then, as now, has not changed.[9] It is any flat and round cake, flat bread, or round flat piece of dough.

Sabina Welser used the term for her noodle dough because, after rolling it out, she cut the dough into little circles. She then put plums in the center of each and folded the dough over to form *Mauldasche*, which she called pies. In Pennsylvania German cookbooks it is very common to find *Mauldasche* called pies rather than their dialect name, one of the most common being "half-moon pies." This is probably the most ancient and most "archaeologically correct" use of the term *pie*, surviving from a time when it referred to a small finger food.

The appropriation of the term *Botboi* for layered noodle preparations in Pennsylfaanisch has effectively narrowed the meaning of *Gumbis* (to the Dutch at least) to deep-dish casseroles using shredded cabbage or some other shredded vegetable as the main layering ingredient. The veal and oyster *Gumbis* (p. 35) and the pork and potato *Gumbis* (p. 138) are examples of this; they would not be mistaken for a potpie.

Gumbis undergoes one further metamorphosis when covered with a top crust; it becomes a *Schlupper* ("SHLOO-per"), or slump in English, as in Anna Moyer's Apple Slump (p. 39) or the Peach and Tomato Slump with Sage (p. 114). Sometimes *Schlupper* is written *Offeschlupper* in Pennsylfaanisch, which points to the Swabian origin of the term, for this very same type of *Gumbis* is still known as *Ofenschlupfer* in many parts of Baden-Württemberg.[10]

To define a *Schlupper*, however, is rather difficult. While the top crust is an obvious departure from the standard *Gumbis*, things also happen inside that alter the character of the dish. It is a nebulous hybrid of a fruit potpie and a dessert *Gumbis*, for it is usually a fruit dish. In essence, it is the original cobbler. In areas of Appalachia where Pennsylvania Dutch settled, *Schluppers* are known as whanges, sonkers, or sonker pies.[11] In Surrey County, North Carolina, for example, the local historical society sponsors a Sonker Festival each September.

Above: Stuncher, or Dummes *paddle, Somerset County, Pennsylvania (1820–1850).*
Right: The Ritscher *was once the basic deep casserole dish of Pennsylvania Dutch cookery.*

SCHALES: *THE PENNSYLVANIA DUTCH GRATIN*

Another type of baked dish is the *Schales* ("SHAH-less"), the Pennsylvania German equivalent of the shallow-dish casserole. A range of recipes fall into this category. On the one hand, there are baked salads similar to the *tian* of Provence; on the other are shallow casseroles of layered ingredients over which an egg- or milk-based sauce is poured to bake and set.

Schales is assumed by Palatine linguists to derive from the Palatine Yiddish *Schalet* or *Scholet*, a meatless dish baked on Friday to serve on the Sabbath. In the Pfalz, *Schales* is generally made with potatoes, reflecting the post-1770 influence of the "Potato Revolution" on German cookery.[12] *Schales* came to Pennsylvania long before that and therefore preserved an older, more fluid identity. We know it as a turnip dish or even as a grain dish, like the spelt and cauliflower combination (p. 37).

Furthermore, the accepted origin of the Yiddish is open to question, for both *Schales* and *Schalet* appear to derive not from strained etymologies leading off into French but from the simple shape of the dish in which the recipe is baked: a flattish shell.

SCHAUMKUCHE: *BREAKFAST CAKE OR PANCAKE?*

In several old cookbooks from the Union County area there is a popular dish called bread omelet, which is neither bread nor omelet. It is a baked dish known in Pennsylfaanisch as *Schaumkuche*, for which there is no better translation than the word *pancake*. The dish is sometimes characterized in old Pennsylvania High German sources as an *Auflauf* (soufflé), since the chief aerating agent is stiffly beaten egg whites.

In the larger context of food history, the *Schaumkuche* of Pennsylvania Dutch cookery belongs to a family of egg dishes known in southern Germany as *Schmarren*. The most famous of these is the Austrian *Kaiserschmarrn*, a fluffy dessert dish that is slashed or torn apart with forks into large pieces right before it is served. This same serving technique is used for *Schaumkuche*, which is why this dish is always at its best the moment it is brought to the table.

Most of the *Schaumkuche* recipes that I have located come from the western sections of the Pennsylvania Dutch Homeland or from Ohio. This suggests to me that the *Schaumkuche* tradition is quickly disappearing in the most urbanized parts of the Pennsylvania Dutch country. With the renewed interest in meatless dishes and health foods, perhaps the *Schaumkuche* will revive itself in new and creative ways. The same may be said for the homely dish called *Dummes*.

DUMMES: *THE PENNSYLVANIA DUTCH "CHOPPED" OMELET*

Dummes ("DOO-miss") is prepared in a skillet. It is a variation of the omelet in which ingredients such as diced bread or potatoes are fried, chopped, and stirred continuously with beaten eggs until the dish has set. Other Pennsylfaanisch terms for it are *Schtarrumpel* and *Huddelstraa*. *Dummes* derives from Pfälzer dialect nouns created from the verb *stampfen*, "to stamp or chop."[13]

Dummes is a Pennsylfaanisch term first recorded in Carbon County, where a large variety of *Dummes* recipes has been preserved.[14] While *Dummes*, like *Schaumkuche*, has no precise English equivalent, both the Quakers and the Welsh Baptists who settled among the Germans made a Welsh dish similar to *Dummes* called *stwnch*. In English, the term is written as *stunch* and pronounced "stoonch." The special wooden stick used to stir and chop the dish was called a stuncher, or in Pennsylfaanisch a *Dummesscheifle* (*Dummes* paddle). A small spatula will serve the same purpose.

Some cooks owned sets of small spatulas and two-tined forks designed specifically for *Dummes* cookery, for making gribble (discussed in the next chapter), and for tearing apart *Schaumkuche* prior to serving. These spatulas and forks were also combined into one implement, with the special fork on the handle end. This was generally known as a gribble iron in English and a *Dummeseise* (*Dummes* iron) in Pennsylfaanisch. The tines of these forks were rather flat, not bowed and sharply pointed like old-fashioned flesh forks.

TIEGELS AND RUTSCHERS: *EQUIPMENT OF THE HEARTHSIDE*

Aside from these special forks and spatulas, our cookery has a rich variety of hearthside equipment dating back to Roman times. For many of their raised-hearth dishes, the Romans employed a lidded cookpot with three legs, which they called a *tripus*. This was the same type of earthenware vessel used for *Gumbis* by medieval cooks in the Rhineland. Such a *stollichte Hafe* (legged pot) was called for specifically in a *Gumbis* recipe for *Ein Krumpus-Kraut* (cabbage *Gumbis*) in the 1691 *Vollständiges Nürnbergisches Koch-Buch* (*Complete Nuremberg Cookbook*).[15] A pot very like the one in the 1691 recipe appears as figure 16 in the 1788 engraving on page 46. The old Pennsylvania Dutch name for such a stewpot was *Tiegel*. The most practical modern equivalent of a *Tiegel* would be a porcelainized iron stewpot with a tight-fitting lid or any porcelainized Dutch oven.

Another Roman cooking vessel, called the *angularius*, produced its own line of progeny, including the Pennsylvania Dutch *Rutscher* or *Ritscher*. Like the *angularius*, the *Rutscher* is flat on the bottom, rounded on the sides, and is often provided with a spout and handle. The Pennsylfaanisch name, which Abraham Brendle recorded in the 1890s, derives from the verb *rutschen*, "to shove or push to and fro"or, more specifically, "in and out of the oven."

Interestingly, there is a Roman bronze *Rutscher* with a long handle in the collection of the British Museum, clear evidence that the form evolved during classical antiquity. The *Rutscher* became a basic utensil in the Pennsylvania German kitchen and lent its peculiar shape to a whole family of baked dishes, like the shad and cabbage recipe (p. 40). Not only have archeological sites in Pennsylvania produced hundreds of *Rutscher* shards, but whole examples have been unearthed as well. Eighteenth-century Moravian potteries in particular seem to have specialized in *Rutscher* production for sale in Pennsylvania and in settlements in North Carolina.

Many eighteenth-century Pennsylvania Dutch cooked on raised hearths very much like the hearths used by the Romans. Often built into these hearths, either along one side or in the fireplace wall, were small, drawerlike ovens used for baking food in a *Rutscher*. Several ovens of this type are still intact in Moravian buildings in Bethlehem, Pennsylvania, and Old Salem, North Carolina. Since these ovens were not constructed for baking bread, they were known in dialect as *Brodeoffe*, or roasting ovens, from the verb *brode*, "to roast."

Deep *Rutschers* with spouts on one end for pouring off fat were used for baking fatty foods like goose, suckling pig, or duck. They could also be used for baking *Dampgnepp* (steam-baked dumplings), yeast-raised cakes, and puddings, as well as *Gumbis*. Some *Rutschers* were supplied with lids specifically for steam baking and braising. In the nineteenth century cast-iron *Rutschers* came into fashion and can still be found at flea markets in regions where Pennsylvania Germans settled.

FLAVORS FROM THE HEARTHSIDE

In the 1857 summer and fall issues of the Allentown *Bauern-Journal*, a Pennsylvania German agricultural monthly, there is a delightful series of articles beginning with "What Every Farmer Should Have at Home." The series, actually written for the farmer's wife, is full of important culinary hints such as where to find juniper berries, how to prepare trout in saffron sauce, and how to avoid bread-baking errors in the brick oven, as well as a call to female readers to establish a recipe exchange. It is source material like this that brings many of the basic flavors in Pennsylvania Dutch cookery into focus, for the cook's hand is not always obvious in printed recipes.

Throughout this book I have made a conscious effort to use these basic flavors and food combinations with the proviso that Pennsylvania Dutch cookery is geographically large and therefore subject to multitudes of subdivisions and nuances keyed to *Bodegeschmack* and local taste.

CORNMEAL, SPELT, AND OTHER GRAINS

The ancient diet of the rural Swiss, the core foods eaten from pre-Roman times down to the late seventeenth century, centered on three groups of foods: goat milk and goat cheese; pears, fresh, dried, and cooked down into pear butter; and barley and millet, both as grains and as bread flours.[16] These are the foods that the Swiss today associate with the *Gaisbauer* (goat farmer), their term for hillbilly. Yet these were also the primary foods of the rural Anabaptists before they left Switzerland and eventually settled in Pennsylvania under the label of Mennonites. Standing behind millet and barley were two other grains—oats and spelt—as well as buckwheat, which became an important crop in German-speaking countries during the 1400s.[17]

Since all of the grains just mentioned produce coarse flours or are difficult to mill because of their hard husks, it was a common practice to "parch" (dry-roast) whole grains to create finer-textured flours. This practice was widespread

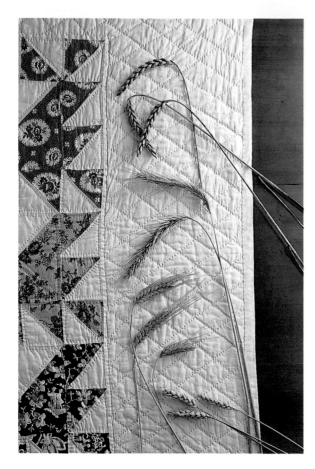

Four basic grains from top to bottom: spelt, rye, barley, and wheat.

among the Celts of western Europe and has persisted in the peasant cookeries of Europe from the Stone Age to the present day. The Pennsylvania Dutch preference for roasted yellow cornmeal is a holdover of this old culinary pattern, further reinforced by the fact that American Indians also parched corn and other foods for meal and flour.

The labor-intensive millet was one of the first grains to be dropped from the diet of the Swiss who came to America, replaced by yellow corn grits and yellow cornmeal. Throughout those parts of Europe where millet was a primary grain food, yellow cornmeal has gradually replaced it.[18]

In terms of Pennsylvania Dutch foodways, corn cookery may be divided into two distinct regional types—yellow cornmeal east of the Susquehanna River and white corn-

meal to the west of the Susquehanna. The Swiss Mennonites who settled east of the Susquehanna prior to the Revolution preferred yellow cornmeal to white because of its direct association with older millet dishes.

Pennsylvania Germans in Maryland and Virginia almost exclusively cook with white cornmeal. This taste preference was assimilated from Anglo-Americans, for white cornmeal is the predominant grain food of the Tidewater South. On the other hand, in Ohio, where the New England preference for yellow cornmeal predominates owing to early Yankee settlement, especially from Connecticut, the Pennsylvania Dutch use yellow cornmeal in their cookery.

It was never necessary for the Pennsylvania Dutch to develop an elaborate cornbread cookery because they possessed a large repertoire of hearth breads made with other grains, primarily oats and rye but also buckwheat. For household bread the primary grain was spelt, more often than not mixed with rye to create maslin bread. The real secret to the fame of Pennsylvania German rye bread was spelt, of which there were two varieties, one resembling wheat, the other with a black groat or berry. Black spelt, called *Schwatzedinkel* in Pennsylfaanisch, was used in cookery like wild rice.

Spelt is called *Dinkel* in Pennsylfaanisch. It was known as German wheat in colonial America because of its association with the Pennsylvania Dutch. The Germans raised wheat as a cash crop, which they shipped to Philadelphia or Baltimore, and raised spelt for their own consumption. The yield of spelt per acre is similar to that of oats, but spelt gives far superior straw, a trait important to farmers with livestock.

Spelt is also higher in nutrients than wheat and contains far more gluten, which is why it produces such remarkable bread. The gluten in spelt, however, is more water soluble than the gluten in wheat; thus, people who have gluten allergies find that they can eat spelt products without trouble. The Germans have recognized the health aspects of spelt since the Middle Ages, particularly its digestibility.

Of all the grain foods, spelt defined the historic cookery of the Pennsylvania Dutch more than any other, even cornmeal, which was eaten everyday in the form of mush. Spelt flour was considered the *only* acceptable flour for gingerbread, so much so that in Germany today the large commercial gingerbread bakeries subsidize farmers to produce a reliable spelt supply. Likewise, the German pretzel bakeries have a vested interest in spelt, for it is spelt gluten that has made Germany the center of pretzel baking for more than a thousand years.

Spelt was used in Pennsylvania Dutch cookery as a form of grits, as a whole grain cooked like rice, as a whole grain harvested green and smoked for use in soups, as a meal in porridges, and as a flour in breads, pastries, and dumplings. Spelt and barley meal were used to make square-shaped johnny cakes that were wrapped in cabbage leaves and baked on hot coals. Spelt and barley flour, mixed with saffron and honey, are still the primary ingredients of the Christmas gingerbread men made in the New Berlin area of Union County. With applications as varied as those of wheat, spelt is set apart by its rich flavor.

I have restored spelt flour to recipes throughout this book in ways used in traditional Pennsylvania Dutch cookery, sometimes as a thickener, sometimes as a primary ingredient. Whole-wheat flour may be used as a substitute, but the equation is not equal because spelt and wheat flours taste different and absorb water at different rates.

Whole-grain spelt (spelt groats) and spelt flour were also parched like cornmeal, primarily as flavoring ingredients to give certain dishes a nutty taste or a crunchy texture. Toasted spelt and rye grains were often plunged into boiling water to create meatless cooking stocks similar in flavor to infusions made with dried mushrooms. These formed the basis of meatless soups eaten by Pennsylvania-German Lutherans and Catholics

during Lent. Today these meatless soups are fertile territory for vegetarian cookery.

Likewise, spelt flour can be parched in a skillet in a process of slow scorching that creates a dark, nutty thickener for soups and stews. This old Pennsylvania Dutch cooking technique, outlined on page 31, is worth reviving not only because of its taste but also because it is an effective replacement for roux (flour fried in fat) and can be used by people whose dietary requirements demand a reduction of fatty or fried foods.

Today spelt is receiving renewed attention as a health food. The old German wheat of the Pennsylvania Dutch, long scorned by our "English" neighbors, may at last return on the scene not as a passing fancy of the food set but as a long-term remedy to modern diets gone awry.

I have more to say about oats and buckwheat in my discussion of soup cookery on page 47 and have reserved comments about wheat and rye for the chapter about breads. But there is one more grain that deserves mention, and it is wild rice.

The Pennsylvania Dutch call wild rice *Wasserhawwer* (water oats), and at one time it was used extensively in our cookery. It grew along all of the rivers in the East well into the nineteenth century but was gradually pushed out of its natural habitat by overharvesting and by invasive marsh plants naturalized from Europe. Now wild rice must come from the upper Midwest, where it still grows in quantities large enough for commercial production. Wild rice was an important feature of our historical cuisine that is

Beans special to historic Pennsylvania Dutch cooking, from left to right: Mostoller Wild Goose beans, Hutterite Soup beans, Grandma Stober's Chow-Chow beans, Fisher beans, Amish Nuttle beans, and Lazy Wife beans.

worth reviving in such old-style dishes as Black Mush (p. 30). Furthermore, since black spelt is now virtually impossible to locate in specialty food stores, wild rice must serve as its substitute.

Except for wild rice and corn, the grains I have just mentioned were all imposed on the Pennsylvania landscape by Europeans. The various flavors and textures that these grains gave to Pennsylvania Dutch cookery were in part a continuation of Old World preference patterns. There is another body of tastes, however, which are not European but which play a vital role in the distinctive flavors of Pennsylvania Dutch cookery. These are ingredients from the other Americas.

Above: Frost on the blackberries and saffron in bloom.
Right: Saffron in my Pennsylvania garden.

THE CARIBBEAN CONNECTION

The salting of shad and herring, and to a lesser degree of rockfish, was once a major industry along the Delaware, Schuylkill, and Susquehanna rivers. Shad, herring, and rockfish formed the "spring trinity" of the Pennsylvania diet between the end of March and the end of June; this was one of the major regional differences between the cookery of the Pennsylvania Dutch Homeland and that in areas settled by the Dutch beyond Pennsylvania. These three fish were often depicted in our regional folk art, one laid over the other as though they were spinning like rays of the sun. The importance of this imagery to the Dutch cannot be overstated because it was toward the sun that all those fish were shipped.

Packed in barrels and sent downriver to Philadelphia or Baltimore with sacks of roasted cornmeal, these fish—and the cornmeal—became articles of commerce in the extensive West Indian trade network. The returning boats brought back pineapples, limes, allspice, ginger root, molasses, rum, coconuts, vanilla beans, cocoa beans, guavas, and peppers. By the 1770s most of these foods were fully assimilated into the urban diet of southeastern Pennsylvania and were available in county market towns to any farmer who could afford to buy them. By degrees these exotic foods found their way into Pennsylvania Dutch kitchens, and over time certain taste combinations evolved that may be characterized as peculiarly Dutch.

Among these is the combination of fresh ginger and rosemary, often with tart apples, as in Anna Moyer's Apple Slump (p. 39). Another is the blend of green (unripe) fruit, limes, and cayenne pepper that is found in Green Apple Pap (p. 38). Habañero or poblano peppers were also used in spicy mixtures of this sort.

Ground cayenne pepper gave heat to another flavoring combination known as Picoso Sugar (p. 129), which entered Pennsylvania Dutch cookery via the Caribbean French who settled in Philadelphia, Lancaster, and York in large numbers during the 1790s. Picoso Sugar is a blend of sugar, cayenne pepper, and cassia. It is used by the Dutch mostly in summer cookery to heighten the flavor of acidic fruits. One typical application is in dishes combining tomatoes and peaches, an invention of Pennsylvania Dutch Maryland cookery dating at least from the 1850s if not earlier. Cassia was extremely cheap in Philadelphia and Maryland because of the large number of German chocolate makers in Philadelphia and Baltimore. These Germans processed chocolate with cassia rather than with cinnamon, and the country people used cassia in all recipes in which cinnamon might otherwise have been used, even in hot chocolate.

Pennsylvania Dutch chocolate was often sweetened only with dark molasses, as in the case of the intensely flavored Chocolate Gingerbread (p. 93). And somewhere along the way, a Pennsylvania Dutch pastry baker discovered the natural marriage of dark rum, honey, and vanilla as a flavoring for cakes, pies, and even pretzels. Honey Jumbles (p. 160) can only be described as deliciously fragrant.

There is a whole cookery based on molasses itself: molasses cookies, molasses pies, molasses fruit cakes, and the now famous molasses crumb cake called Shoofly Pie. The original recipe (p. 96) for this breakfast cake, dating from the 1876 United States Centennial, is published here after a long hibernation in an Ephrata, Pennsylvania, attic.

Lastly, the Caribbean Connection provides one final piece in a puzzle of flavors not indigenous to Pennsylvania or to any of the places where the Dutch subsequently settled. That piece is saffron, called *Safferich* in Pennsylfaanisch. In all of the regions in Europe from which the Pennsylvania German people originated, saffron was a luxury associated with the food of the nobility or with foods connected to certain life-turning events, such as weddings or funerals. It was not an herb of everyday fare.

While it is true that there were saffron dealers among the Pennsylvania Germans as early as the 1730s, the real impetus to saffron agriculture in Pennsylvania came in the 1790s from the Pennsylvania-German Jews. At that time Philadelphia merchants banded together to create a monopoly over trade in the Caribbean at the expense of England and Spain. Distance and fast sailing ships were in

Philadelphia's favor, and the network of Quaker and Jewish merchants throughout the Caribbean provided the necessary agents on location to pull off the scheme. One of the trade goods in that scheme was saffron, an important herb to Spanish and Portuguese cooks in the Caribbean. Philadelphia commodity exchanges for the period before 1812 often listed saffron on a weekly basis, and in general one pound of saffron was quoted at one pound of gold.

The War of 1812 turned the scheme topsy-turvy and left Dutch farmers with a glut of saffron. Some localities fell into a permanent saffron habit that is now, 180 years later, beginning to disappear only because saffron is once again nearly worth its weight in gold. The last large local grower of saffron was a two-acre farm owned by Martha and Myron Dupple at Reistville, Pennsylvania.

The culture of the saffron crocus did not spread beyond Pennsylvania, for it shared with millet a similar fate of abandonment and subsequent substitution when cooks took their passports and went over the mountains. This time, instead of crossing the Atlantic, the Dutch weathered the storms of the Alleghenies. When they laid out their kitchen gardens from Lancaster, Ohio, to Kitchener, Ontario, one plant they certainly left out was saffron. In its place they planted rows of prickly safflower, not just for the petals, which provide a saffronish yellow, but for the seeds as well, for safflower seeds give oil.

SEED OILS

The Pennsylvania Dutch have always used and valued olive oil, but costliness limited its use to those who could afford it. It is not unusual to find olive oil called for in eighteenth- and nineteenth-century recipes in which cost was no object. For the people in the country, however, the olive was an elusive berry. On the other hand, there was another trinity that supplied Dutch cooks with the cooking oils they needed. It was a trinity that consisted of safflower oil, rapeseed oil (the primary ingredient in modern canola oil), and sunflower oil.

Dr. Johann David Schoepf, the German physician who traveled through Pennsylvania in the 1780s, was amazed to find the sunflower so firmly embedded in our foodways. Schoepf noted that sunflowers beyond the Alleghenies grew lustier in virgin soil than in cultivated parts of Pennsylvania and "not less than twenty feet tall."[19] Who would deny themselves of such untroubled abundance?

In 1830, Charles Barnitz of York began manufacturing and selling cold- and hot-pressed sunflower oil "far superior to the best Olive Oil, for table and family use," according to period newspaper announcements.[20] The success of Barnitz's sunflower oil was evident in a gradual shift in Pennsylvania Dutch cookery away from safflower oil, which was expensive to produce, and away from rapeseed oil, which required special presses.

Sunflower oil was particularly favored for steamed foods as a seasoning and for frying, particularly in chop-and-stir-fry preparations like *Dummes*. Sunflower, safflower, and rapeseed oils do not share the advantage of lard or peanut oil in having a high burning temperature, and thus their application for deep frying was always limited. Yet they were popular as salad oils and even, in limited ways, for sautéing and light frying.

I have heard it said that Pennsylvania Dutch cookery is dead without lard. However, it was only when commercial lard became cheaper after the Civil War that cooks switched to it in large numbers. If anything, lard nearly killed our cookery. Perhaps a healthy reversion to the old trinity of sunflower, safflower, and rapeseed oils would be welcomed not only by doctors but also by pigs.

Organic cabbage and camomile in my Pennsylvania garden.

GREEN CUISINE

The kitchen garden has yielded up many special flavors for the Pennsylvania Dutch cook. Ripeness is one of the key ingredients to creating a Pennsylvania Dutch "taste," and it helps to be a gardener, for plants have a language of their own.

Peaches that still have "snap," apples sour enough to pucker the lips, gooseberries as hard as marbles—unripe fruit was an old Middle European taste preference often noted by travelers through the Pennsylvania Dutch country. With the upsurge of sugar consumption in our cookery since the 1880s, this green cuisine has almost disappeared, yet it is preserved here and there in certain recipes that do not work with ripe ingredients.

Green Apple Pap (p. 38) is one of them. But so too are green apple pies, green currant pies, and puddings in which green peaches are first poached in Madeira. Green peaches are mixed with green tomatoes to make raw chutneys or fiery mandrams, those spicy West Indian relishes that go so well with white meats.

This greenness was further accentuated with certain green herbs that give very specific flavors to food. I am thinking here of the green (unripe) seeds of coriander, which taste neither like the leaves nor like the dried ripe seeds. Green coriander seeds are crucial to the success of many pickle recipes.

The green seeds of fennel were used in pickles for this same special taste. It is green fennel seed that gives Kutztown Jar-Jar (p. 116) its delightful boost. In fact, fennel was at one time so common in Pennsylvania Dutch cookery, even to flavor apple butter, that many writers considered it a defining taste in our cuisine.

Garlic chives also provided a special flavor. The green (unripe) seeds were dried and saved for winter. When a little frying was done, a few of these seeds were popped into the oil to give it a pungent flavor fit to warm the heart on even the coldest days of winter. An alternative to this was garlic oil, that is, sunflower or safflower oil flavored with garlic (p. 128). The Dutch used a great deal of garlic and onions in their food until the 1860s.

The "other garlic" that we use in our cookery, and one that is happily still extant in many kitchen gardens, is the Catawissa onion. Called *Winterzwiwwele* (winter onions) in Pennsylfaanisch, this native American onion is known as the perennial tree onion or top onion (*Allium cepa,* var. *proliferum*) in many herbals. It has a distinctive growing habit, with red bulblets forming on the stem rather than in the ground, and it yields an excellent shallot-like flavor ideal for making herb vinegars.

VINEGAR COOKERY AND SOUR BRAISING

The reigning monarch of all our flavored vinegars is raspberry vinegar. Its use was so much a part of Pennsylvania Dutch cookery in the eighteenth and nineteenth centuries that virtually all the cookbooks printed in our part of the country contain recipes for this preparation. Raspberry vinegar was used in sauces for meats like smoked tongue, in salad dressings, in marinades, even in pickles. When mixed with sugar and mineral water, raspberry vinegar was also a popular summer drink.

The popularity of fruit-flavored vinegars is doubtless an extension of the Pennsylvania Dutch preference for sweet-sour combinations in cookery: the interplay of fruit and meat, the counterpoint of tastes like quince and honey, and the use of black vinegars for sauces. Black vinegars are old, barrel-aged vinegars that become excessively sharp and what we call smoky in reference to the oak taste. Black vinegars are seldom used alone, except perhaps in mince-meat pies. Rather, they are reduced through hard boiling to a semi-syrup with dried fruit, raisins, brown sugar, molasses, or a combination of any of these.

Black vinegars are excellent in meat cookery and are the real secret behind our sour braised hams. Sour braising is an extremely old cooking technique in which meat is steam-baked in a tightly sealed pot. It offers a tasty, low-fat alternative to other methods of preparing meat, especially pork. It has the added benefit of acting as a tenderizer, a great boon to cooks who want to spend less money on cheaper cuts of meat.

Most of all, vinegars are used in our cookery to flavor soups. This was a common practice in German Renaissance cookbooks. The added interest that dill vinegar or horse-radish vinegar gives to a very plain soup cannot be appreciated until tried. It is so economical that I do not see why it ever fell out of fashion. Furthermore, the addition of smoked meat such as goose or capon can turn an unpretentious meal into an experience worth repeating.

The green seeds of garlic chives are dried for use in cooking.

Spelt Bread Stunch.

SPELT BREAD STUNCH
(DINKELBROD DUMMES)

This typical breakfast Dummes is still made among older generations of Pennsylvania Dutch cooks, especially in the spring when goose eggs are abundant.

YIELD: 4 SERVINGS

¼ cup (60 g) unsalted butter or cooking oil
4 cups (330 g) diced Spelt Bread (p. 84) or rye bread
  without caraway seed
½ cup (30 g) chopped scallion or leek
3 cloves garlic, minced, or 3 tablespoons (30 g) finely
  chopped Catawissa onion
2 goose eggs or 4 large chicken eggs
¾ cup (180 ml) plain whole-milk yogurt
2 tablespoons (5 g) coarsely minced fresh parsley
2 tablespoons (5 g) coarsely minced fresh lovage or a mix
  of chopped dark green outer celery leaves and chervil
sea salt and freshly grated pepper to taste

Heat the butter or cooking oil in a large skillet. Add the bread and stir-fry until the bread begins to brown (2 to 3 minutes), then add the scallions and garlic. Beat the eggs until lemon colored. Combine with the yogurt and the chopped herbs. Pour this over the bread and onion mixture and let stand for about 1 minute. Take a sharp spatula and quickly chop and stir the mixture until all of the egg is set and the *Dummes* is broken up into tablespoon-size pieces. Season and serve immediately.

BLACK MUSH
(SCHWATZE BREI)

In colonial times Black Mush was viewed as a poverty food, a winter emergency dish when stores of meat were gone. That attitude has long since disappeared now that wild rice has become a luxury.

YIELD: 6 TO 8 SERVINGS

1 cup (175 g) uncooked wild rice
1½ cups (210 g) roasted yellow cornmeal
¾ cup (125 g) organic buckwheat flour
2 teaspoons sea salt
2½ quarts (2.5 liters) Spelt Stock (p. 81) or water
6 tablespoons (90 ml) canola oil
2 teaspoons ground fennel seed
1½ teaspoons cayenne pepper or hot chili powder
8 ounces (250 g) shredded Amish farmer's cheese or
  Gruyère
thin slices of Amish farmer's cheese or Gruyère

Put the uncooked wild rice in a blender or food processor and process until the grains are broken up into small grits. Combine this with the cornmeal and buckwheat flour. Dissolve the salt in 6 cups (1.5 liters) of spelt stock and bring to a hard boil in a heavy saucepan. Add the canola oil and reduce the heat to a gentle boil.

Combine 2½ cups (600 ml) cold spelt stock with the flour mixture to form a smooth batter. Pour this gradually into the boiling stock, whisking at intervals to avoid lumps. Reduce the heat to a low simmer and cook the mush for about 10 minutes, stirring often to keep it from sticking to the bottom. Heat the remaining 1½ cups (360 ml) spelt stock and add this to the mixture. Cook and stir until the mush is thick and porridge-like (about 20 minutes), then add the ground fennel and cayenne pepper.

Stir the shredded cheese into the mush until completely melted. Stir continuously until the mush attains a thick, creamy consistency, then serve hot with a garnish of sliced cheese.

PARCHED FLOUR
(GEBRANNTES MEHL)

Parching can be done to any type of flour. Parched flours will turn rancid if stored too long, especially in hot weather.

YIELD: ¹/₂ CUP

½ cup (60 g) spelt flour or all-purpose flour

Place a 12-inch (30-cm) iron skillet over high heat until it begins to smoke. Add the flour, spreading it evenly on the bottom of the pan. Stir constantly with a wooden spoon or spatula until the flour turns a dark brown color (at most, 10 minutes). The flour will smoke as it parches and ball into small lumps. Break these up with the back of the stirring spoon. The degree of darkness is a matter of personal taste. The darker the flour, the more intense the nutty flavor.

When the flour has reached the desired brownness, pour into a wooden bowl to cool. When cool, store in an airtight container.

WHITE CASSOULET
(SCHWEIZER RITSCHER)

The cheese originally used in this recipe was called ball cheese (Ballekees) and was hung in bags and aged in the attic. It had a small, soft interior and a thick, hard, yellow rind. Since this cheese is no longer made, I have substituted pecorino romano, which is similar in saltiness and sharp taste.

YIELD: 6 TO 8 SERVINGS

2 cups (450 g) dried white beans
2½ cups (500 g) pearl barley
1 cup (100 g) chopped leek, white part only
2 cups (200 g) chopped leftover roasted pork or veal
3½ cups (875 ml) Basic Pork Stock (p. 68) or Basic Veal Stock (p. 69)
2 cups (500 ml) whole milk or heavy cream
1 cup (250 ml) dry white wine
1 cup (75 g) grated pecorino romano cheese
sea salt and freshly grated pepper to taste
6 tablespoons (20 g) minced fresh chervil
2 tablespoons (5 g) minced fresh chives

Cook the beans in 1 quart (1 liter) of salted water for 25 minutes or until tender. Drain and discard the water.

Preheat the oven to 350°F (175°C). Mix the cooked beans, uncooked barley, leek, and pork in a covered casserole or baking dish. Add the pork stock, cover, and bake 1 hour. Remove from the oven and stir the ingredients. Add the milk, wine, and cheese, and mix until the cheese is completely melted. Cover and return to the oven for another 25 minutes. Adjust seasonings and stir in the chervil. Serve garnished with chives.

WHITE MUSH OR SWISS POLENTA
(WEISSEBREI ODDER SCHWEIZER BREI)

YIELD: 6 TO 8 SERVINGS

2 cups (400 g) pearl barley
1 ½ quarts (1.5 liters) milk, scalded
½ cup (125 ml) sunflower oil or clarified butter
6 tablespoons (35 g) grated sapsago cheese
2 ½ teaspoons sea salt
⅔ cup (25 g) minced fresh dill

Put the barley in a food processor or blender and process until the groats are broken down into small pieces. Bring to a boil 5 cups (1.25 liters) of milk in a large heavy saucepan and add the barley grits, including any powder that formed during processing. Reduce the heat, cover, and simmer for 30 minutes over low heat or until the barley is tender. Then add the remaining cup (250 ml) of hot milk, the sunflower oil or drawn butter, the cheese, and the salt. Cover and simmer an additional 15 minutes or until thick. Stir occasionally so that the mush does not stick to the bottom. Right before serving, add the dill. Serve hot as a one-pot breakfast dish or as a dinner side dish like mashed potatoes.

Alternate Serving Hint: The cooked mush can be poured hot into a greased bread pan and allowed to cool and set. Once it is set, turn it out on a clean work surface and cut into slices. Dip the slices in cornmeal or cracker crumbs and fry in peanut oil or Garlic Oil (p. 128) in a heavy skillet until golden brown on both sides.

DRIED FRUIT AND DUMPLINGS
(SCHNITZ UN GNEPP)

Known throughout southwestern Germany, Alsace, and Switzerland by a variety of local names, this pleasant mixture of stewed dried fruit and dumplings has only one name among the Pennsylvania Dutch: Schnitz un Gnepp. It is one of those filling Sunday dinner dishes that from one pot feeds many.

YIELD: 4 TO 6 SERVINGS

2 2-pound (1-kg) meaty smoked ham hocks
3 quarts (3 liters) Basic Ham Stock (p. 66) or Basic Pork Stock (p. 68)
2 cups (500 ml) apple wine
2 cups (150 g) dried sweet apples (apple Schnitz)
10 (150 g) dried pear halves, cores and seeds removed
½ cup (75 g) coarsely chopped prunes
1 recipe Limburger Dumplings (recipe follows)

Cover the ham hocks in a deep saucepan with ham or pork stock and apple wine. Simmer 1 hour or until the liquid is reduced to 3 quarts (3 liters) and the meat is tender. Remove the hocks, trim off the fat, and pick the meat from the bones. Discard the bones and reserve 2 cups (300 g) of coarsely chopped meat.

Add the dried fruit and reserved meat to the meat stock, cover, and simmer 35 minutes or until the fruit is soft. Then add the cheese dumplings. Cover and simmer an additional 10 minutes. Serve immediately.

Schnitz un Gnepp in a redware bowl by Dorothy Long. On the pewter dish in front are Snippled Beans and Pickled Pearl Onions. Wild persimmons ornament the gridiron.

LIMBURGER DUMPLINGS
(LIMBARRIER GNEPP)

For this recipe use only authentic natural Limburger cheese, not processed Limburger spreads.

YIELD: 4 TO 6 PORTIONS

4 ounces (125 g) ripe Limburger cheese
2 tablespoons (30 ml) cream or whole milk
1 large egg
¾ teaspoon sea salt
⅔ cup (90 g) all-purpose flour

Chop the cheese into coarse crumbs, then put it into a food processor. Add the cream, egg, and salt. Purée until smooth, then add the flour and process to form a thick, sticky paste. Transfer the paste to a well-floured board or cookie sheet and pat it out until ½ inch (1 cm) thick. Slice into 1-inch (2-cm) strips. Cut off ½-inch (1-cm) pieces of dough and add them to the stewing *Schnitz un Gnepp*. Cook 10 minutes, then serve immediately.

PIGEON POTPIE
(DAUWWE BOTBOI)

"Wild pigeons – Immense flocks of these beautiful birds have been flying about this neighborhood for several days. Our sportsmen have not lacked in industry, and nearly everyone has by this time had a taste of Pigeon Pot-Pie," reported the Bucks County Intelligencer for March 29, 1830. Pigeon cookery, for which our region was famous in the eighteenth and nineteenth centuries, has now shifted to domestic squab. Though squab is not quite the same as wild passenger pigeon, every section of the Pennsylvania Dutch region still has its own local version of pigeon potpie. This hearty Shippensburg recipe is a good match for Pennsylvania pinot noir or chambourcin wine.

YIELD: 8 TO 12 SERVINGS

½ cup (100 g) dried black-eyed peas
½ cup (85 g) split green peas
2¼ cups (300 g) fresh green peas
1 recipe Saffron Noodles (p. 51, note)
3 squabs, cut into quarters, necks and giblets reserved
10 crushed juniper berries
1 cup (150 g) diced slab bacon
½ cup (65 g) chopped hearts of celery (yellow stems and leaves)
1½ cups (150 g) sliced leek
3 tablespoons (25 g) parched spelt flour (p. 31)
1½ teaspoons ground fennel seed
sea salt and freshly grated pepper to taste

Put the black-eyed peas in a bowl and cover with 1 cup (250 ml) boiling water. Cover and let stand 2 to 3 hours or until swollen. Drain off the excess liquid and put the peas in a saucepan with enough water to cover. Cook until tender (about 30 minutes). Drain the peas and, while still hot, combine with the split peas. Cover and let the steam from the black-eyed peas soften the split peas. When cool, combine this mixture with the fresh peas.

While the peas are cooking, prepare the saffron noodle dough. Roll out the dough as thin as possible or use a pasta machine with a lasagna attachment. The thinner the potpie noodles, the more tender they will be when cooked. Cut the dough into small squares or lozenge shapes. Set aside to dry while preparing the broth.

Put the reserved necks and giblets from the squabs in a small saucepan with 3 cups (750 ml) of water and 10 juniper berries. Let the broth simmer 30 minutes. Strain and reserve 2 cups (500 ml) of the broth. Coarsely chop the cooked livers and set aside.

While the broth is simmering, put the slab bacon in a large skillet and fry until it begins to brown. Add the quartered squabs and brown for 20 to 25 minutes or until cooked but not falling from the bone. Drain and reserve both the squab and the bits of fried bacon.

Preheat the oven to 350°F (175°C). Mix the celery and leek and spread half over the bottom of a deep baking dish or Dutch oven. Cover with the bits of reserved bacon, the reserved chopped livers, and half of the pea mixture. Make a layer of saffron noodles, then arrange the cooked squab on top. Cover the squab with the remaining celery and leek mixture and the rest of the peas.

Combine the reserved broth with 2 cups (500 ml) water, the parched spelt flour, and the ground fennel. Beat with a whisk so that the flour and fennel are completely blended and free of lumps, then pour over the squab. Cover tightly and bake for 1 hour. Adjust seasonings and serve.

VEAL AND OYSTER GUMBIS
(KALWEFLEESCH-UN-AUSCHTER GUMBIS)

YIELD: 6 TO 8 SERVINGS

⅓ cup (60 g) diced slab bacon
8 ounces (250 g) coarsely chopped cooked veal
1 turnip, peeled and diced (about 4 ounces/125 g)
4 ounces (125 g) coarsely chopped prunes
9 cups (765 g) finely shredded cabbage, resembling angel hair noodles
2 medium onions (250 g), sliced into rings
20 stewing oysters with ½ cup (125 ml) oyster liquid
2 hard-cooked large eggs, sliced
⅓ cup (25 g) minced fresh parsley
1 cup (250 ml) whole milk
freshly grated pepper
1 tablespoon minced fresh rosemary

Preheat the oven to 350°F (175°C). Lightly brown the bacon in a skillet over medium heat for about 4 minutes. Lift out with a slotted spoon and put the bacon in a large bowl with the veal, turnip, and prunes. Make a layer with half of the cabbage in the bottom of a deep 8-quart (8-liter) baking dish, and scatter the onions on top. Spread the veal mixture on top of the onions. Then make a layer of oysters and sliced eggs. Cover with the remaining cabbage. Scatter the parsley over the top, add the milk and the liquid from the oysters, and season with pepper. Cover and bake 45 minutes. Stir the contents and serve immediately with a garnish of minced rosemary.

Turnip Casserole with pickled eggs.

TURNIP CASSEROLE
(RIEWE SCHALES)

There are a number of tasty turnip Schales recipes in circulation among the Amish of eastern Ohio and Lawrence County, Pennsylvania, which abuts the Ohio border. This recipe comes from Lawrence County.

YIELD: 6 TO 8 SERVINGS

fine breadcrumbs
1½ cups (230 g) grated raw turnip
1½ cups (260 g) grated raw potato
¾ cup (45 g) chopped scallion
2 tablespoons (5 g) minced fresh parsley
¼ cup (60 g) unsalted butter, melted
1 cup (250 ml) whole milk
½ cup (125 ml) sour cream
1 teaspoon sea salt
½ teaspoon freshly grated pepper
½ cup (70 g) sifted fine *Semmede* (p. 52) or ½ cup
   (60 g) fried breadcrumbs

Lightly grease a 9-inch (23-cm) shallow casserole or gratin dish and dust it with fine breadcrumbs. Preheat the oven to 375°F (190°C).

To prepare the vegetable batter, combine the grated turnip, potato, scallion, and parsley. Melt the butter and add it to the mixture. Combine the milk and sour cream with a whisk and fold into the vegetables. Taste and season with salt and pepper, then pour the filling into the baking dish. Pat the mixture down with a spatula or spoon so that it is smooth on top. Scatter sifted fine *Semmede* or fried breadcrumbs evenly over the top. Bake for 40 minutes. Serve immediately.

CAULIFLOWER AND SPELT CASSEROLE
(BLUMMEGRAUT SCHALES MIT DINKEL)

YIELD: 6 TO 8 SERVINGS

1 medium cauliflower (2 pounds/1 kg)
1 cup (175 g) spelt groats (whole berries)
¼ teaspoon ground saffron
½ cup (100 g) salt mackerel
½ cup (125 ml) whole milk
¼ cup (60 ml) sunflower or vegetable oil
1 cup (200 g) finely chopped onion
2 tablespoons (15 g) grated sapsago cheese
2 tablespoons (25 g) Dijon-style mustard
3 tablespoons (10 g) minced fresh parsley
½ cup (30 g) chopped scallion
¾ cup (100 g) pumpkin seed
2 tablespoons (15 g) breadcrumbs
2 tablespoons (30 g) unsalted butter

Wash and divide the cauliflower into florets. Chop the stem and place it in a deep saucepan with 1 quart (1 liter) boiling water. Put the florets in a vegetable steamer and set this inside the saucepan. Cover and steam over medium heat for 15 minutes. Drain and reserve the florets, cooking liquid, and chopped stems in separate containers.

Bring 1 cup (250 ml) of the reserved cooking liquid to a boil in a medium-sized saucepan. Rinse the spelt and put it in the boiling liquid with the saffron. Cover and boil 2 minutes. Remove from the heat and set aside to cool. When the cauliflower, cooking liquid, and spelt are cool, refrigerate overnight. Chop the salt mackerel, cover with the milk, and refrigerate overnight.

The next day, add 1 cup (250 ml) of the reserved cooking liquid to the spelt. Cover and simmer over medium heat for 50 minutes. Do not remove the lid or stir the spelt. At the end of 50 minutes, uncover and cook off any remaining liquid. Remove from the heat and set aside.

Preheat the oven to 375°F (190°C). Drain and rinse the mackerel. Chop into very fine bits or, if preferred, to a paste consistency. Sauté the mackerel in the sunflower oil for 3 minutes, then add the chopped onion. Cook until the onion is soft (about 4 minutes). Purée the reserved cauliflower stems with 1 cup (250 ml) of the reserved cooking liquid and add this to the chopped onion mixture. Combine the onion and the reserved cooked spelt. Add the sapsago cheese, mustard, parsley, scallion, and pumpkin seed. Spread this mixture evenly in a greased casserole dish. Scatter breadcrumbs over the top and dot with butter. Bake for 45 minutes. Serve immediately.

BREADCRUMB SCHAUMKUCHE
(GRIMMELE SCHAUMKUCHE)

This perfect hot-weather dish comes from the Bottner family of Petrolia in western Pennsylvania.

YIELD: 4 SERVINGS

3 large egg yolks
1 cup (100 g) fine breadcrumbs or *Mutschelmehl*
½ teaspoon sea salt
¼ teaspoon dried marjoram or ½ teaspoon minced fresh marjoram
1 teaspoon caraway seed, bruised with the back of the spoon
1 tablespoon (15 g) unsalted butter
5 large egg whites

Beat the yolks until lemon colored, then combine with the crumbs, salt, marjoram, and caraway. Using a pastry cutter, work the egg mixture to a uniform crumb texture. Heat the butter in a skillet or, better, a crepe pan. Beat the egg white with a whisk until stiff peaks form and fold the crumb mixture into it. Pour this into the skillet and cook over medium heat. When one side is golden brown, turn it over to brown the other side. Serve immediately with freshly made Green Apple Pap (recipe follows).

GREEN APPLE PAP
(GRIENE EBBELBREI)

Pap *is an old-fashioned word for any food that is soft and purée-like. In this case the pap is served as a relish with poultry, such as cold fried chicken, or as a sauce.*

YIELD: 4 TO 6 SERVINGS

14 ounces (440 g) unripe green apples, peeled and cored (see note)
⅔ cup (160 ml) dry white wine
3 tablespoons (45 ml) extra-virgin olive oil
½ teaspoon ground mace
½ cup (100 g) sugar
grated zest of 1 lime
¼ teaspoon cayenne pepper

Put the apples, wine, olive oil, mace, sugar, lime zest, and cayenne in a food processor and purée to a smooth, creamy consistency. Serve immediately

Note: Unripe Summer Rambos, Yellow Transparents, and Gravensteins are excellent choices for this recipe.

ROASTED CORNMEAL AND RYE BRAN SCHAUMKUCHE
(SCHAUMKUCHE FUN WELSCHKARN UN KARNKLEE)

This recipe comes from the Viger family of Clarendon, Pennsylvania, who serve it as an accompaniment to roast pork.

YIELD: 6 TO 8 SERVINGS

1 cup (125 g) roasted yellow cornmeal
1 cup (100 g) rye bran (wheat bran may be substituted)
2 teaspoons sea salt
2 teaspoons ground fennel seed
1 teaspoon ground cumin

4 large eggs, separated
¼ cup (60 g) unsalted butter, melted
2 cups (500 ml) whole milk
Browned Onions (recipe follows)
sea salt and freshly grated pepper to taste

Preheat the oven to 350°F (175°C). Combine the cornmeal, rye bran, salt, fennel, and cumin with a whisk in a bowl. Beat the egg yolks until lemon colored, then add the melted butter and milk and continue beating until thoroughly combined. Add the dry ingredients to form a thick batter. Beat the egg whites until they form stiff peaks, then gently fold them into the batter mixture. Do not overfold or the batter will deflate.

Pour the batter into a greased baking dish and bake for 45 minutes. When the *Schaumkuche* is set, remove from the oven and tear into large pieces with two forks. Let the steam escape, then serve on hot plates with Browned Onions. White wine may be served as a beverage.

BROWNED ONIONS
(ZWIWWELBRIEH)

YIELD: 6 TO 8 SERVINGS

4 medium onions (1 pound/500 g), sliced or chopped
3 tablespoons (45 ml) sunflower or vegetable oil
2 tablespoons (25 g) brown sugar
2 tablespoons (15 g) spelt flour or whole-wheat flour
1 cup (250 ml) Basic Beef Stock (p. 66) or more to taste
2 tablespoons (25 g) Dijon-style mustard

In a large skillet, sauté the onions in the sunflower oil until they begin to turn brown. Add the sugar. Cook 1 minute, then add the flour and continue sautéing until the onions become thick and dark colored (about 3 minutes). Thin with the beef stock, then add the mustard. Serve hot over fresh baked *Schaumkuche.*

Anna Moyer's Apple Slump
(Der Anni Moyer ihr Ebbelschlupper)

Yield: 6 to 8 servings

Slump Crust (Schlupperdeeg)

¾ cup (90 g) all-purpose flour
¼ cup (30 g) spelt flour or whole-wheat flour
1 teaspoon baking powder
¼ teaspoon sea salt
1 large egg
½ cup (125 ml) whole milk
1 tablespoon (15 g) unsalted butter, melted

Preheat the oven to 375°F (190°C).

Sift together the all-purpose flour, spelt flour, baking powder, and salt in a large bowl. Make a well in the center of the flour mixture. In a separate bowl, beat the egg until lemon colored, then mix in the milk and butter. Pour into the well in the flour and work into a dough with the consistency of biscuit dough.

Dust a clean work surface liberally with spelt flour. Roll out the dough to form a lid for a casserole dish measuring 8 by 12 inches (20 by 30 cm) and about 6 inches (15 cm) deep. Let the dough rest while preparing the apples.

Apple Filling (Ebbelg'fillsel)

6 cups (750 g) pared and sliced tart apples
1 tablespoon grated fresh ginger root
1 tablespoon minced fresh rosemary
1 cup (200 g) sugar
½ teaspoon sea salt

Grease the interior of a casserole dish. Mix the apples, ginger, and rosemary and spread evenly in the casserole. Dissolve the sugar and salt in ¼ cup (60 ml) water. Bring to boil and cook hard for 2 to 3 minutes to create a thick syrup. Pour over the fruit, then cover with the slump crust. Make 3 slashes at 3-inch (7.5-cm) intervals to create vents for steam, then bake 35 to 40 minutes or until the crust turns to golden brown. Serve hot or cold.

Potato Pattycakes
(Grumbiere Batsche)

Among the Pennsylvania Germans this popular dish has two names: Batsche and Offekuche (stove cakes). The latter name comes from the fact that the pattycakes were often prepared on the hot surface of a five- or ten-plate stove.

The oldest of our Batsche recipes originate from Westphalia along the border of northwestern Germany and Holland. Today Batsche continue to be popular as a snack food and as a dinner side dish, particularly with ham and stewed fruit. Batsche on Good Friday are almost a ritual.

Yield: About 18 cakes, or 4 to 6 servings

2 cups (400 g) coarsely shredded raw potato
3 cups (400 g) coarsely shredded raw turnip
1 cup (100 g) thinly slivered raw carrot, resembling toothpicks
3 large eggs
¼ cup (30 g) spelt flour or whole-wheat flour
sea salt and freshly grated pepper to taste
peanut oil

Mix the potato, turnip, and carrot. In a separate bowl, beat the eggs, then gradually beat in the spelt flour. Combine the potato and egg mixtures. Add salt and pepper to taste.

Heat a griddle or skillet and grease liberally with peanut oil. When the oil begins to smoke, drop heaping tablespoonfuls of the potato mixture onto the griddle, press flat with the back of a spoon, and fry until golden brown. Turn and brown on the other side. Continue until all the potato mixture is used.

Serve the *Batsche* as soon as they are made, or lay them on a cookie sheet and keep warm in an oven preheated to 300°F (150°C). Minced fresh rosemary is very good as a garnish.

BAKED SHAD WITH CABBAGE AND TOMATOES
(G'BACKENER MOIFISCH MIT GRAUT UN TOMATTS)

This delightful shad dish comes from Dauphin County. The recipe belonged to Mrs. Carl Adam, who lived in Harrisburg at the turn of this century. Since Mrs. Adam's recipe makes quite a fulsome dinner, this may be treated as a one-pot meal.

YIELD: 4 TO 6 SERVINGS

3 tablespoons (45 g) unsalted butter
1 cup (100 g) plain breadcrumbs
1½ tablespoons minced fresh parsley
2 tablespoons (5 g) minced fresh chives
1 teaspoon minced fresh winter savory or ½ teaspoon dried savory
1 3- to 4-pound (1.5- to 2-kg) buck shad, gutted and cleaned but with head and tail left on
6 cups (550 g) finely shredded cabbage, resembling angel hair noodles
1 cup (65 g) shredded sorrel
1 cup (250 g) chopped onion
1 cup (150 g) peeled, seeded, and chopped fresh tomatoes
⅔ cup (160 ml) dry white wine
4 slices country smoked slab bacon

Preheat the oven to 350°F (175°C). Melt the butter in a skillet and fry the breadcrumbs until straw colored, stirring constantly to prevent scorching (3 to 4 minutes). Add the parsley, chives, and savory, and remove from the heat.

Open the shad and cut the cavity from the head toward the tail with a sharp knife so that the fish opens out flat when lying on its back. To accomplish this, press down with the point of the knife under the neck and follow the backbone so that all the "rib" bones are cut at their bases. Fill the cavity with the browned breadcrumb mixture, then sew it up with trussing thread.

Poach the cabbage in salted water for 3 to 4 minutes to tenderize it, then drain and combine with the sorrel, onion, and tomatoes. Cover the bottom of a shallow roasting pan with the cabbage mixture, then lay the stuffed shad on top of it. Pour the wine on top, then drape the bacon slices diagonally at even intervals over the fish. Bake for approximately 40 minutes, depending on the size of the fish. Baste from time to time with liquid from the pan. When the fish tests done, serve immediately.

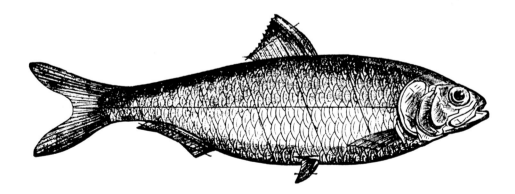

Opposite: Ball cheese filled with dry curds (foreground); pot cheese in earthenware cups; Amish farmer's cheese, a domestic version of Gruyère; and sapsago, a green cone-shaped grating cheese flavored with melilot.

CUP CHEESE
(ZIEGERKEES)

The first requirement for this recipe is raw milk from certified animals. For readers unable to obtain high-quality raw milk or who are reluctant to use it, please refer to my Shortcut Method following this recipe.

The Grube family of Lancaster County, from whom this recipe comes, originally prepared their cheese in stoneware crocks. In calculating the amount of cheese needed, keep this rule of thumb in mind: 1 gallon (4 liters) of raw whole milk will yield approximately 1 pound (500 g) of fresh curd. The Grube method does not use rennet, which is a plus for those who are strict about vegetarian concerns.

YIELD: 6 DEEP CUSTARD CUPS, 3 INCHES (7.5 CM) IN DIAMETER BY 2 1/2 INCHES (6 CM) DEEP, OR 18 TO 24 SERVINGS

1 gallon (4 liters) certified raw whole milk
3 cups (750 ml) certified raw goat milk
1 gallon (4 liters) scalding-hot water
¼ cup (60 ml) high-acid vinegar (optional)
2½ teaspoons sea salt
1 cup (250 ml) heavy cream
6 tablespoons (90 g) unsalted butter, room temperature
½ teaspoon baking soda
3 large eggs
½ cup (40 g) minced fresh chives or chervil
2 teaspoons ground sage
caraway seed

Mix the whole milk and goat milk and place in a sterilized glass container. Cover and set in the refrigerator for 5 to 10 days or until it begins to sour and form clabber. Clabber has a junket-like consistency and the flavor of natural yogurt.

Pour the clabbered milk mixture into a clean stainless-steel 3-gallon (12-liter) pan and bring to a boil over high heat. As the milk begins to heat, pour scalding water around the inside edge of the pan. If curds do not form and pull away from the sides of the pan, scatter vinegar over the center of the hot clabber, only enough to make it separate and form curds. Once the curdling process begins, the clabber will separate into curds and whey very quickly. Use as little vinegar as possible, no more than ¼ cup (60 ml).

Once the curds form, they will draw together in a cake toward the center of the pan, leaving the yellowish whey around the edges. Skim off the curds with a fine strainer and put them in a colander lined with clean cheesecloth. Discard the whey. Pull the cheesecloth up to shape the curds into a tight ball. Let this drain at room temperature in the colander overnight.

The next day, work the salt into the curds to form a spongy crumb. Pack this into a sterilized wide-mouthed container, cover, and age 3 to 5 days in the refrigerator or until the curd turns yellow and smells strongly of cheese. The longer the curd is ripened, the sharper the cheese.

Put the ripened curd in a double boiler with the cream, butter, and baking soda, and warm gradually over medium heat. Once the cheese has melted and is thoroughly combined with the other ingredients, beat the eggs until lemon colored and fold them in. Cook about 15 minutes or until thick, then fold in the chives or chervil and the sage. Pour into glass or glazed earthenware custard cups. Scatter caraway seed on top as a garnish, then set in the refrigerator to cool.

Once the cheese has set, it is ready to use. It will keep under refrigeration for as long as 2 weeks. Serve as a spread on bread or crackers.

Shortcut Method

This will make a cheese similar in taste and character to the preparation described in the preceding recipe. Eliminate the raw milk, scalding water, and vinegar and substitute the following:

1¼ pounds (625 g) small-curd cottage cheese

8 ounces (250 g) goat cheese

4 ounces (125 g) Limburger cheese

Put the cheeses into a food processor with the cream, butter, and soda, and process until smooth. Put this in a double boiler as directed above for the ripened curd and warm it gradually over medium heat. Once the mixture has melted, add the beaten eggs and cook about 15 minutes or until thick. Fold in the herbs and pour the mixture into custard cups. Scatter caraway seed on top and set in the refrigerator to cool.

Above: Oxen plowing, from an eighteenth-century woodcut.
Overleaf: Ingredients and basic stocks for soup cookery.

SOUP AND NOODLE COOKERY

Enter the impish *Bucklich Mennli,* "Little Humped-Back Man," the eternal bane of the Pennsylvania Dutch kitchen, the designing elf who inhabits each and every Pennsylvania Dutch household. He is responsible for such mishaps as scorched toast, overturned wastepaper baskets, dumplings that fall apart, dripping faucets, chipped canning jars, and a host of other irritations, including his favorite: throwing ashes into soup.

The precautions that the Pennsylvania Dutch housewife undertook in order to create a perfect soup cannot be underestimated. Soup cookery was the centerpiece of her art, just as a hearth at worktable height was the centerpiece of the old Pennsylvania Dutch kitchen. In fact, the history of our soup cookery and the raised hearth go hand in hand.

5 Feuerzange 6 Dreyfus 7 Caster ol. 8 Hackemesser
9 Reibeisen 10 Pfanne 11 Rost 12 Schaumlöffel 13 Fleisch-
gabel 14 Bratspies 15 Mörsel 16 Tiegel.   Schwarz Sc.
N° 32.

*Above: Copper engraving from a popular 1788 Pennsylvania German
school book showing a soup hearth (7), a* Rutscher *(10), and a* Gumbis
pot *or* Tiegel *(16).*
Opposite: Cookpot or Breihaffe *(1865–1880) by Willoughby Smith,
Womelsdorf, Pennsylvania.*

The Pennsylvania German house was organized around a specific arrangement of rooms in the seventeenth and eighteenth centuries, as plans in German architecture books of the period reveal.[1] Houses were built to face south or east to take advantage of the sun. The front door opened directly into the kitchen, or the *Kich* in Pennsylfaanisch. To the left of the *Kich* stood the stove room, or what we call a *Schtupp*.

The stove room was heated by a stove of cast iron, tile, or brick that was fed hot coals through the back of the fireplace wall in the kitchen. The Pennsylvania German family took its meals in the stove room, not the kitchen. Cooking was done both on the raised hearth and on the stove in the *Schtupp*. A restored hearth and stove are in place at the 1719 Hans Herr House in Lancaster County, which is maintained by the Lancaster Mennonite Historical Society and open to the public. The raised hearth at the Herr House (see p. 135) appears as it would have while in use during the eighteenth century.

The raised hearth traces back to classical antiquity, but there is disagreement among German architectural historians about whether this hearth left the Rhine Valley at the close of the Roman Empire or whether it simply receded into small cultural pockets where Celto-Latin languages continued to be spoken down into the late Middle Ages. One of these areas included a large section of Bavaria; another included eastern Switzerland. Whatever the case, the raised hearth regained its central place in southern German cookery toward the end of the 1500s, determining not only the type and shape of cooking equipment but also the type of dishes prepared on it.

The raised hearth was popular because it eliminated stooping, it required less fuel and was therefore more energy efficient than down-hearth fireplaces, and it stayed warm long after the fires died down, allowing cooks to create dishes that were slow cooking. While dinner was simmering, the housewife was freed to devote her attention to other chores. Thus, hearth technology promoted the development of soups and stews.

The raised hearth was often called the *Suppehaerd* (soup hearth) in Pennsylfaanisch, particularly when special compartments were cut into it for kettles and pots. The engraving on the left shows a German raised hearth with all of its equipment, including the hole in the top where a stewpot would go. Stewpots set into the raised hearth were used primarily to cook down bones to create stocks and broths, which became the basis for soups and sauces, as well as components in dishes like *Gumbis* and potpie.

One of the most important adjuncts to the evolution of raised-hearth cookery was the development of foods that served as extenders for stocks and broths. Liquids salvaged from boiling vegetables, for example, could be added to the stockpot and reduced with bones to form a rich broth. To give the broth interest or to create a meal out of it, various preparations of flour were used. We call them *Deegwarrick* in Pennsylfaanisch, from the German word *Teigwerk*. Literally, both terms mean "things created out of flour." It is the essence of frugal cuisine.

In the previous chapter I mentioned parched flour as a substitute for flours fried in oil or fat. Throughout middle Europe fried flour (roux) still forms one of the cornerstones of peasant cookery. In America it is a feature of both Pennsylvania Dutch and Cajun cooking, and many soups in both cultures are based on the flavor of different types of roux, from pale golden yellow to nearly black.

In my recipe for Oat Flour Soup (p. 58), I have chosen to move back in time to a roux cookery that existed before it became associated with French haute cuisine, to a vegetarian fasting dish of great age, as preserved by Marcus Rumpolt in his 1581 classic German cookbook, *Ein New Kochbuch*.[2] Rumpolt's Oat Flour Soup not only is a medieval prototype for later roux soups made with wheat flour but is also a model for various later potato soups, including vichyssoise. Unlike its potato descendants, however, Oat Flour Soup has an almost silken texture.

In terms of texture, the next grade of soup extender above roux is *Semmede* ("ZEH-meh-dah"), which comes in two forms: fine and coarse. During the late 1300s, buckwheat *Semmede* became a common peasant food in the Rhineland.[3] It is still made in some parts of Germany and in Pennsylvania. The technique for making it is unique and belongs to an old family of European peasant dishes made by simultaneously stirring, chopping, and frying in a skillet. A stiff lump made of buckwheat flour and water is chopped and stirred into dry buckwheat flour in a scorching-hot skillet. The parched flour is then gradually incorporated into the dough to form coarse, crispy crumbs.

The Pennsylvania folk term for this cooking technique is the verb *gribble*, which is also used as a noun. Thus, when a cook "gribbles" buckwheat dough, she produces *Semmede*. She does this with a tool called a gribble iron, a combination spatula-and-fork with special flattish tines, designed specifically for stirring gribble to keep it loose.

The Pennsylvania Dutch treat *Semmede* either as a quick meal (like a breakfast cereal) or as a component of other dishes, for example, sifted over casseroles as a topping. It can also be used in stuffings in place of chopped nuts.

Sadie Kriebel, an elderly Schwenkfelder from Montgomery County, still remembers *Semmede* as a traditional family breakfast dish served like kasha with milk and brown sugar.[4] For the uninitiated, the best way to visualize *Semmede* is to

Gribbling set, including spatula and specialized fork.

Spätzle are created by chopping dough into little dumplings rather than by grating or rubbing. *Spätzle* are common in Pennsylvania Dutch cookery, but we call them *Oiergnepplin* (plural form of *Oiergnepp*), meaning "little egg dumplings." In the Pennsylfaanisch of Ohio, they are called *Schpetzel*.

Out of the *Oiergnepp-Riwwel* tradition evolved a number of larger, similarly shaped forms of pasta, among them *Schupf* or *Schupfnudle*, which may be equated roughly with French *quenelles*. In Pennsylfaanisch, *Schupf* dumplings are humorously referred to as *Buwweschpitzle* (boys' bits) and are made almost exclusively for such festive occasions as Christmas dinner, weddings, and family reunions.

In Pennsylfaanisch, round dumplings of any size are called *Gnepp* (pronounced "NEPP"), from the German *Knöpfe*, meaning "buttons," and buttons are what the dumplings should resemble. The large meat or marrow dumplings, sometimes the size of cannon balls, that are still popular in Bavaria and Austria were never common among the Pennsylvania Dutch. We seem to favor small dumplings, perhaps because they are more practical as dish extenders.

As a more substantial extender, we have noodles in a great variety of shapes. The *Nudelholz*, a rolling pin with sharp ridges, cuts dough into strips of various widths, some

think of the commercial breakfast cereal called Grape-Nuts, although *Semmede* is not quite as hard and granular.

For a coarser texture, rivels, or *Riwwele* in Pennsylfaanisch, are little dumplings (or large crumbs) produced by rubbing or grating dough against the small holes of a colander, wire screen, or vegetable grater. The root idea comes from the German word *reiben*, "to rub or grate." The dough for both *Riwwele* and a larger dumpling called *Spätzle* originated as refined substitutes for whole-grain dishes and were therefore classified as luxury foods during the early Middle Ages.

Rivels are sometimes boiled, then fried until crisp. When they are added hot to soup, the hissing and popping sound provides an obvious explanation of why they are called poprobins in English. Poprobins can also be made by deep-frying cooked whole-grain spelt.

*Noodle rolling pin (*Nudelholz*) and potpie cutter (*Nudelreedel*), both dating from circa 1810–1825.*

resembling linguine, others in the shape of wide ribbons. The dough can also be cut into squares for potpies or into rounds that are filled and folded over to make *Mauldasche*, our form of ravioli.

Buwweschenkel (boys' thighs) are stuffed long noodles bent into the shape of boomerangs and pinched at the ends "to look like the knobs of a bone," according to Katie Hoffman Slonaker (1903–1983), who used to make them that way at her Sassamansville home. One of Katie's *Buwweschenkel* made with spelt dough is shown beside a bowl of spelt soup on page 57.

Buwweschenkel are now prepared in a variety of shapes in local restaurants, but Katie's is the oldest shape and the one that resembles the *Buwweschenkel* breads that are made for All Saints' Eve in Hessia even to this day.[5] That connection suggests an older, perhaps pre-Christian meaning to all forms of *Buwweschenkel*.

As Malinda Stoltzfus and her daughter Miriam Beiler pointed out while making noodles (p. 51), there are corollary recipes that always accompany noodle-making. The average batch for them consumes twelve egg yolks (three times the yield of my recipe). Because they *never* waste egg whites, the whites left over from noodles are used to make angel food cakes. Annie Wampole's Cornstarch Cake (p. 89) was probably invented for this very reason. Consider making it the same day noodles are planned.

Harvest fields in York County.

"BOYS' BITS" STUNCH
(BUWWESCHPITZLE DUMMES)

The recipe on which this is based appeared in a 1918 Reading almanac and produced enough dumplings for 30 people. Such large quantities were popular for Sunday dinners, church suppers, and similar gatherings. The morels, however, were suggested to me by some Perry County friends who serve a fresh morel Dummes at their annual morel picnic early each May. The picnic is one of those informal, front-porch affairs that assume the dimension of a feast as friends and neighbors return from morel harvesting in the hills. Poke, wild asparagus, and shad also figure in their menu, and hearty red wines are a must.

YIELD: 4 TO 6 SERVINGS

5 dried small morels (enough to fill ½ cup/125 ml)
1 cup (250 ml) boiling water
⅓ cup (60 g) diced lean slab bacon
½ recipe *Buwweschpitzle* (p. 173)
½ cup (50 g) chopped leek
2 tablespoons (25 g) chopped prunes
4 large eggs
1½ tablespoons minced fresh parsley
1½ tablespoons minced fresh marjoram
sea salt and freshly grated pepper to taste

Put the morels in a heatproof jar. Add the boiling water, cover, let stand overnight. The next day, remove the morels and set aside to drain. Strain the morel water through a fine sieve and reserved for use in soups or freeze and use as an alternative to meat stock.

Follow the directions for making *Buwweschpitzle*. Boil the dumplings, then drain and reserve. Heat the bacon in a skillet and fry until it begins to brown. Add the dumplings and sauté until they turn a golden color. Then chop the reserved morels into small pieces and add to the dumpling mixture along with the leek and prunes. Beat the eggs until lemon colored and combine with the fresh herbs. Pour this over the sautéed dumpling mixture and cook until the eggs set. When golden brown on the bottom, turn the *Stunch* over to brown the top. Chop into large irregular pieces, season with salt and pepper, and serve immediately.

COTTAGE CHEESE SPÄTZLE
(SCHMIERKEES OIERGNEPPLIN)

In 1906, Cooking Club Magazine featured a midwestern Pennsylvania Dutch lunch menu with cottage cheese Spätzle, a side dish once quite popular in the Pennsylvania German counties of central and southern Ohio.[6]

YIELD: 4 TO 6 SERVINGS

1 cup (250 g) cottage cheese
1 large egg
1¼ cups (155 g) all-purpose flour
1 teaspoon salt or 1 tablespoon grated Parmesan cheese

Put the cottage cheese, the egg, 1 cup (125 g) of the flour, and the salt in a food processor and pulse intermittently until a smooth paste forms. Scatter the remaining ¼ cup (30 g) flour over the surface of a small cutting board and spread the paste on this until about ¼ inch (½ cm) thick. Bring a large pot of salted water to a hard boil, then reduce to a gentle simmer. Taking a sharp knife or spatula, chop off small bits of dough and drop them into the water. Cook 10 minutes or until they float. Skim off with a slotted spoon and serve with breadcrumbs fried in butter or sunflower oil.

Opposite: Malinda Stoltzfus and Miriam Beiler preparing egg noodles.

Egg Pasta
(NUDELDEEG)

YIELD: 4 TO 6 SERVINGS

1 tablespoon plus 1 teaspoon (20 g) cold unsalted butter
1½ cups (185 g) all-purpose flour
⅛ teaspoon sea salt
2 large eggs
2 large egg yolks

Cut the butter into the flour and salt to form fine crumbs. Beat the eggs and egg yolks together until lemon colored. Make a well in the center of the crumb mixture and add the eggs. Work together until a dough forms. Roll out the dough as thin as possible or run it through a pasta maker, then drape it over a clothesline, the back of a wooden chair, or some other clean, sturdy prop.

Let the dough dry for 15 to 20 minutes, then cut it into strips for noodles, squares for potpie noodles, or circles for pocket dumplings. For cooking instructions, refer to specific noodle recipes. In general, the dough is ready when it is *al dente* (3 to 4 minutes) after cooking in gently boiling salted water.

Note: To make Saffron Noodles *(Safferich Nudle)*, add ¼ teaspoon of ground saffron to the beaten eggs before combining with the flour. Be certain the saffron is very dry and brittle before grinding or there will be flecks of yellow in the dough. The easiest way to grind saffron is to work it to a powder with a mortar and pestle.

GRIBBLE, OR STIR-FRIED BUCKWHEAT CRUMBS
(SEMMEDE)

YIELD: 2 CUPS (275 G) FRIED CRUMBS OR 2 TO 4 SERVINGS

1½ cups (210 g) organic buckwheat flour
½ teaspoon sea salt
approximately 3 tablespoons (45 g) cooking fat or oil
   (see note)

Sift ¾ cup (105 g) of the buckwheat flour and the salt into a deep mixing bowl. Add 1½ cups (375 ml) boiling water and stir until thick. Place an ungreased large skillet over medium-high heat. When the pan is hot, add the remaining ¾ cup (105 g) buckwheat flour and let it begin to scorch. Put the thickened buckwheat flour on top and, using a spatula, stir and chop until all of the buckwheat batter is worked into the flour and small crumbs have formed (about 30 minutes). Keep the crumbs loose and constantly moving so that they do not burn. *Semmede* should consist of crumbs of nearly uniform size, so pour the crumbs into a sieve and separate into two textures: fine and coarse. The fine texture should resemble celery seeds.

Once separated, the *Semmede* can be cooled and stored in jars or even frozen for later use.

To prepare *Semmede* for serving, put a skillet over high heat. For each 1½ cups (210 g) of prepared crumbs, melt 1 tablespoon (15 g) of butter with 1 tablespoon (15 g) of lard; or melt 2 tablespoons (30 g) of bacon drippings; or use 2 tablespoons (30 ml) peanut oil. Stir to coat the crumbs evenly, then stir and fry until brown and crispy.

Serve in bowls with hot milk, meat stock, or clear soup. The cold fried crumbs may also be served with sour milk and fruit as a hot-weather supper dish.

Note: Butter and bacon drippings impart particular flavors, but peanut oil gives just as crisp a texture. In fact, some cooks like the crumbs just as they are, without frying.

MEAT DUMPLINGS
(FLEESCHGNEPP)

This highly adaptable recipe was discovered in a collection of recipes assembled by Johannes Reisner of Hereford, Berks County, during the 1860s.[7] It will work with any type of cooked meat as long as the meat weighs exactly 4 ounces (125 g). Otherwise, the dumplings will fall apart.

YIELD: 14 MINI-DUMPLINGS, OR 4 TO 5 SERVINGS

4 ounces (125 g) cooked meat
1 teaspoon unsalted butter, melted
2 tablespoons (15 g) white breadcrumbs (*Mutschelmehl*)
1 large egg yolk

Put the meat in a food processor and chop until it forms a fine crumb. Pour the crumbs into a bowl and add the melted butter. Stir thoroughly, then work in the breadcrumbs. Add the egg yolk and mix until a stiff paste forms. Using the hands, break the paste into 14 equal pieces and roll into balls about the size and shape of a chestnut. Let them stand 30 minutes before cooking.

Bring a pot of salted water to a hard boil, then reduce the heat to a gentle simmer. Add the dumplings and let them cook 10 minutes or until they float. As soon as the dumplings float, they are ready to serve.

POPROBINS, OR RIVELS
(RIWWELE)

There are two distinctly different methods for making rivels, with two very different results.

The first method, which is probably the oldest — and by many German cooks considered the most correct — calls for rubbing the dough against a grater or colander with small holes to produce a form of pasta resembling rice.

The other type of rivel is made by rubbing flour and egg between the fingers to form little wormlike bits of dough, which are sometimes given further shaping, such as pressing to form "flakes." Perhaps because it is handled and thus more compressed than the other, this type of rivel tends to be tough and doughy, even though it has an avid following among many Dutch cooks. My recipe advocates the classic technique. It comes from my distant cousin, Liselotte Weber Paul, of Steinwenden in the Pfalz.

YIELD: 6 TO 8 SERVINGS

1¾ cups (215 g) unbleached all-purpose flour
⅛ teaspoon sea salt
2 large eggs
2 tablespoons (30 ml) effervescent mineral water or
    plain seltzer water
2 tablespoons (30 ml) sunflower or vegetable oil
8 cups (2 liters) meat stock

Sift the flour and salt into a large bowl. Make a well in the center. In a separate bowl, beat the eggs until lemon colored, then add the mineral water. Pour this into the well in the flour and stir to form a soft dough. Break off pieces of dough and dip them in flour. Then rub through the holes of a vegetable grater or colander. Spread the crumbs on a cookie sheet or cloth to dry (about 25 minutes).

Classic rivels (Riwwele) are made by rubbing dough through a sieve or colander.

Bring 8 cups (2 liters) of salted water to a hard boil, then reduce to a simmer. Add the sunflower oil and prepared rivels. Cook 3 to 4 minutes. When all the rivels are floating—a sign they are done—drain and transfer to hot meat stock for rivel soup or reserve for later use as a side dish. A vegetarian rivel soup can be made with Spelt Stock (page 81) flavored with chopped scallions and herbs.

Poprobins are made by pan-frying cooked rivels in butter or by deep-frying in oil or lard preheated to 375°F (190°C) until golden color and crisp. They are then scattered piping hot over the surface of soups right before serving.

Ingredients for Saffron Noodles with Yellow Tomato Sauce.

SAFFRON NOODLES WITH YELLOW TOMATO SAUCE
(SAFFERICH NUDLE MIT GEELTOMATTS-SOSSE)

Easy to make, this dish can be served hot as a side dish or cold as a salad.

YIELD: 4 TO 6 SERVINGS

1 cup (250 ml) puréed raw yellow tomato
1 cup (250 ml) Basic Chicken Stock (p. 68)
2 fresh bay leaves, bruised
20 pearl onions, cut in half lengthwise
½ cup (65 g) diced carrot
¼ cup (25 g) chopped dried peaches
1 recipe fresh Saffron Noodles (p. 51, note)
2 tablespoons (30 ml) sunflower or safflower oil
1 cup (200 g) chopped raw yellow tomato
1 teaspoon minced fresh tarragon
1 tablespoon (15 ml) Garlic Vinegar (p. 128)

Put the puréed tomato, chicken stock, and bay leaves in a saucepan and bring to a gentle boil over low heat. Cook for 10 minutes, then remove from the heat and reserve.

While the tomato purée and stock are cooking, put the onions, carrot, and peaches in a separate saucepan. Pour in 1 cup (250 ml) boiling water, cover, and simmer over low heat for 5 minutes. Remove from the heat and reserve.

Bring a large saucepan of salted water to a rolling boil over high heat. Reduce the heat to medium and add the noodles and sunflower oil. Cook for about 3 minutes or until tender but not soft. Drain and return the noodles to the saucepan. Add the reserved purée mixture, the onion and carrot mixture, and 1 cup (200 g) chopped tomato. Set over medium heat and cook only until hot. Add the tarragon and garlic vinegar and serve immediately.

NOODLE SOUP WITH ROCKFISH DUMPLINGS
(NUDELSUPP MIT FELSEFISCHGNEPP)

George Girardey published several traditional recipes using noodles in soup, as well as a simple recipe for fish dumplings, in his Handbuch über Kochkunst. I am using his dumpling recipe here in combination with a noodle soup recipe from the Horstmeier family of Huntingdon, Pennsylvania. Rockfish dumplings should be light and about the size of large marbles. Where striped bass (rockfish) is unavailable, any fish with a firm flesh may be substituted.

YIELD: 6 TO 8 SERVINGS

Before preparing the soup, make the noodles and dumplings as directed below and set them aside to dry.

Spelt Noodles (DINKELNUDLE)

1 large egg
2 tablespoons (30 ml) milk
¼ teaspoon sea salt
1 cup (140 g) spelt flour

Beat the egg until lemon colored, then add the milk and salt. Sift in the spelt flour and work into a stiff dough. Knead a few minutes to make it soft and pliant, then roll out as thin as possible on a work surface lightly dusted with all-purpose flour. If using a pasta machine, feed the dough through the rollers as though making very thin lasagne. Cut the noodle dough into thin strips resembling linguine, then cut into diagonal pieces. Spread the noodles on a cookie sheet to dry while preparing the dumplings and soup.

Fish Dumplings (FISCHGNEPP)

YIELD: 14 DUMPLINGS

½ cup (4 ounces/125 g) cooked rockfish, picked of bones
2 tablespoons (15 g) white breadcrumbs (*Mutschelmehl*)
1 large egg yolk
1 teaspoon unsalted butter, melted
¼ teaspoon sea salt
¼ teaspoon grated nutmeg
⅛ teaspoon white pepper

Put the fish, breadcrumbs, egg yolk, butter, salt, nutmeg, and pepper in a food processor and pulse until a light paste forms. Using the fingers, break off pieces of paste and gently roll into 14 balls of equal size. Set aside on a cookie sheet to dry while preparing the soup.

The Soup (DIE SUPPEBRIEH)

2 tablespoons (30 ml) Garlic Oil (p. 128)
1 cup (4 ounces/125 g) diced country cured ham
1 cup (145 g) chopped scallion
6 cups (1½ liters) Basic Veal Stock (p. 69)
1 teaspoon sea salt
⅛ teaspoon cayenne pepper
2 tablespoons (5 g) minced fresh parsley
2 tablespoons (5 g) minced fresh chervil
1 cup (45 g) shredded lettuce
¼ cup (60 ml) Sage Vinegar (p. 129)

To assemble the soup, heat the garlic oil in a heavy saucepan and sauté the ham until it begins to brown (about 4 minutes). Add the scallion and cook until soft. Add the veal stock, 4 cups (1 liter) of water, salt, and cayenne. Bring the soup to a gentle boil. Add the reserved spelt noodles and cook 2 minutes, then add the fish dumplings. Continue cooking until the dumplings float (about 5 minutes), then add the parsley, chervil, and lettuce. Test the noodles and dumplings for doneness, then add the sage vinegar and serve immediately.

Spelt Soup with Hickory Nut Dumplings
(Dinkelsupp mit Hickerniss-Gnepp)

In the Pfalz the Germans prepare a spelt soup considered a delicacy as well as a health food. The spelt is harvested while still green, then lightly smoked. This green, smoked grain is then ground into flour for soup. Historically, the Pennsylvania Dutch also made Grienkannsupp, but today only the ripe grains are available in our shops. Nonetheless, the green spelt tradition lingers in other ways, for example, in Chicken Corn Soup (p. 60), in which the sweet green spelt has been replaced with corn.

In this recipe the flavor of spelt flour is contrasted with the taste of hickory nuts. Hickory nut dumplings — a thoroughly Dutch addition — are at their best the day after they are made.

YIELD: 4 TO 6 SERVINGS

3 tablespoons (45 g) unsalted butter
¾ cup (60 g) spelt flour
5 cups (1.25 liters) Basic Ham Stock (p. 66)
¼ teaspoon sea salt
⅛ teaspoon freshly grated pepper
¼ teaspoon grated nutmeg
2 large egg yolks
3 tablespoons (45 ml) heavy cream
1 recipe Hickory Nut Dumplings (recipe follows)
grated nutmeg

Melt the butter in a large heavy saucepan and fry the spelt flour over medium-high heat. The roux will form a lumpy mass, which should be chopped to a coarse meal consistency with a spatula, then stir-fried in a way similar to the technique for making *Semmede* (p. 52). Once the spelt is dark brown and nutty, heat the ham stock and pour it boiling hot over the flour. Whisk vigorously to create a smooth, creamy texture, then simmer 10 minutes. Season with salt, pepper, and nutmeg. Right before serving, beat the egg yolks with the cream and add to the soup. Serve as soon as the egg thickens. Add the dumplings as prepared below and garnish each serving with a dash of grated nutmeg.

Hickory Nut Dumplings
(Hickerniss-Gnepp)

YIELD: 24 DUMPLINGS, OR 6 SERVINGS

1¼ cups (100 g) ground hickory nuts (see note)
¼ cup (30 g) white breadcrumbs (*Mutschelmehl*)
¼ teaspoon sugar
¼ teaspoon ground mace
¼ teaspoon baking soda
1 large egg
⅓ cup (80 ml) milk
spelt flour
oil or fat for deep frying

Combine the ground hickory nuts, breadcrumbs, sugar, mace, and baking soda. Beat the egg and milk together. Combine with the crumb mixture. Form into 24 small dumplings. Roll in spelt flour and let stand, uncovered, for 15 minutes before cooking. Heat the oil or fat in a deep fryer to 375°F (190°C) and fry the dumplings until golden brown (about 2 minutes). Drain and set aside to cool. Store overnight for use the next day. Use as directed in the soup recipe above.

Note: The hickory nuts must be ground to a cornmeal texture. The best tool for this is a Swedish *mandelkvarn*, a small hand grinder that can be mounted to the top of a table. A coffee grinder will work, but not a food processor, which will not reduce the nuts to a fine enough texture.

Fresh hickory nut dumplings have a hard crust, which softens as they stand overnight. Fresh, crispy hickory nut dumplings can be rolled in confectioners' sugar and served like doughnuts or served with stewed peaches and sugar.

Spelt groats (in basket), Spelt Soup (center), Spelt Bread (bottom right), and Buwweschenkel (a form of stuffed noodle) beside the bowl.

Oat Flour Soup
(Hawwermehlsupp)

This soup is just as good reheated the next day and can be served as a sauce under poached asparagus or poke. In the original 1581 recipe, Marcus Rumpolt also suggested several nonvegetarian alternatives, such as goose fat or lard for the rapeseed (canola) oil, and meat stock for the spelt stock. A meat-flavored stock made with dried mushrooms can be used instead of true meat stock.

Yield: 4 to 6 servings

5 tablespoons (75 ml) canola oil
¾ cup (105 g) organic oat flour
8 cups (2 liters) Spelt Stock (p. 81)
1½ cups (375 g) puréed cooked chick-peas
1 teaspoon sea salt
½ teaspoon freshly grated pepper
¼ cup (60 ml) Garlic Vinegar (p. 128)

Heat the canola oil in a deep saucepan and stir-fry the oat flour in it for about 4 minutes over high heat. The flour should smoke and begin to smell nutty; it will not darken like wheat flour. Add the spelt stock and simmer 15 minutes, stirring from time to time to remove lumps. Add the puréed chick-peas, salt, and pepper. Right before serving, add the vinegar. Serve hot or cold.

Potato Soup with Parched Spelt Flour
(Grumbieresupp mit G'brannte Dinkelmehl)

This type of potato soup has always been popular among the Dutch as a winter dish. The smooth texture harks back to medieval soups prepared with bean purées. Since this recipe comes from Northampton County, and a similar version appeared as an "heirloom" recipe in The Bethlehem Cook Book *in 1900, the recipe here is probably of Moravian origin.*

Yield: 4 to 6 servings

2 pounds (1 kg) red potatoes (weight after peeling)
1 quart (1 liter) whole milk
2 tablespoons (30 g) unsalted butter
2 tablespoons (15 g) parched spelt flour (p. 31)
1½ teaspoons sea salt
⅛ teaspoon cayenne pepper
sapsago cheese

Boil the potatoes until tender, then rice or mash them so that there are no lumps. Heat the milk and butter in a deep saucepan over medium heat. When the butter has melted, add the potatoes. Whisk until completely smooth, then add the parched flour, salt, and pepper. Reduce the heat and simmer for 10 minutes or until the soup thickens. Serve hot, liberally garnished with grated sapsago cheese.

SMOKED EEL SOUP WITH HOMINY
(G'SCHMOKTE-OHLESUPP MIT HAHMINI)

This is a Pennsylvania Dutch version of a much less elaborate native American smoked eel and hominy porridge. The Lenni-Lenape who inhabited the Delaware River valley were particularly fond of stewed smoked eel during the winter. It is often mentioned in diaries of Moravian missionaries. Eel dishes are still popular in York County and the other Dutch counties along the western shores of the Susquehanna.

YIELD: 8 TO 10 SERVINGS

1½ pounds (600 g) whole smoked eel
1 large carrot, cut in half lengthwise
4 fresh bay leaves, bruised
3 large cloves garlic, crushed
20 juniper berries
3 tablespoons (45 ml) walnut oil
2½ cups (250 g) chopped leek
4 cups (760 g) cooked large hominy
1 cup (175 g) cooked wild rice
2 large smelts (6 ounces/185 g) or any similar small fish
1 tablespoon sea salt

2 tablespoons (30 ml) Garlic Vinegar (p. 128)
minced fresh parsley

Trim the head, tail, and fins from the eel and reserve. Remove the skin, carefully pulling it away from the meat, and discard. Fillet the fish by cutting along the spine with a sharp knife. Separate the fish into halves. Remove the bones. Reserve the bones and meat in separate containers.

Put the reserved head, tail, fins, and bones into a heavy saucepan with 1 gallon (4 liters) of water, the carrot, bay leaves, garlic, and juniper berries. Bring the water to a gentle boil over medium heat, cover, and simmer continuously for 2 hours. Skim off any foam that forms on the surface of the stock. At the end of 2 hours, strain the stock and reserve. Discard the head, bones, and other solids.

Heat the walnut oil in a heavy stewpan, add the leeks, and cover. Sweat the leeks for 3 minutes, then add the reserved stock. Bring to a gentle boil over medium heat and cook 10 minutes. Add the prepared hominy, wild rice, and 1½ cups (250 g) of the chopped reserved eel. Cook 15 minutes or until the hominy is thoroughly hot.

Trim the tails and fins from the smelts and remove the bones. Cut the fish into 1-inch (2-cm) pieces and add to the stew. When the fish is hot, add the sea salt and garlic vinegar. Serve immediately with a liberal garnish of minced parsley.

Pounding hominy (Potter County, Pennsylvania) in the 1840s.

CHICKEN CORN SOUP
(HINKELSUPP MIT WELSCHKANN)

This dish has its historical roots in whole-grain porridges that were once standard fare among the German peasantry, particularly in the sweet green spelt soups of the Rhineland. The exclusive use of chicken (not an everyday food until this century) and the addition of corn freshly scraped from the cob evoke images of large sit-down feasts at the height of summer.

It is the milk from fresh corn that gives this soup its unique, slightly sweet flavor. By implication, this means go lightly with the sugar. For a truly rich corn flavor, see the note below about boiling the cobs.

YIELD: 6 TO 8 SERVINGS

4½ to 5 pounds (2.5 to 3 kg) stewing chicken
2 cleaned chicken feet (optional)
1½ cups (225 g) chopped onion
3 tablespoons (15 g) minced fresh lovage or celery leaves
  (outer green leaves)
1½ tablespoons minced fresh parsley
½ teaspoon ground saffron
12 ears fresh corn (see note)
3 hard-cooked large eggs, chopped
1 to 2 tablespoons sugar
sea salt and freshly grated pepper to taste
minced fresh lovage

Put the chicken in a deep saucepan and cover with 3 quarts (3 liters) of water. Add the chicken feet and onion. Stew 1 hour, then add the lovage and parsley. Continue to cook another hour or until the meat is tender and falling from the bones. Remove the chicken and discard the feet. Strain the stock and discard the herbs and onion. Return the stock to the pot and add the saffron.

Debone the chicken and discard the skin and gristle. Chop the meat into small irregular pieces and add to the stock.

Score and cut the kernels from the ears of corn. Add the corn to the soup. Simmer until the corn is cooked (about 10 minutes), then add the eggs. Test the broth for sweetness. Add 1 tablespoon of sugar or more if necessary, but only enough to enhance the flavor of the corn. Season with salt and pepper and serve with a garnish of minced lovage.

Some cooks choose to add rivels (p. 53) to this soup, which to my mind makes it thick and overly starchy. If rivels are used, I think ½ recipe should be sufficient.

N o t e : Rather than adding sugar to enhance the corn flavor of the soup, try this old Pennsylvania Dutch cooking trick. After cutting the corn from the cobs, break 6 cobs in half and add to the strained chicken stock along with 2 cups (500 ml) of water. Cook the cobs 25 minutes, then strain the stock. Return the stock to the pot, add the onion and ground saffron, then proceed as directed above.

Chicken Corn Soup with corn cobs to enrich the flavor of the stock.

GREEN APPLE SOUP
(GRIENE EBBELSUPP)

Green apple soup is really an herb soup — unripe apples are only part of it — geared for hot, humid weather. The Reinoehl family of Lebanon County, from whom I collected the recipe many years ago, serves it with chopped tomatoes.

YIELD: 6 TO 8 SERVINGS

3 tablespoons (45 ml) vegetable oil
½ cup (60 g) white breadcrumbs (*Mutschelmehl*)
2 cups (200 g) sliced leek
8 ounces (225 g) unripe green cooking apples, peeled and cored
3 cups (750 ml) apple wine or a fruity white wine such as a Vidal
3 fresh bay leaves
½ cup (100 g) finely chopped sorrel
1 cup (100 g) finely chopped lettuce
1 cup (150 g) finely chopped purslane (leafy part only, see note)
1½ teaspoons sea salt
1 cup (250 ml) heavy cream
minced fresh mint or lemon thyme

Put the oil in a deep saucepan and brown the breadcrumbs in it over medium-high heat. Add the leek and cook 3 minutes or until soft. Purée the apples in a food processor and add them to the crumb and leek mixture. Add the apple wine, 5 cups (1.25 liters) of water, and the bay leaves. Cover and cook over medium heat for 20 minutes. Then add the sorrel, lettuce, and purslane. Cook no more than 2 or 3 minutes, just enough to heat the herbs. Taste and season with salt, then set the soup aside to cool.

Once the soup has cooled, refrigerate until cold. Just before serving, add the cream and garnish with minced mint or lemon thyme. Or serve with chopped tomatoes, allowing ½ cup (100 g) per serving, as shown opposite.

Green Apple Soup served over chopped tomatoes.

Note: Where purslane is unavailable, double the amount of sorrel and add 2 tablespoons (30 ml) of lemon juice as a substitute.

CHERRY SOUP
(KAERSCHESUPP)

I have never made an eighteenth-century Pennsylvania Dutch soup that has translated across the barrier of time as gracefully as this one. The secret is simple: use sweet cherries.

The recipe comes from the second edition of Friederike Löffler's Oekonomisches Handbuch, *from a copy brought to Pennsylvania in 1795 by Rosina Epting.*

YIELD: 4 TO 6 SERVINGS

2½ pounds (1.25 kg) fresh sweet cherries (weight after pitting)
¼ cup (60 g) unsalted butter
2 tablespoons (15 g) all-purpose flour
6 tablespoons (90 g) sugar
2 cups (500 ml) dry red wine, such as Zinfandel or Petite Sirah
grated zest of 1 lemon
¼ teaspoon ground clove
½ teaspoon ground cinnamon
½ teaspoon sea salt
sour cream (optional)

Pit the cherries and weigh them. Reserve the excess juice from the fruit. Chop the cherries into pea-size pieces and mix with the reserved juice.

Melt the butter in a deep saucepan and fry the flour until straw colored. Add the cherries and sugar. Stir thoroughly to cover all the fruit with roux. Cover the pan and simmer gently for 10 minutes. Then add 2 cups (500 ml) of water, the wine, lemon zest, spices, and salt. Once the liquid has begun to boil, the soup is ready to serve. Serve hot or cold with sour cream as a garnish.

GROUNDCHERRY SOUP
(JUDDEKAERSCHE-SUPP)

Clara Behmer of Neffsville, Pennsylvania, was well known in the 1920s for her yellow tomato soups. The Pennsylvania Dutch refer to the small, cherry-size yellow tomatoes used in cookery as Oiertomatts ("egg" tomatoes), since they resemble bird eggs, in shape at least. Most of our egg tomato recipes are actually adaptations of much older recipes using groundcherries (Physalis heterophylla Nees), a member of the nightshade family that grows in abundance along the edges of local fields and orchards. This recipe is a variation of one of Mrs. Behmer's most popular soups.

2 teaspoons sea salt
3 pints (1 kg) groundcherries or yellow cherry tomatoes
1 cup (250 ml) heavy cream
¼ cup (60 g) unsalted butter
2 tablespoons (30 g) finely chopped scallion
1½ tablespoons minced fresh dill
1 teaspoon minced fresh coriander
2 tablespoons (5 g) minced fresh chives
minced or fried parsley

Remove the groundcherries from their husks, rinse, and place in a deep saucepan. Bring 6 cups (1.5 liters) of salted water to a boil and pour over the groundcherries. Cover and simmer over medium heat for 20 to 25 minutes or until all the groundcherries are soft. Purée the fruit and liquid together in a blender or food processor, then add the cream. Melt the butter and add it to the soup.

Reheat the soup mixture in a clean pan, but do not boil it. Add the onion and fresh herbs. Serve hot, garnished with minced or fried parsley.

Serving Hint: This soup is at its best when made 2 to 3 hours in advance of serving. Standing brings out the subtle, slightly pineapple-pumpkin flavor of the groundcherries.

Shopping Hint: Groundcherries are commonly found throughout the United States east of the Rocky Mountains. They are available for sale in Pennsylvania farm markets from late July through September. A closely related plant, the Cape gooseberry *(Physalis peruviana)*, a native of South America, has been introduced to areas of the West Coast and Pennsylvania, where it is sold commercially. In fact, several members of the groundcherry family have been naturalized in Pennsylvania, including the large-berried Mexican tomatillo. The groundcherries shown in the picture on this page are the ones most commonly used in our cookery, but there is also a pink variety that is native and tastes a bit like strawberries. It is used in pies.

The flavor of groundcherries suggests a mixture of pumpkin and pineapple.

Pretzel Soup with Peanut Roux
(*Bretzelsupp mit g'reeschte Grundnussmehl*)

YIELD: 6 TO 8 SERVINGS

8 to 10 3-inch (7.5-cm) unsalted pretzels (8 ounces/225 g)
3 quarts (3 liters) apple cider
¼ cup (60 g) unsalted butter
2 teaspoons sea salt
¾ cup (90 g) unsalted blanched peanuts
3 tablespoons (45 ml) peanut oil
sea salt to taste

Break the pretzels into small pieces and put them in a deep bowl. Cover with 3 cups (750 ml) of the cider and soak 1 to 2 hours. Transfer to a saucepan and add another 4 cups (1 liter) of cider, the butter, and the salt. Cover and cook over low heat until reduced to mush. Purée in a food processor until smooth, then pour the batter into a clean saucepan and thin to a vichyssoise consistency with 5 cups (1.25 liters) of hot cider—or hot water if the cider is too sweet. Bring to a gentle boil and serve hot with peanut roux drizzled over the top.

To make peanut roux, chop the peanuts in a blender until reduced to a powder. (Do not overprocess or they will turn to peanut butter.) Sift if necessary to remove the large pieces. Heat the oil in a skillet and fry the peanut flour 2 to 3 minutes or until it begins to brown. Drizzle over the top of the soup. Do not stir. The roux may be salted slightly to create a greater contrast of flavors.

Note: If the pretzels are not highly toasted, the soup may lack its characteristic nutty flavor. It may be necessary to toast the pretzels in the oven before using in soup. A little scorching will not hurt them.

Country store at Hinkeltown, Pennsylvania.

STOCKS FOR SOUPS AND MEAT DISHES

BASIC BEEF STOCK WITH ONIONS
(GRUNDREZEPT FER OCHSEFLEESCHBRIEH MIT ZWIWWELE)

By itself, this stock makes a passable onion soup, although its real purpose is to provide contrasting stock for dumplings and noodles. When cooking oxtails, add a few venison bones to strengthen the flavor.

YIELD: 2 TO 2 ½ QUARTS (2 TO 2.5 LITERS)

2 pounds (1 kg) oxtails
2 small onions, sliced
2 small turnips, peeled and sliced
10 whole allspice
10 peppercorns
2 cloves garlic, sliced
1 tablespoon unsalted butter
1 tablespoon sunflower oil
3 medium onions (1 pound/500 g), chopped
2 tablespoons (30 g) brown sugar
2 teaspoons sea salt

Put the oxtails in a deep saucepan with 1 gallon (4 liters) of water, the sliced onions, turnips, allspice, peppercorns, and garlic. Bring to a slow boil, then reduce the heat and simmer 2 hours or until the meat falls from the bone and the stock is reduced to 2½ quarts (2.5 liters). Skim off any fat that forms while the meat is cooking.

Strain the stock, reserving the meat to use in pocket dumplings, meat dumplings, or soup. Discard the other cooked ingredients.

Heat the butter and sunflower oil over high heat in a saucepan. Add the chopped onions and stir-fry for 2 minutes. Add the brown sugar and salt, and coat the onions thoroughly, then reduce the heat to a slow simmer. Cover and sweat for 20 minutes. Add the strained beef stock and boil gently for 15 minutes. Pour the stock through a fine sieve and set aside to cool. When cool, skim off any fat that may have formed on top, then freeze or use as needed.

BASIC HAM STOCK
(GRUNDREZEPT FER SCHUNKEBRIEH)

The flavor of smoked ham or capon should predominate, and if some bacon rinds or fatty skin from the capon is tossed in for added flavor, so much the better. The fat comes out of the stock in the end anyway.

YIELD: 3 QUARTS (3 LITERS)

2 medium ham hocks (2 pounds/1 kg) or the picked carcass of a smoked capon
2 medium onions, cut in half
4 fresh bay leaves, lightly bruised

Put the ham hocks or capon in a deep saucepan with the onions and bay leaves and cover with 4 quarts (4 liters) of water. Bring to a boil over medium-high heat, then reduce to a simmer and cook gently for 2 hours or until the stock is reduced to 3 quarts (3 liters). Skim off any scum that may form. Strain the stock through a fine sieve or a piece of cheesecloth. Reserve the meat from the ham hocks or capon for soup or dumplings. Discard the bones, bay leaves, and cooked onion. Put the strained stock in the refrigerator to cool and jell. When it jells, skim off any fat that has formed on the top. Freeze or use as needed.

From left to right: Green Tomato Mandram; gribble or Semmede, both fine and coarse; and Basic Beef Stock with Onions. In the stock, Egg Pasta in the form of ribbon noodles and Meat Dumplings garnished with calendula petals.

BASIC PORK STOCK
(GRUNDREZEPT FER SEIFLEESCHBRIEH)

YIELD: APPROXIMATELY 3 ½ QUARTS
(3.5 LITERS)

3½ pounds (1.75 kg) meaty pork bones
1 small carrot, cut in half lengthwise
1 medium onion, cut in half and stuck with 6 cloves
2 dried cayenne peppers
1 bouquet garni (5 small sprigs fresh marjoram, 1 sprig fresh rosemary, 3 sprigs fresh parsley)
5 fresh bay leaves, bruised

Put all the ingredients in a saucepan with 1 gallon (4 liters) of water and bring to a boil over medium-high heat. Reduce to a simmer and cook gently for 2 hours. Remove any scum that may form as the stock begins to boil. Strain the stock and pick the meat from the bones. Reserve the meat for soups or dumplings. Put the stock in the refrigerator to cool and jell, then skim off the fat. Freeze or use as needed.

BASIC CHICKEN STOCK
(GRUNDREZEPT FER HINKELBRIEH)

Die Geschickte Hausfrau (1848) contains a straightforward recipe for chicken soup calling for the heads, bones, and feet, the secrets to any well-flavored soup. Since chicken feet are quite inexpensive in our farmers' markets — nearly every country butcher sells them — it is possible to make the stock far more cheaply than buying it ready-made in tins.

YIELD: APPROXIMATELY 3 QUARTS (3 LITERS)

16 chicken feet, cleaned and declawed
3 small onions, cut in half
1 6-inch (15-cm) carrot, cut in half lengthwise
1 8-inch (20-cm) celery stalk with leaves
6 whole allspice
16 juniper berries

Put all the ingredients in a deep saucepan with 1 gallon (4 liters) of water and simmer 2 hours or until the skin falls from the bones. Strain and set aside to cool. Skim off any fat that forms on the top, then freeze for later use.

BASIC VEAL STOCK
(GRUNDREZEPT FER KALBSFLEESCHBRIEH)

During the latter part of the nineteenth century, Meadville, Pennsylvania, became a center of regional cookery. Many of the best Pennsylvania German recipes preserved from that period come from the Meadville Cooking School. This is one of them.

YIELD: 2 QUARTS (2 LITERS)

2 pounds (1 kg) meaty veal bones
1 cup (100 g) chopped onion
¼ cup (50 g) chopped carrot
1 cup (150 g) chopped turnip
1 6-inch (15-cm) celery stalk with leafy top
6 whole cloves
6 peppercorns
½ teaspoon ground mace

Put the veal bones in 3 quarts (3 liters) of water in a deep saucepan and gradually bring to a simmer over medium heat. Cook gently for 1 hour, skimming frequently. Add the remaining ingredients and cook another 2 hours. Strain the stock and discard the bones and vegetables. Reserve the meat for soups or the Veal and Oyster Gumbis (p. 35). Measure the stock. If there is more than 2 quarts (2 liters), return it to the pan and reduce to 2 quarts (2 liters) over high heat. Cool and skim off any fat that may have formed, then freeze or use as needed. Do not store in the refrigerator for more than 2 days.

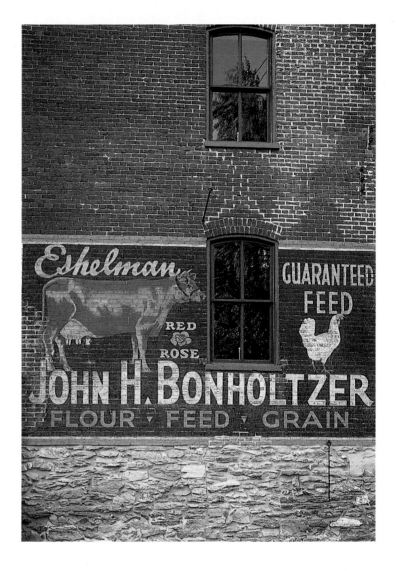

Old mill at Fertility, Pennsylvania.
Overleaf: Buckeye Bread (in kettle by fire), Spelt Bread (left of table), Potato Bread with "hex sign" decoration (on chair), Bucks County Rye Bread (on floor), and Weaverland Wedding Bread (six-pointed star).

RUSTIC BREADS & BAKEOVEN CAKES

Bread is so basic to Pennsylvania German culture that it amazes me to see such little attention devoted to it in our popular cookery books. The only author to take a serious look at traditional Pennsylvania Dutch breadbaking was Edith Bertels Thomas in her *Mary at the Farm and Book of Recipes* (Norristown, Penn., 1915). Thomas based her recipes on informal interviews with country cooks and bakers, which she combined with photography to create a semi-ethnographic look at the Pennsylvania Dutch and their foods. Her photographs of a "potato pretzel"—a large braided loaf shaped like a pretzel—and a sliced loaf of rye bread are invaluable records.

Food writer Florence Fabricant recently pointed out in the *New York Times* that Americans are finally rediscovering old-style bread. I hope that this renewal will spread to the Pennsylvania Dutch, not simply because the Dutch established

America's first bread basket in colonial times, but also because they were among the last to give up traditional bread-baking practices. In fact, these methods never fully disappeared, and there are little pockets here and there where the art is still flourishing.

In the Mahantongo Valley, for example, where folk art and old foodways still abound, the brothers at Christiansbrunn Cloister still bake their daily bread in an outdoor bakeoven, and crusty breads they are. The last Mahantongo housewife known to have used an outdoor oven regularly was Sallie Wiest Troutman (1882–1972) of Klingerstown. Sallie was proud of her wheat bread and baked twelve to sixteen loaves weekly for her family well into the 1960s. Her bakeoven is still lovingly maintained by the Troutmans in full working order with all the required tools. Most of the other bakeovens in the valley have been demolished.

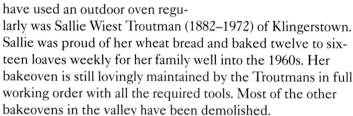

Above: Sallie Troutman's bakehouse near Klingerstown, Pennsylvania.
Right: Old bakehouse at the Landis Valley Museum.

Nearly all Pennsylvania Dutch bread-baking in the eighteenth and early nineteenth centuries was done in bakehouses situated safely away from the main dwelling. Built of brick or stone, the large beehive-shaped ovens were heated by a fire that was built inside. Applewood, dogwood, white oak, maple, and other dense woods with intense heat-producing properties were always preferred. Since the temperature of the fire could exceed 900°F (460°C), it is not difficult to imagine the danger to a dwelling if such an oven cracked open or collapsed while being fired. For this reason, ovens were placed outside at a safe distance from the house. Quite often, as on other Pennsylvania Dutch outbuildings and the farmhouse itself, the roof was covered with fireproof clay pantiles, similar to those on the bakeoven pictured on the opposite page.

After the fire died down in the bakeoven, the coals were raked out and the oven swabbed as clean as possible with a wet wad of rye straw or a rag on a long pole. Rye straw emitted a special steam that would turn bread crusts a golden-yellow, as though they had been brushed with egg yolk.

When the heat in the oven dropped to about 450°F (230°C), the unbaked bread, which had been allowed to rise in rye straw baskets, was turned out onto a board or peel and slipped into the oven to bake in the heat radiating from the oven walls. The bread was placed either directly on the hot floor of the oven or on well-floured earthenware plates. The Chickweed Pie shown on page 90 was baked in one of these old-style dishes.

In another baking method, small loaves or single loaves were baked on a raised-hearth with the wood coals used for meal preparation or general heating. The loaves were placed in shallow Dutch ovens or on special raised hearth griddles with three legs (see p. 80). A pot or skillet could be turned over the bread and covered with hot coals to create the type of multi-directional "soaking" heat needed for bread-baking.

The Pennsylvania Dutch had to modify their specialized baking techniques when cast-iron stoves came into fashion in the nineteenth century. The stoves not only changed the shape of loaf bread by introducing tin and iron bread pans but also led to a multitude of adjustments to accommodate processed flours, ready-made yeasts, and yeastless breads leavened with chemical compounds.

It is not my intention to teach the basics of bread-baking because there are plenty of books on that subject. Beginners should be aware of a book by Brother Peter Reinhart called *Brother Juniper's Bread Book* (1991), which I highly recommend as an introductory text. I have instead provided procedures to replicate in a modern oven the old-style Pennsylvania German breads using liquid yeasts, hops, and all the specialized flours.

Brother Peter refers to his baking technique as the slow-rise method. This is the method used by traditional Pennsylvania Dutch cooks. Furthermore, most of our old-style breads are sourdough of one form or another because we use liquid yeast, which contributes to the flavor.

Elmira Layton sorting hops in her Slatedale garden.

Elmira Layton of Slatedale in Lehigh County, well known in her day for excellent rye breads, was an expert at yeast-making and the cultivation of hops. Elmira would infuse about seven or eight hops flowers (depending on their size) in 1 cup (250 ml) of boiling water to make her hops "tea" for yeast. That proportion is sufficient for all the bread recipes in this book.

In yeast-making, hops act as a selective disinfectant, killing off naturally occurring unwanted yeasts and thereby creating less competition for the "good" yeasts that do the actual leavening. The commercial yeasts sold in supermarkets or sold wholesale to bakeries are yeast cultures that have been reduced by various processing methods to one or two yeast species. These yeasts are monochromatic, for they produce only one kind of flavor—one shoe, so to speak, that must fit all feet. I use these commercial yeasts—the active dry yeast, in any case—mostly for the convenience of my readers to reactivate liquid yeasts. This saves time and frustration, but commercial yeasts, given a chance, will kill off many of the natural yeasts in starters.

Old-style liquid yeasts take advantage of many species of yeast to create different flavors, giving cooks a wide range of baking choices. Instead of hops, for example, peach leaves might be used, or buttermilk whey. The finished yeast can be further flavored with tansy leaves, a popular treatment among the Pennsylvania Dutch of Somerset County, or with wild grape stems. With endless possibilities the creative bread baker can derive considerable pleasure from baking

Historically, the Pennsylvania Dutch used four basic kinds of yeast: hard yeast, hop yeast, milk yeast, and potato yeast. In Pennsylfaanisch the word for any type of liquid yeast is *Satz*, often written in English as *sots*. The root meaning of the word is "starter," something that jumps to life. In music a *Satz* can be a composition. I like to think of yeast musically; the sound of its bubbles is a chorus getting ready to sing.

LIQUID YEASTS AND YEAST STARTERS

The key to traditional yeasts is a plant known as hops, a perennial vine that reaches almost twenty feet (six meters) in height. It is the flower that is collected in late summer and dried for making yeast.

Right: Hops from my Pennsylvania garden.
Opposite: Spleenwort growing on an old wall.

bread that actually *tastes* of its ingredients.

Yeasts work by their own clocks, and while they can be hurried along, they will not be rushed. When dealing with old-style breads, we must throw off many of the paradigms that shape our present-day ideas about baking. Old bread recipes often take twice as long to rise as modern ones, but the results are usually better. Rather than concentrating bread-baking into one or two hours, the older methods spread it out over several days, a little yeast-making here, a little flour preparation there, a watchful eye keeping tabs on the progress of the dough.

Not every Dutch housewife had luck in getting her dough to rise. Thunderstorms were always considered a great threat because a quick change in air pressure could affect yeast dramatically. So could gusts of frigid air, and it never ceases to amaze me how the bread made it from the house to the bakehouse in the dead of winter without falling flat.

Witchcraft, which still has its following up in the hills, was also a problem. When the dough was placed in rye straw baskets to rise, the bottom of each basket was lined with a cloth. I use old salt bags that have been trimmed square and hemmed. The cloth was dusted with flour and the dough laid on top, then covered with another cloth to protect it from drafts. If the bread refused to rise and witchcraft was the suspected cause, the Pennsylvania Dutch had an effective remedy in a little plant called spleenwort, or *Widderkumm* in Pennsylfaanisch, which means "come again," in the sense of recharging something with vitality.[1]

Spleenworts, any sweet fern in the family *Asplenium*, are mostly small, delicate plants that grow on rocks or stone walls. For their small size, they possess uncommonly large powers against witches. It has been explained to me that witches work on bread via the ground, using the rocks below to "confuse the yeast and pull it down." Therefore a sprig of spleenwort placed beneath the cloth under each

ball of dough will rechannel the spell and break the force holding back the yeast.

Spleenwort works along the same principle as the *Hexebese*, or "witch brooms," tacked over the entrance to bakehouses. Consisting of little sprigs of juniper that have developed ball-like growths on the end, the brooms look very much like the old-fashioned brushes used by chimney sweeps. When tacked over entrances, the brooms are said to create a force field that witches cannot penetrate. "The *Hexe* stare at the brooms," explained one old informant, "and they see all the little strands, which whirl about in their heads so they cannot think. They lose their balance, fall down, and will go crazy if they look at the brooms too much. If you can make them go crazy, you can turn them back into crows."

HARD YEAST (*SATZKUCHE*)

Hard yeast, or cake yeast, is made by infusing hops flowers in boiling water, straining the tea, then mixing it with coarse spelt flour, whole-wheat flour, or rye meal and a liquid yeast like the Hagerstown yeast (p. 77). This mixture is allowed to proof (foam up) in a warm place, then it is stirred down and mixed with cornmeal to form a stiff paste. This is patted into a square pancake, cut into strips, and spread on a cloth or baking sheet to dry. When dry, the strips are stored in a muslin bag in a cool, dry cupboard or in an airtight jar if the weather is humid. A day before yeast is required for baking, a piece of dry paste is broken up in lukewarm water and allowed to reactivate. When foamy, it is ready to use. Although slower to activate, this type of yeast is closest in texture to the granulated active yeast now sold in supermarkets, for it can be ground into crumbs and measured out in similar fashion.

In another old method a hard yeast starter was created by saving the scrapings from the dough tray (the wooden

Hops harvesting in 1835.

trough in which the dough was raised and kneaded) or a piece of the raised dough itself. The dough scrapings were rolled out to about ⅛ inch (3 mm) thick, dried until crisp, then broken into small pieces and stored in an airtight container. Like the *Satzkuche*, a piece of this dry dough would be soaked in lukewarm water until reactivated into a foaming yeast. This was the technique used by Elmira Layton for creating her rye bread yeasts.[2] It was generally referred to as the Roman method by professional bakers in eighteenth-century Philadelphia and is so described in the *Farmer's Encyclopedia* of 1844.[3]

HOP YEAST (HOPPESATZ)

A shortcut method, hop yeast is similar to hard yeast. A tea is made by boiling hops flowers in water. This is strained and mixed with spelt or rye flour while still hot. The batter is allowed to cool until lukewarm, then it is mixed with liquid yeast and sweetened with molasses or maple sugar. When frothy, the yeast is ready to use. If properly stored, it will remain active for about ten days. Since baking was generally done on Fridays (to have fresh bread for the weekend), this yeast could be kept going from one week to the next by reserving part of it as a starter for the following batch.

MILK YEAST (MILLICHSATZ)

Considered the "instant" yeast of colonial times, milk yeast was easier to make than the others, but it was also the most unsafe because there were no hops to selectively destroy wild yeasts and bacteria. Country bakers did not know what bacteria were, but through trial and error they were well acquainted with the end results, both good and bad.

To make milk yeast, raw milk was mixed with salt and coarse flour or cornmeal and put in a warm place to ferment. Naturally occurring yeasts in the flour or cornmeal gradually produced enough of a yeast culture to create a foamy liquid. This was often incorrectly called salt-rising yeast on the mistaken assumption that it was the salt that caused the reaction. Once the milk and flour mixture began to foam, it had to be used immediately or it would lose its strength and sour.

Milk yeast that soured was sometimes mixed with active liquid yeast or crumbs of hard yeast to salvage it. This was the basis for what is now known as sourdough starter. Rather than proceed through the unpredictable ups and downs of a raw milk ferment, I have provided a more reliable Sourdough Liquid Yeast recipe (p. 79).

Instead of milk, some Pennsylvania German bakers used whey, particularly when making sweetened breads as dessert cakes, or added rennet to raw milk to separate the curds and whey. They mixed the whey with salt and flour to make a yeast and saved the curds to later beat into the sponge. Rich bread made according to this method was called rennet bread (*Laabbrod*) or, more commonly, cottage cheese bread (*Schmierkeesbrod*) in reference to the curds.

Among the Pennsylvania Dutch, all curd-enriched breads were considered expensive and were eaten only on special occasions. They were often baked in the form of muffins or dinner rolls (*Weck*), or used as the basis for such festive Christmas breads as *Hutzelbrod*, long ornamental loaves of bread stuffed with brandied dried fruit. Recipes of this sort were taught in the cooking classes at the Moravian Seminary during the latter part of the eighteenth century. The Weaverland Wedding Bread (p. 88) is based on this principle.

HAGERSTOWN LIQUID YEAST
(HEEGERSCHTEDDLER SATZ)

This variation of Millichsatz (milk yeast) cultivates naturally occurring yeasts. The recipe appeared in the Pennsylvania Dutch cookbook Die Geschickte Hausfrau (The Handy Housewife) and in numerous regional publications of the pre-Civil War period. However, I have gone back to the Maryland almanac Der Volksfreund und Hägerstauner Calender for 1852 for this particular version of the recipe, since it originated in the Hagerstown area to begin with. The proportions given here are one-half of the original recipe. Whey may be used instead of spring water.

YIELD: 1 GALLON (4 LITERS)

1¾ cups (215 g) whole spelt flour or organic whole-wheat flour
¼ cup (45 g) brown sugar
2 tablespoons (30 g) sea salt
1 gallon (4 liters) spring water

Combine the flour, sugar, salt, and water. Boil over medium heat for 1 hour. Remove from the heat and set aside to cool until lukewarm (98°F/37°C). Pour the liquid yeast into sterilized wine bottles or quart jars. Cover the jars with cheesecloth or some other loose material that will keep out dust and insects—gnats and flies are attracted to yeast. Put the jars in shallow pans or trays to catch the overflow and store in a warm place. When the yeast becomes active (allow 2 to 3 days), it will overflow the jars. It is then ready to use.

N o t e : If for some reason the yeast has not begun to ferment after 3 days, add ½ teaspoon active dry yeast or ¼ cup (60 ml) hops tea to each jar.

POTATO YEAST (GRUMBIERESATZ) AND POTATO BREAD

As a variation of milk yeast, potatoes were boiled in water with molasses or brown sugar, then puréed to a batter consistency. Wild yeasts in the potatoes and in the air would cause the slurry to ferment. Once foamy, it had to be used immediately or it would become beery.

Another method, popular among the Moravians, was to boil potatoes in whey rather than water, especially for Moravian Sugar Cake (p. 95). Mashed potatoes replaced curds in the sponge to create more economical recipes for feeding many people. Like curds, potatoes increased the bulk and moisture content of baked goods and therefore extended their freshness, an important factor for the huge communal meals once prepared by Moravian cooks.

One would assume from the liberal way the Pennsylvania Dutch use potatoes in baking that this tuber is as essential to our bread as the yeast. Historically, potatoes figured largely only where economy seems to have been the controlling factor. Exactly when this happened in Pennsylvania Dutch cookery cannot be dated precisely, but the majority of the Pennsylvania Germans came to America prior to the 1770s, when widespread food shortages forced the German farmers to turn to potatoes as a means of survival. Thus, the early settlers did not bring with them the elaborate potato recipes associated with German cookery today. The Dutch learned about potatoes on this side of the Atlantic.

One of the earliest recipes for potato bread appeared in the writings of Jakob Guyer (1716–1785), known as Kleinjogg in his native Switzerland, a rural philosopher who published extensively on agricultural reform.[4] Guyer's essays on farming were reprinted in Pennsylvania German almanacs and newspapers. Although Guyer never visited America, his influence was pervasive, and it is fair to say that he helped to put potato bread on the Pennsylvania Dutch table.

Many methods of making potato bread evolved, since the age-old challenge of producing more bread from less flour faced rural cooks everywhere. One of the best known in Pennsylvania was the "Swabian" technique, so called by Johann Halle in his *Magie, oder, die Zauberkräfte der Natur* (*Magic, or the Marvelous Powers of Nature*, Berlin, 1786).[5] Halle's compendium dealt with "natural science," not magic, and it was extremely popular among the Pennsylvania Dutch intelligentsia, particularly the chapters devoted to home economy.

According to the Swabian method, unpeeled potatoes were boiled until soft. They were then peeled, chopped, grated, reduced to a loose meal, and dried out overnight. The following day the potato meal was mixed with spelt flour, salt, and yeast and worked into a sponge, which was formed into dough for bread.

This was similar to another so-called Swabian technique in which peeled potatoes were cut into thin slices, or *Schnitz*, and dried either on a stove or in an outdoor bakeoven after bread-baking was done. The dried potatoes—which looked like potato chips—were then taken to a grist mill and ground into meal or flour. This was mixed with spelt flour as an extender in making bread. If the dried potatoes were toasted or "parched" before they were milled, the bread developed a delightfully nutty flavor.

The mechanics for making a potato sponge were outlined in a counterpart to Halle's *Magie* called *Noth-und Hülfs-Büchlein* (*Primer for Emergencies and Relief*), published in the 1780s in the form of a heart-wrenching story about the tribulations of the village of Mildheim in Saxony. Written in a simple pedagogical style, the book was in fact a survival guide for teenage readers, emphasizing scientific farming and progressive housekeeping. Hugely popular among the farmers of Pennsylvania, the primer was printed in Germany, with entire editions expressly for our market. Copies still turn up at farm sales today.

SOURDOUGH LIQUID YEAST
(SAUERDEEG SATZ)

This form of Grumbieresatz (potato yeast) was normally prepared two days before baking. A new batch was started every week with residue from the last. In place of residue to activate it, I suggest active dry yeast. The starter can be kept dormant in the refrigerator for as long as ten to twelve days, but to keep it active it is best to store it in a warm place.

YIELD: APPROXIMATELY 2 QUARTS (2 LITERS)

4 medium potatoes (650 g), peeled and chopped
1 teaspoon (5 g) sea salt
7 cups (1.75 liters) spring water or whey
⅓ cup (50 g) organic white cornmeal
2 tablespoons (30 ml) unsulfured molasses
¼ ounce (7 g) active dry yeast
1¼ cups (155 g) whole spelt flour or organic whole-wheat flour

Boil the potatoes in 6 cups (1.5 liters) salted spring water or whey until soft. Strain the liquid and pour it while still hot over the cornmeal. Reserve the leftover potatoes for use in another recipe or put them in soup. Warm the remaining cup (250 ml) of spring water or whey over medium heat and dissolve the molasses in it. Remove from the heat and set aside until lukewarm (98°F/37°C). Add the dry yeast and let it proof.

While the yeast is proofing, simmer the cornmeal mixture over low heat for 20 minutes, then strain it through a fine sieve and discard the meal. Measure the strained liquid and add boiling spring water or whey if there is less than 6 cups (1.5 liters). Beat in the spelt flour with a whisk to create a thick, smooth batter resembling heavy cream. Then add the proofed yeast and set in a warm place to ferment. The *Satz* is ready to use when it is light and foamy, a bit like frothy pancake batter. Allow 2 days, weather conditions permitting.

FROM RYE BREAD TO WHITE BREAD

The popularity of rye bread among the Pennsylvania Dutch farming classes is supported by a vast number of reminiscences, casual references in letters and journals, and here and there actual working recipes.

The basic bread of survival, rye bread came in many forms, from black breads made with a mix of black spelt and rye flours to very light loaves made with as much as 80 percent spelt flour and as little as 20 percent rye. Among the English in Pennsylvania, rye bread usually consisted of one-third wheat flour, one-third barley flour, and one-third rye. The Bucks County Rye Bread recipe (p. 81) actually follows the English pattern, but uses spelt instead of wheat.

Spelt was not universally grown by the Pennsylvania Germans, and in many areas where farming was near subsistence level, rye alone often sufficed. In cookery it was often mixed with cornmeal and other extenders, as in Buckeye Bread (p. 82) from Ohio. Although spelt did not move west on the same massive scale as the Pennsylvania Dutch themselves following the Revolution, its cultivation has continued in limited areas. All of the spelt shown in this book that is still in the husk came from Leon Hoernchemeyer's farm near Norwalk in Huron County, Ohio.

Rye production among the Pennsylvania Dutch declined dramatically during the Civil War, when emphasis was placed on wheat production for the military. Because the market networks for wheat remained in place when the war was over, consumption shifted from rye bread to wheat, and spelt agriculture nearly became extinct.

While many Pennsylvania Dutch women continued to use their outdoor bakeovens simply because they could bake anywhere from eighteen to twenty-four loaves of bread at a time, the post–Civil War shift to white wheat bread was a permanent one. This reflected similar changes taking place in mainstream American culture as a result of industrialization and a new working class emphasis on white breads, red meats, and sugar.

The shift to wheat flour was also hastened by the introduction of the cookstove and the ease with which pastries could be baked in it. Thus, the decline of rye bread and other coarse country breads during the latter half of the nineteenth century was counterbalanced with a veritable explosion of newfangled pastries and pies. Cookbooks from the period are crammed with inventions, from Annie Wampole's Cornstarch Cake (p. 89) and Shoofly Pie (p. 96) to Mary Gladfelter Cake and Centennial Pudding. The recipe for Hickory Nut Corn Cake (p. 100) is a twentieth-century example of this continuing trend.

CAKES, PIES, AND CLAFTY PUDDING

As I mentioned earlier, the culinary ancestor of the pie was a noodle or dough envelope stuffed with various fillings, the *Mauldasche* in Pennsylvania Dutch cookery. The oldest German word for a flat, round piece of dough is *Kuchen* ("KOO-ken"), written in Pennsylfaanisch as *Kuche* ("KOO-keh"). In Alsatian German this is pronounced "KEE-sheh," from which the French created the word *quiche*. In any other American cookbook, my recipes for Chickweed Pie (p. 90) and Onion Pie (p. 96) would be called quiches, even though they do not have a French origin.

Regardless, the concept is the same: flat cakes baked under some type of sweet or savory filling. In order to keep the filling from running off, the edges of the dough are turned up; thus the tart is born.

Old-style Pennsylvania Dutch tarts were usually baked in leftover bread dough, exactly like a pizza. If the tart was made for a special occasion, the dough might be enriched with butter or other ingredients such as chopped herbs or even spices like cardamom or ginger. Yeast-Raised Butter Crust (p. 91) is typical of this type of breadlike tart dough. In fact, there is a vast family of tarts requiring a butter crust, from very plain fruit tarts in which halved plums or peaches are stuck directly into the dough, to elaborate preparations with fruit poached in wine or brandy and covered with rich, custardy toppings.

All the pie recipes in this chapter can be baked on Yeast-Raised Butter Crust or simply on bread dough, even pizza dough. That is certainly how they were served in the eighteenth century. However, the Pennsylvania Dutch today use short crusts for most of their pies, something they acquired from Anglo-American cookery.

Until the 1780s, the English in Pennsylvania generally used barley flour for short crusts, what the Dutch refer to as *Breeseldeeg* (from *bröseln*, "to crumble"). Only the very wealthy used pastry flour from wheat. As the Pennsylvania Dutch assimilated Anglo-American foods into their cookery, they tended to copy and retain certain foods at a slower rate than the mainstream culture around them. In some areas of the Pennsylvania Dutch Homeland, barley flour and sour cream butter are still used for short crusts.

It is tempting to look at Pennsylvania Dutch cookery as a mosaic of old foods now long extinct in the American diet, but a few isolated examples do not create a general rule. The red velvet cake associated today with the Amish—a chocolate cake that turns red due to the liberal presence of baking soda—can be found in charity cookbooks from almost any part of the country in the Victorian period. But since the Amish now sell red velvet cake from roadside stands, many food writers have jumped to the conclusion that they also invented it.

Footed iron griddle for use on a raised hearth. Pennsylvania, circa 1790–1820.

ROASTED SPELT AND SPELT STOCK
(GEREESCHTE DINKEL UN DINKELBRIEH)

This recipe can be used for any whole grain, including rye and wheat. Before measuring, always be certain to pick out black or imperfect grains.

YIELD: 2 CUPS (380 G) COOKED SPELT
6 CUPS (1.5 LITERS) SPELT STOCK

1 cup (190 g) spelt groats (whole berries)
8 cups (2 liters) water
1 teaspoon sea salt

Preheat the oven to 375°F (190°C). Spread the spelt on a cookie sheet. Roast 15 minutes, then immediately pour the hot grain into a large kettle of boiling salted water. Cover and simmer over low heat 1 hour or until the spelt groats are tender. Drain, reserving both the berries and the stock for later use.

BUCKS COUNTY RYE BREAD
(BUCKS KAUNDI KANNBROD)

The bread made with this recipe won many prizes at county fairs during the nineteenth century. The design, dividing the bread into eight sections with a ruler, is a traditional pattern dating from medieval times. It served the practical purpose of creating equal portions.

YIELD: 8 TO 16 SERVINGS

OLD-STYLE YEAST
2 cups (500 ml) active Hagerstown Liquid Yeast (p. 77)

SHORTCUT YEAST
½ ounce (14 g) active dry yeast proofed in 2 cups (500 ml) lukewarm spring water (98°F/37°C)

3 cups (750 ml) whole milk
1 tablespoon (15 g) bacon drippings or salted butter
2 tablespoons (25 g) dark brown sugar
¼ cup (50 g) sea salt
4 cups (500 g) organic spelt flour
4 cups (500 g) organic barley flour
4 cups (500 g) organic rye flour
spelt meal, rye bran, or wheat bran

Prepare the old-style yeast or shortcut yeast. Warm the milk over medium heat and add the bacon drippings or butter, sugar, and salt. Stir until the sugar and salt are dissolved, then remove from the heat and set aside to cool.

In a deep 6- to 7-quart (6- to 7-liter) bowl, sift together all of the spelt flour and 2 cups (250 g) of the barley flour. Make a well in the center of the flour mixture. When the milk is lukewarm (98°F/37°C), beat the yeast into it, then pour this into the well. Stir to form a stiff batter. Cover and set in a warm place until doubled in bulk (about 3 hours) or until the sponge has risen to the top of the bowl.

Stir down the sponge and add the rye flour and the remaining barley flour. Work into a dough and knead on a well-floured surface for 15 to 20 minutes.

Optional step: Cover and set aside in a warm place until doubled in bulk. Knock down and knead an additional 15 to 20 minutes.

Shape the dough into a flattish round loaf 12 to 13 inches (30 to 33 cm) in diameter. Grease a 16-inch (40-cm) pizza pan and scatter spelt meal or bran over it. Set the dough on this and, using the edge of a ruler, press 4 incisions into the dough to divide it into 8 equal sections. Stick the end of the ruler into the middle of each section. Then scatter spelt flour over the dough, filling the incisions liberally. Cover and set aside in a warm place to rise, allowing 6 to 8 hours.

When the dough has risen, preheat the oven to 175°F (80°C), uncover the bread, and put it into the oven. Let it "spring" (puff up) in the oven as it warms for 15 minutes. *Do not open the oven door.* Increase the heat to 450°F (230°C) and bake for an additional 15 minutes. Reduce the temperature to 400°F (205°C) and bake for another 15 minutes. Then lower the temperature to 350°F (175°C) and bake for 30 to 35 minutes or until the bread taps hollow. Cool on a rack. Do not cut the bread while it is hot.

Note: To create a crispier crust, lightly brush the bread with ice water as soon as it comes from the oven. For a soft crust, brush the crust with oil or melted butter.

BUCKEYE BREAD
(BUCHSAWEBROD)

From the area around Lancaster, Ohio, this is an excellent example of how light cornbread was made in the 1820s, before the introduction of chemical leaveners. The original recipe was meant to be baked in a cast-iron Dutch oven. To re-create this down-hearth technique, use an 8-quart (8-liter) Dutch oven with lid, preferably one with a porcelainized interior.

YIELD: APPROXIMATELY 10 SERVINGS

OLD-STYLE YEAST
8 dried hops blossoms
1 cup (250 ml) boiling spring water

SHORTCUT YEAST
1 tablespoon sugar
1 cup (250 ml) warm milk (98°F/37°C)
¼ ounce (7 g) active dry yeast

2 cups (500 ml) whole milk, scalded
2 cups (250 g) organic yellow cornmeal
2 cups (500 ml) active Sourdough Liquid Yeast (p. 79)
3 large eggs
3 tablespoons (45 g) sea salt
3 cups (375 g) organic whole spelt flour
5½ cups (685 g) organic white bread flour
organic white bread flour
organic yellow corn grits

To make old-style yeast, infuse the hops in the water for 30 minutes, then strain and discard the blossoms. Reserve the hops tea.

To make shortcut yeast, dissolve the sugar in the milk and proof the yeast in it.

Pour the scalding-hot milk over the cornmeal in a deep bowl. Beat with a whisk until smooth, then add the old-style or shortcut yeast and the sourdough liquid yeast.

Beat the eggs until lemon colored and fold into the cornmeal slurry. Sift together the salt, spelt flour, and bread flour. Measure out 5½ cups (685 g) and stir into the cornmeal mixture. Work into a soft, sticky dough. Cover and set in a warm place until doubled in bulk (about 3 hours).

Stir down the raised dough and beat in the remaining flour mixture. Dust a work surface with bread flour and knead the dough until spongy, working in only enough additional flour so that the dough is no longer sticky.

Grease an 8-quart (8-liter) Dutch oven and scatter yellow corn grits over the bottom. Place the dough in the Dutch oven, cover, and set in a warm place to rise. Allow 3 to 6 hours, depending on the weather; the dough should rise to the top of the pan.

Preeat the oven to 175°F (80°C). Uncover the dough and place the Dutch oven immediately in the oven. Let the dough "spring" (puff up) in the oven for 15 minutes. Then, without opening the door, increase the temperature to 450°F (235°C) and bake 15 minutes. Lower the temperature to 400°F (205°C) and bake an additional 15 minutes. Then lower the heat to 350°F (175°C) and bake 20 to 25 minutes or until the bread taps hollow on the bottom. Cool on a rack.

MILK BREAD
(MILLICHBROD)

Millichbrod *is what good bread should be by definition. It is the white bread that once made Pennsylvania Dutch bakers so universally admired in this country, and its revival is long overdue.*

When molded into a stollen-shaped Feschtleeb *(celebration loaf), there was no white bread of greater esteem on the Pennsylvania German table, for this was the honorary white bread of weddings, baptisms, and funerals. It was the white part of this bread that yielded the crumbs for* Mutschelmehl, *a necessary ingredient in many of our classic folk recipes.*

The recipe published here comes from Johann Raab, a German baker who lived in Philadelphia during the 1790s.

YIELD: 16 TO 20 SERVINGS

1 cup (250 ml) active Sourdough Liquid Yeast (p. 79)
¼ ounce (7 g) active dry yeast
2 cups (500 ml) lukewarm whole milk, buttermilk, or whey (98°F/37°C) (see note)
10 cups (1.25 kg) organic white bread flour
3 tablespoons (45 g) sea salt
cold water

To imitate old-style brewer's yeast, put the sourdough yeast in a cup or jar, set in a bowl of warm water (115°F/46°C), and warm it to 90°F (32°C). Proof the dry yeast in this, then combine with the warm milk. Put this mixture in a deep bowl and stir in 2 cups (250 g) of flour to form a slurry. Cover and set aside to rise until foamy (about 2 hours). Then stir down with a wooden spoon.

Sift together the remaining flour and the salt, then stir into the slurry. Use only enough flour to form a dough that is not sticky when touched. Knead 15 to 20 minutes or until soft and spongy, then cover and set aside in a warm place to double in bulk (about 8 hours). Knock down and knead again for

15 to 20 minutes, then form into 2 round loaves (*boules*) or into one *Feschtleeb* and set on greased 12-inch (30-cm) pizza pans or a well-floured earthenware pie plate.

Cover and let the bread recover until fully risen (about 40 minutes). Preheat the oven to 175°F (80°C). Put the bread in the oven and *do not open the door again* until the bread is done. Let the loaves "spring" (puff up) in the oven for 10 minutes, then raise the temperature to 450°F (235°C) and bake 15 minutes. Reduce the temperature to 400°F (205°C) and bake 15 minutes. Then reduce the temperature to 350°F (175°C) and bake an additional 25 to 30 minutes or until the bread taps hollow on the bottom. Upon removing the bread from the oven, immediately brush it with cold water, then cool on racks.

Note: For a more intense sourdough flavor, substitute cultured buttermilk for part or all of the 2 cups (500 ml) of milk called for in the recipe. If no sourdough starter is on hand, substitute 1 cup (250 ml) lukewarm milk (98°F/37°C) and proof ½ ounce (14 g) active dry yeast in it, omitting the ¼ ounce (7 g) of yeast called for in the recipe.

German Rampion, an old root and leaf vegetable.

SPELT BREAD
(DINKELBROD)

Because spelt gives a higher yield per acre than oats, some Amish farmers raise it as horse feed. Amish horses have been getting a great deal because spelt is rich in nutrients. It is also easier to digest for people allergic to wheat products, and it makes delicious bread.

YIELD: MINIMUM OF 10 TO 15 SERVINGS

OLD-STYLE YEAST
8 dried hops blossoms
1 cup (250 ml) boiling potato water
2 cups (500 ml) active Sourdough Liquid Yeast (p. 79)

SHORTCUT YEAST
½ ounce (14 g) active dry yeast
3 cups (750 ml) lukewarm potato water (98°F/37°C)

1 cup (250 g) cooked mashed potatoes
¼ cup (60 g) butter or shortening
2 tablespoons (30 g) sea salt
13 cups (1.625 kg) organic whole spelt flour
spelt meal or yellow corn grits

To make old-style yeast, infuse the hops in the water for 30 minutes, then strain and discard the blossoms. Combine the hops tea with the liquid yeast in a wide-mouthed jar. Set the jar in a pan of warm water (115°F/46°C) and proof the yeast until it begins to overflow.

To make shortcut yeast, proof the dry yeast in the potato water until foamy.

Combine the mashed potatoes, butter, and salt, then add the yeast (either old-style or shortcut) and 3½ cups (435 g) of spelt flour. Whisk to form a thick slurry, cover, and set in a warm place until doubled in bulk (about 2 hours).

Stir down with a wooden spoon and add the remaining flour. Knead for 20 minutes and form into a round loaf (*boule*). Grease a 16-inch (40-cm) pizza pan and scatter spelt meal or grits over it. Put the molded loaf on this, dust the top with spelt meal or spelt flour, and cover with a cloth. Set in a warm place to rise at least 6 hours, preferably overnight.

Preheat the oven to 175°F (80°C). Remove the cloth from the bread and put it in the oven immediately. Let the bread "spring" (puff up) for 15 minutes, then increase the temperature to 450°F (235°C) and bake for 15 minutes. Reduce the temperature to 400°F (205°C) and bake another 15 minutes. Then lower the temperature to 350°F (175°C) and bake for 30 to 35 minutes or until the bread taps hollow on the bottom. Cool on a rack.

Note: Traditional Pennsylvania German spelt bread was also baked in 8-inch (20-cm) crescents that were brushed with a mixture of 1 tablespoon molasses thinned with 1 tablespoon of saffron water as soon as the bread was taken from the oven. This is the same glaze used on St. Martin's Horns (p. 164).

POTATO BREAD FOR BRICK OVENS
(GRUMBIEREBROD FER DIE BACKOFFE)

This recipe comes from the Broadwater (Breitwasser) family of Lonaconing, Maryland, but actually traces to an 1830 Germantown, Pennsylvania, almanac.[6] In the late nineteenth century it was widely circulated among members of the Church of the Brethren in the Mid-Atlantic states and the Midwest. This bread is most like the white breads of rural Alsace and the Pfalz: crusty, chewy, with a delicious nutty flavor.

YIELD: 10 TO 20 SERVINGS

OLD-STYLE YEAST
8 dried hops blossoms
½ cup (125 ml) boiling potato water
1 cup (250 ml) active Hagerstown Liquid Yeast (p. 77)

SHORTCUT YEAST
½ ounce (14 g) active dry yeast
1½ cups (375 ml) lukewarm potato water (98°F/37°C)

2 cups (500 g) cooked mashed potatoes
½ cup (125 g) sugar
6 tablespoons (90 g) sea salt
15 to 16 cups (1.875 to 2 kg) organic white bread flour

To make old-style yeast, infuse the hops in the water for 30 minutes, then strain and discard the blossoms. Combine the hops tea with the liquid yeast in a wide-mouthed jar. Set the jar in a pan of warm water (98°F/37°C) and proof the yeast mixture until it overflows.

To make shortcut yeast, proof the dry yeast in the potato water until foamy.

Combine the mashed potatoes, sugar, and salt with 3 cups (750 ml) of boiling water. Stir in 8 cups (1 kg) of bread flour to form a thick slurry. Add the proofed yeast (either old-style or shortcut), then cover and set aside to rise until doubled in bulk (about 2 hours). Stir down and add the remaining flour. Knead 20 minutes on a clean work surface dusted liberally with flour.

Optional step: Cover and set aside to rise again until doubled in bulk. Knock down and knead 20 minutes.

Form the dough into a round loaf (*boule*) and set on a greased 16-inch (40-cm) pizza pan.

Optional step: Stamp the center of the loaf with a traditional Pennsylvania German carved wooden bread mold or a greased iron trivet with a hex sign pattern. If a wooden bread mold is used, leave it on the loaf while it rises. A butter print with a hex sign motif may be substituted for a bread stamp. Bread stamps and butter prints can be purchased directly from the carvers listed in A Cook's Guide to Regional Shopping (p. 184). Most of those craftspeople will also carve special mold patterns on commission.

Cover the dough and let it rise in a warm place for 2 to 3 hours or until the loaf is roughly 5 inches (13 cm) high. (Remove the optional wooden bread stamp.)

Preheat the oven to 450°F (235°C). Bake the bread 15 minutes, then reduce the temperature to 400°F (205°C) and continue baking for another 15 minutes. Reduce the temperature to 375°F (190°C) and bake for 30 to 35 minutes or until the bread taps hollow on the bottom. Cool on a rack. Do not cut the bread until it is room temperature.

PINCH-DECORATED FLAT BREAD
(PETZKUCHE)

Many Pennsylvania Dutch trace their ancestry to the Odenwald, a thickly forested region in the modern German state of Hessen. There, as in Pennsylvania, this folk bread is still baked by those few holdouts who cherish their heirloom brick bread ovens.

There is no English equivalent for Petzkuche, at least no name that is neatly translatable. In German the verb petzen means "to pinch," and the distinctive patterns on the surface of this rich, crispy, buttery bread are made by doing precisely that. Historically, Petzkuche was eaten at meals like breadsticks or crackers, or when stale, toasted and served like croutons in soup.

YIELD: 30 TO 40 SERVINGS

OLD-STYLE YEAST
8 dried hops blossoms
1 cup (250 ml) boiling spring water
1¼ cups (310 ml) active Hagerstown Liquid Yeast
  (p. 77)

SHORTCUT YEAST
½ ounce (14 g) active dry yeast
2¼ cups (560 ml) lukewarm water (98°F/37°C)

8¾ cups (1.09 kg) organic white bread flour
1 tablespoon (15 g) sea salt
12 ounces (375 g) unsalted butter
butter to fill the pinches (at least 4 ounces/125 g)
6 tablespoons (90 g) cold unsalted butter

To make old-style yeast, infuse the hops in the water for 30 minutes, then strain and discard the blossoms. Combine the hops tea with the liquid yeast in a wide-mouthed jar. Set the jar in a pan of warm water (98°F/37°C) and let the yeast proof until it overflows.

To make shortcut yeast, proof the active dry yeast in the lukewarm water.

While the yeast is proofing, sift the flour and salt together in a large bowl. Then cut the butter into small pieces and mix with the flour. Either rub the butter and flour through a sieve to form a fine crumb or process the mixture in a food processor.

Make a well in the center of the crumbs and add the proofed yeast. Work into a stiff dough but do not knead. Cover and allow to double in bulk (about 2 hours). When doubled in bulk, knock the dough down and roll out to roughly 2 inches (5 cm) thick. Then fold the dough over twice. "Brake" the dough by striking it vigorously with a rolling pin at least three times. Then roll the dough out 1 inch (2.5 cm) thick, fold it over twice, and brake it again. Repeat this at least 5 times or until the dough becomes soft and pliant.

Divide the dough into 3 equal portions and roll them out ½ inch (1 cm) thick on 3 greased baking sheets measuring roughly 12 by 18 inches (30 by 46 cm). As the dough is rolled, try to keep it in a rectangular shape.

Starting along one edge of the dough, use the fingers to make a row of deep pinches, spacing them about 1 inch (2 cm) apart. Repeat by making another row about 3 to 4 inches (7.5 to 10 cm) from the first. Cover all the sheets of dough with rows of pinches in this same manner. The most important point is that the rows be parallel and evenly spaced, regardless of number. This is what gives the bread its decorative appearance.

With a fork, prick a line down the center of the spaces between each row of pinches. Do this between all the rows of pinches, and be certain to press down hard enough to touch the baking sheet with the tines of the fork.

Fill each pinch hole with a tiny dot of butter. Cover the doughs and let them recover for approximately 30 minutes. While they are rising, preheat the oven to 400°F (205°C). Bake the bread for 25 minutes or until golden brown. As the bread is removed from the oven, rub it liberally with cold butter, at least 2 tablespoons (30 g) per bread sheet. *Petzkuche* is best served hot on the day it is baked.

Weaverland Wedding Bread and Pinch-Decorated Flat Bread.

WEAVERLAND WEDDING BREAD
(WEBERDAALER HOCHZICHBROD)

My old friend Ivan Glick and I were in the back reaches of the Conestoga Valley, deep in the Welsh Mountains that straddle the border of Chester and Lancaster counties, when we came upon a remarkable 1740s stone cabin. The setting is still quite vivid in my mind: early April, new grass in the fields, a hint of green in the surrounding woods, cows in the distance wearing bells, and near the foundation of the old house, a wonderful cold brook overgrown with the crispest watercress I have ever tasted.

The ancient Mennonite woman who lived there spoke Pennsylfaanisch of the purest and most nasal kind — like old French, virtually a voice out of the eighteenth century. It developed that she was born a Weber (Weaver), as I was, and this fortuitous bit of Freindschaft was enough to break the ice. She had heard of my grandfather Weaver through Ira Landis, a Mennonite genealogist, and finally, or should I say long at last, with an impish sparkle in her eyes, she passed over to me a recipe that was truly a Weaver family heirloom.

Many years later, while investigating the collections of the Swiss National Museum in Zurich, I discovered a 1527 embroidered tablecloth depicting dishes and all the accoutrements of a meal. One of the breads embroidered onto that tablecloth was cousin Mary Hildebrand's bread.

I am now satisfied to imagine that Swiss-born Margarethe Weber, whose husband bought up the Lancaster County valley known as Weaverland in 1721, was the great progenitrix of this wedding bread recipe, which has been passed down from Weaver mother to daughter for at least ten generations. This is the bread they served as wedding cake. The recipe makes two flower-shaped loaves or one large (16-inch/40-cm) loaf, as shown on page 87.

YIELD: 16 TO 20 SERVINGS (see note)

OLD-STYLE YEAST
8 dried hops blossoms
½ teaspoon ground saffron (contents of one 10-grain vial)
½ cup (125 ml) milk or whey, scalded
1 cup (250 ml) active Sourdough Liquid Yeast (p. 79)

SHORTCUT YEAST
2 teaspoons honey
1 cup (250 ml) lukewarm milk (98°F/37°C)
½ ounce (14 g) active dry yeast
½ teaspoon ground saffron (contents of one 10-grain vial)
½ cup (125 ml) whole milk, scalded

½ cup (125 g) unsalted butter, cut up
8 cups (1 kg) organic white bread flour
1 tablespoon aniseed
1 cup (250 g) small-curd cottage cheese
½ cup (125 ml) honey
1 tablespoon (15 g) sea salt
2 large eggs
whole cloves
1 large egg yolk
3 tablespoons (45 ml) milk

To make old-style yeast, infuse the hops and saffron in the scalding-hot milk for 20 minutes, then strain and discard the blossoms. Combine the infusion with the liquid yeast in a wide-mouthed jar. Set the jar in a pan of warm water (115°F/46°C) and proof the yeast until it begins to foam.

To make shortcut yeast, dissolve the honey in the lukewarm milk and proof the dry yeast in it. While the yeast is proofing, infuse the saffron in the scalding-hot milk for 20 minutes. Then add the saffron infusion to the proofed yeast.

Place the cut-up butter in a large bowl and sift the flour over it. Rub the mixture through a sieve or colander to form a fine crumb or process it in a food processor. Add the aniseed, then make a well in the center of the crumb mixture.

In a separate bowl or a food processor, beat the cottage cheese to a smooth purée with the honey and salt. Beat the eggs until lemon colored and combine with the cheese purée. Then add the saffron-flavored yeast (either old-style or shortcut). Pour this mixture into the well in the crumb mixture and work into a soft dough. Knead 10 to 15 minutes or until pliant and spongy, dusting with additional flour only if the dough is sticky to touch. Cover and set aside in a warm place to rise until doubled in bulk (about 2 hours).

For 2 loaves, knock the dough down and divide it into 2 equal portions. Divide each portion into 7 equal pieces, allowing 1 piece for the center of each flower and 6 for the surrounding petals. Knead the center pieces into balls. Lay them on the greased baking sheets. Knead the pieces for petals individually about 5 minutes, then mold into petal shapes. Attach the petals to the centers to form flowers. Cover and allow the flowers to recover for about 35 to 40 minutes or until fully risen.

Preheat the oven to 375°F (190°C). When the dough has recovered, slash each petal in a zigzag pattern lengthwise down the center with a sharp knife. Cut a ring in the middle piece of each flower with knife or round cookie cutter. Stick cloves into the flower centers.

Bake for 30 minutes. At the end of 30 minutes, beat the egg yolk and milk together to form a glazing mixture. Remove the bread from the oven and brush with the glazing mixture, then bake an additional 5 to 8 minutes or until the glaze is set and the bread taps hollow on the bottom. Cool on racks.

Historical note: This old-style curd bread was traditionally made in large batches. Several women would work together from scratch, starting with raw milk, and produce the necessary yeasts, curds, fresh butter, ground saffron, and specially prepared flour. They would bake perhaps as many as twenty or thirty loaves at a time, in addition to the other baked things required for a large wedding feast.

ANNIE WAMPOLE'S CORNSTARCH CAKE
(DER ANNI WAMPOLE IHR WELSCHKANNKUCHE)

During the 1850s, Mrs. Charles L. Wampole of Norristown was considered one of the leading home cooks in Pennsylvania. At state fairs she usually took prizes for her apple butters, peach butters, and homemade soaps.[7] But it was her cornstarch cake that made her famous.

Annie Wampole first exhibited her cake at the Montgomery County Agricultural Show in 1855, where it took first prize. Her clever recipe was published soon afterward in the popular almanac Der Neue Amerikanische Landwirtschafts-Calender and quickly became a Pennsylvania Dutch favorite because it made use of egg whites left over from noodle-making. This recipe may be the original angel food cake.

YIELD: 10 TO 12 SERVINGS

½ cup (120 g) unsalted butter
1 cup (250 g) superfine sugar
5 drops essence of bitter almond
1 cup (110 g) cornstarch
1 cup (125 g) pastry flour
1 teaspoon cream of tartar
½ teaspoon baking soda
8 large egg whites
⅓ cup (45 g) slivered almonds

Preheat the oven to 375°F (190°C). In a large bowl, cream the butter and sugar, then add the almond essence. In a separate bowl, sift together the cornstarch, flour, cream of tartar, and baking soda twice. Beat the egg whites with a whisk until they form stiff peaks, then fold them into the butter and sugar mixture. Gently fold in the flour mixture a little at a time, then the almonds. Pour the batter into a greased 10-inch (26-cm) tube pan and bake 40 minutes or until the cake tests done. Cool on a rack before removing from the pan. Serve without icing.

CHICKWEED PIE
(HINKELDARREMKUCHE)

This very old recipe was never written down until I convinced an elderly cousin of mine to work through it so that I could weigh and measure step-by-step. I am certain that the pie was originally baked in a yeast-raised crust, but sometime in the nineteenth century there was a shift to short pastry. I now have the redware dish that my cousin used all her life to bake the pie in. After I had baked in it myself several times, I was startled to learn from a ceramics specialist that it dated from the 1790s. Had the Bucklich Mennli known, surely it would have cracked in half right before my eyes.

Although it is best served hot, Chickweed Pie will keep for 1 to 2 days in the refrigerator and can be reheated in a microwave oven.

Some advice about harvesting chickweed. Stellaria media grows like a mat against the ground. It is at its peak for culinary purposes right before it blooms. When the plant blossoms, it is covered with tiny white starlike flowers. These go to seed, and in the early fall another crop appears.

YIELD: 6 TO 8 SERVINGS

3 cups (250 g) finely chopped chickweed
1 cup (185 g) diced slab bacon
½ cup (75 g) finely chopped onion
3 large eggs
1½ cups (375 ml) sour cream
1 tablespoon all-purpose flour
½ teaspoon grated nutmeg

*Common chickweed (*Stellaria media*) makes a delicious lunch pie in early spring or fall.*

Preheat the oven to 325°F (165°C). Line a 10-inch (26-cm) pie dish with short crust. Make a raised border around the rim to prevent the filling from overflowing during baking. Pick the chickweed clean of dead leaves and twigs that may have become tangled in it as it grew. Trim off the root ends of the stems, reserving only the greenest and leafiest parts. Rinse thoroughly in a colander, then pat dry with paper towels.

Bunch the chickweed together into a ball and chop it with a sharp knife, or put it into a food processor and process with the chopping blade until reduced to a confetti texture. Measure out 3 cups (250 g) and place into a large bowl.

Fry the diced bacon in a skillet until it begins to brown, then add the onion. Cook until the onion wilts (about 3 minutes). Remove the bacon and onion mixture with a slotted spoon and add to the chickweed. Discard the drippings from the pan. Beat the eggs until lemon colored, then add the sour cream, flour, and nutmeg. Combine the egg mixture with the chickweed and bacon.

Spread the filling evenly in the prepared pie shell and pat down firmly with a spoon. Bake for 1 hour. The pie is done when it has set in the center and has developed a golden tinge across the top.

Note: Less adventuresome cooks may substitute 4 cups (260 g) finely chopped spinach for the chickweed. This, of course, changes the recipe to *Schpinatkuche* (Spinach Pie).

YEAST-RAISED BUTTER CRUST
(BUTTERDEEG)

This is the basic yeast-raised dough for old-style Pennsylvania Dutch fruit and onion pies. Before tin baking sheets came into general use in the nineteenth century, most of our traditional pies were made round, about 12 to 14 inches (30 to 35 cm) in diameter.

YIELD: 10 TO 12 SERVINGS

OLD-STYLE YEAST
8 dried hops blossoms
½ cup (125 ml) boiling spring water
1 cup (250 ml) active Sourdough Liquid Yeast (p. 79)

SHORTCUT YEAST
¼ ounce (7 g) active dry yeast
1½ cups (375 ml) lukewarm water (98°F/37°C)

3½ cups (430 g) organic white bread flour
½ teaspoon sea salt
¼ cup (60 g) cold unsalted butter, cut up
3 large eggs

To make old-style yeast, infuse the hops for 20 minutes in the water, then strain and discard the flowers. Combine the hops tea and liquid yeast in a wide-mouthed jar. Set the jar in a pan of warm water (115°F/46°C) and proof the yeast until it begins to overflow.

To make shortcut yeast, proof the dry yeast in the lukewarm water.

Sift the flour and salt into a deep bowl. Add the butter and rub the mixture through a sieve or colander to form a fine crumb or process it in a food processor. Make a well in the center of the crumbs.

Beat the egg yolks into the yeast (either old-style or shortcut) and pour into the well in the crumb mixture. Stir and work into a stiff dough. Knead 5 to 10 minutes on a well-floured work surface until the dough is soft and spongy and no longer sticks to the fingers. Cover and set aside in a warm place to rise until doubled in bulk (about 1½ hours).

Knock down the dough and roll it out until ½ inch (1 cm) thick. Lightly grease a round baking pan measuring approximately 12 inches (30 cm) in diameter and line it with the dough. Push the dough about ¾ to 1 inch (1.5 to 2 cm) up the sides of the pan. (If the side crust is lower than this, the filling may overflow.) Prick the bottom of the dough with a fork to prevent it from blistering during baking. Then set aside and let the dough recover for 10 to 15 minutes.

Preheat the oven to 375°F (190°C). Fill the crust with the pie filling as directed and bake for 40 minutes or until the filling is set in the middle and the crust is golden brown.

Note: Any sort of pie filling may be baked in this crust as long as the volume of the prebaked filling does not exceed 1 to 1½ quarts (1 to 1.5 liters).

APPLE BUTTER PIE
(LATTWAERRICK-KUCHE)

Cider Pie in New England, Apple Butter Pie in the Mid-Atlantic states, there are innumerable names and regional nuances for this early American classic. The original Pennsylvania Dutch method of making it, however, is similar to that for the traditional flat fruit tarts of southwestern Germany and France. The filling for this recipe comes from a member of the Zion Mennonite Church in Souderton, Pennsylvania.

YIELD: 24 SERVINGS

1½ cups (185 g) pitted sun-dried cherries
3 tablespoons (45 ml) kirsch or pear schnapps
1 recipe Yeast-Raised Butter Crust (p. 91)
2 cups (510 g) unsweetened, unspiced apple butter
½ cup (90 g) brown sugar
½ teaspoon sea salt
1 teaspoon ground cinnamon
3 large eggs
¼ cup (60 ml) whole milk
1½ tablespoons cassia sugar or vanilla sugar (see note)

The night before baking, combine the dried cherries and kirsch in a small bowl. Cover and infuse 8 hours.

Prepare the crust. Grease an 11½- by 17-inch (28- by 42.5-cm) baking sheet. After the dough has risen, knock it down and spread it evenly on the baking sheet. Push up the dough along the sides to form a 1-inch (2-cm) rim. Prick the bottom with a fork and set aside to recover for 15 minutes.

While the dough is recovering, preheat the oven to 375°F (190°C). Mix the apple butter, brown sugar, salt, and cinnamon. Beat the eggs until lemon colored, then combine with the milk. Stir into the apple butter mixture to form a thick batter. Strain the infused cherries from any remaining liquid and scatter them over the unbaked crust. Then add the batter. Bake for 40 minutes. Cool on a rack. When cool, scatter cassia sugar or vanilla sugar over the surface of the pie. Cut the pie into 3-inch (7.5-cm) squares and serve.

Note: To make cassia sugar, combine 1½ teaspoons of ground cassia with 1½ tablespoons of sugar. For directions on making vanilla sugar, refer to the note on page 100.

GREEN APPLE PIE
(GRIENE EBBELKUCHE)

For this excellent recipe, which was published in 1887, I suggest Winesap or Smokehouse apples, slightly unripe of course.[8]

YIELD: SERVES 8 TO 10

short pastry crust
5½ cups (1.1 kg) shredded raw apple (about 6 apples, pared and cored)
6 tablespoons (90 g) unsalted butter
1 cup (170 g) dark brown sugar
¾ cup (95 g) chopped pitted sun-dried cherries or chopped dried pears
¾ cup (95 g) chopped hickory nuts
¼ cup (60 ml) lime juice
1 teaspoon ground allspice
4 large eggs
candied angelica or citron (optional)

Preheat the oven to 350°F (175°C). Line a 12-inch (30-cm) tart pan (approximately 1½ to 2 inches/3 to 5 cm deep) with short crust. Prick the bottom with a fork. Shred the apples and put them in a deep bowl. Cook the butter and sugar together in a saucepan over medium heat until the mixture bubbles and begins to smell like butterscotch (about 5 minutes). Add the dried cherries and plump them in the sugar mixture. When the cherries are soft, add them together with the butter mixture to the shredded apples. Then add the hickory nuts, lime juice, and allspice. Beat the eggs until lemon colored and fold them into the apple mixture. Pour into the pastry shell, pat down with a knife or spatula to smooth the surface, then bake for 60 minutes or until set in the center. Cool on a rack and decorate, if desired, with candied angelica or citron.

CHOCOLATE GINGERBREAD
(WEICHE LEBKUCHE MIT TSCHAKLETT)

The Pennsylvania Dutch make two types of gingerbread: a cake like the recipe here and a cookie. The cookie is by far the older of the two. The cake evolved in the nineteenth century with the coming of the cookstove and the invention of baking powder. Called Weiche Lebkuche (soft gingerbread) in Pennsylfaanisch, this is the cake most Americans now associate with the word gingerbread.

Johanna Portman's Union County recipe for chocolate-flavored gingerbread is notable in several regards. It is intensely chocolate, not too sweet, and it is meant to be served in small portions.

Yellow Transparent apples (foreground) and Summer Rambos in baskets from the 1840s.

The best news is that, as cakes go, the Portman recipe is relatively low in fat, and molasses is the only sweetener. Because of the low fat content, the cake tends to become dry if kept too long, so it is best served the day it is made.

Lastly, do not use ground ginger. Use grated fresh ginger root as directed.

YIELD: 16 PORTIONS

1 cup (250 ml) unsulfured molasses
½ cup (125 ml) sour cream or buttermilk
1 tablespoon grated ginger root
1 tablespoon grated orange zest
1 teaspoon ground cassia or cinnamon
½ teaspoon sea salt
¼ cup (60 g) unsalted butter
2 ounces (60 g) unsweetened baking chocolate
1 teaspoon baking soda
1 teaspoon water
2 cups (250 g) organic spelt flour (or substitute double-sifted whole-wheat flour)
fine cake crumbs or white breadcrumbs
white sand sugar (see note)

Preheat the oven to 375°F (190°C). Combine the molasses, sour cream, ginger, orange zest, cassia, and salt in a deep bowl. Melt the butter and chocolate in a double boiler over simmering water, then fold it into the batter. Dissolve the baking soda in the water and add to the liquid mixture, folding and sifting a little at a time until thoroughly combined.

Grease two 7-inch (18-cm) pie pans and dust with fine stale cake crumbs or breadcrumbs. Add the batter and scatter sand sugar over the top.

Bake for 35 to 40 minutes or until the cakes test done in the center. Cool on racks. Serve at room temperature.

N o t e : Sand sugar is a white granular sugar that is sold in many supermarkets for cake and cookie decoration. It often comes in mixed or single colors.

MORAVIAN SUGAR CAKE
(HANNHUTTER ZUCKERBROD)

After visiting Bethlehem, Pennsylvania, in 1906, food writer Julia Davis Chandler observed that Moravian sugar cake was baked throughout the area on Saturday so that it could be served for Sunday evening supper.[9] Each Moravian community, be it Bethlehem or Lititz in Pennsylvania or Old Salem in North Carolina, made sugar cake in slightly different ways. Regardless of those variations, the oldest and most traditional shape for the cake was round, the same size as the wooden peels on which they were raised. The quantity given here will make one 16-inch (40-cm) round cake, or it will fill a 2-inch (5-cm) deep rectangular pan measuring 8 by 14 inches (20 by 35 cm).

YIELD: 15 TO 20 SERVINGS

OLD-STYLE YEAST
8 dried hops blossoms
1 cup (250 ml) boiling potato water
1 cup (250 ml) active Sourdough Liquid Yeast (p. 79)

SHORTCUT YEAST
¼ ounce (7 g) active dry yeast
2 cups (500 ml) warm potato water (115°F/46°C)

¾ cup (185 g) unsalted butter
1 cup (250 ml) whole milk
1 cup (250 g) cooked mashed potatoes
8 cups (1 kg) organic white bread flour
1 teaspoon sea salt
2 large eggs
2 tablespoons (20 g) ground cinnamon
1 cup (170 g) brown sugar
½ cup (125 g) superfine sugar

Moravian Sugar Cake baked in its traditional round shape.

To make old-style yeast, infuse the hops in the potato water for 20 minutes, then strain out the blossoms. Combine the tea with the liquid yeast in a wide-mouthed jar. Set the jar in a pan of warm water (115°F/46°C) and proof the yeast until it begins to overflow.

To make shortcut yeast, proof the dry yeast in the potato water until foamy.

Chop ½ cup (125 g) of the butter and put it in a saucepan with the milk. Warm over medium heat until the butter melts. Remove from the heat and let the mixture cool until lukewarm (98°F/37°C), then combine it with the yeast (either old-style or shortcut). Put the mashed potatoes in a deep bowl with 3 cups (375 g) of flour and the salt. Add the yeast mixture and stir to form a thick slurry. Cover and set aside in a warm place until doubled in bulk and covered with bubbles (about 2½ hours).

Beat the eggs until lemon colored and fold into the slurry. Add 1 tablespoon of cinnamon and ½ cup (85 g) of brown sugar that has been sifted to remove lumps. Then stir in the remaining flour. Beat the dough vigorously for about 5 minutes.

For a traditional round sugar cake, spread the dough on a greased 16-inch (40-cm) pizza pan. Make it thicker in the center than around the edges and leave about 1 inch (2.5 cm) between the edges and the rim of the pan to allow for rising. Set aside in a warm place and let the dough rise until about 3 inches (7.5 cm) high in the middle (about 1½ hours).

Once the dough has risen, preheat the oven to 350°F (175°C). Cream the remaining ½ cup brown sugar and ¼ cup butter with 1 tablespoon of cinnamon. Grease the index finger and press holes into the raised dough at even intervals. Fill each hole with ½ teaspoon of the butter paste. Pinch the holes together and bake 30 to 35 minutes or until the cake tests done in the center.

If the cake is baked in a deep rectangular pan, extend the baking time by 10 minutes. When the cake is done, remove from the oven and cool on a rack. Sift the superfine sugar over the cake to create a "snowy" appearance. Do not cut the cake until it is room temperature.

ONION PIE
(ZWIWWELKUCHE)

Of all the old-style Pennsylvania Dutch "pies," this was basic. It was served as a snack to field hands during harvesting breaks. It appeared at virtually every gathering where large numbers of people needed to be fed, and in many households it was a favorite dish for evening supper.

This recipe is the one my family uses. It is much like the "classic" recipes found in old cookbooks, even though it comes directly out of my grandmother's head — it was one of the first things she learned to make for my grandfather when they were married.

While country-smoked slab bacon certainly gives Zwiwwelkuche a unique flavor, vegetarian alternatives abound, like the one I have provided made with prunes.

YIELD: 10 TO 12 SERVINGS

1 recipe Yeast-Raised Butter Crust (p. 91) or any pizza dough
4 cups (500 g) sliced onion
3 tablespoons (45 ml) safflower oil or butter
⅔ cup (125 g) diced slab bacon
4 large eggs
1 cup (250 ml) sour cream or organic yogurt
1 teaspoon caraway seed

Prepare the butter crust as directed. Cover and set aside to double in bulk.

While the dough is rising, put the onions and the oil in a heavy skillet, cover, and sweat over medium heat until soft and beginning to brown (about 15 minutes). Fry the bacon in a separate pan until golden, then drain and reserve.

Preheat the oven to 375°F (190°C). Press down the raised dough and roll it out to ¼ inch (6 mm) thick. Line a baking pan measuring 8½ by 14 inches (21 by 35 cm) with the dough. Roll the edges of the dough down and tuck under to form an even rim about 2 inches (5 cm) high along the sides. Let the crust recover for about 15 minutes, then spread the cooked onions and bacon evenly over the bottom.

Beat the eggs until lemon colored, then combine with the sour cream. Spread over the onions, then scatter caraway seed over the top. Bake 30 to 40 minutes or until the filling has set and begun to turn golden brown on the surface. Serve hot or at room temperature.

For a meatless alternative, omit the bacon and scatter 1 cup (150 g) chopped prunes over the cooked onions when filling the pie. Cover this with the sour cream mixture and scatter caraway seed over the top. Bake as directed above.

SHOOFLY PIE
(MELASSICH-RIWWELKUCHE)

Shoofly Pie is a breakfast cake meant to be eaten early in the morning with plenty of hot coffee. It first appeared in 1876 at the Centennial in Philadelphia under the name Centennial Cake. Recipes for Centennial Cake were circulated many years afterward among upcountry cooks, but it was the alternate names — Granger Pie and Shoofly Pie — that became the most popular, the latter doubtless in reference to the brand name of molasses that went into the original recipe.

Today there are many versions of Shoofly Pie — wet bottom, dry bottom, chocolate flavored. I firmly believe that the original recipe is by far the best. In the early 1930s my grandmother Weaver obtained the Centennial recipe from Mrs. Miles Fry of Ephrata, whose family had preserved it from the 1870s. Regardless of personal preferences about Shoofly Pie, remember just one thing: it is not Shoofly Pie unless it is made with molasses.

Onion Pie (Zwiwwelkuche), the classic Pennsylvania Dutch "pizza." Pie crimper by Thomas Loose.

short pastry crust
1½ cups (185 g) all-purpose flour
½ cup (125 g) sugar
½ cup (125 g) unsalted butter
1 teaspoon ground cinnamon
½ teaspoon grated nutmeg
¼ teaspoon sea salt
½ teaspoon baking soda
¾ cup (180 ml) warm water
¾ cup (180 ml) unsulfured molasses

Preheat the oven to 425°F (220°C). Line a 9-inch (23-cm) pie dish with short pastry and set aside. Using a pastry cutter or food processor, work the flour, sugar, and butter to a loose crumb, then add the cinnamon, nutmeg, and salt. In a separate bowl, dissolve the baking soda in the warm water and combine with the molasses. Pour the liquid into the unbaked pie shell, then fill with the crumb mixture. Be certain that the crumbs are spread evenly along the sides; this will help prevent overflow during baking.

Bake the pie in the middle of the oven for 15 minutes, then reduce the temperature to 350°F (160°C) and bake 35 to 40 minutes or until the center of the pie is firm and cakelike. Serve hot from the oven or cool on a rack and serve at room temperature.

Note: Shoofly Pie is delicious when served with cooked puréed pawpaws *(Asminia triloba)*—the green fruit is shown on page 116—or with "apple butter" made from wild May apples *(Podophyllum peltatum)*. As a dessert it goes well with raspberry or strawberry wine or even with pear brandy.

Shoofly Pie may be served either as a breakfast cake with coffee or as a dessert with fruit wine.

YORK COUNTY PEPPERMINT PIE
(YARRICK KAUNDI PEFFERMINZKUCHE)

Several years ago I was pleased to discover a short piece about peppermint pies in Der Reggeboge, *a publication of the Pennsylvania German Society.*[10]

Even though this York County specialty is only one member of a large family of custardy milk pies known among the Pennsylvania Germans as Easter Pies (Oschterkuche), Peppermint Pie is not a typical custard. It is fluffy, airy light, and virtually melts in the mouth, very much like a soufflé.

Another important point is flavor. The intensity of baked peppermint varies with soil and a multitude of other factors affecting the plant, not the least being that some of the volatile oils in peppermint always cook out when subjected to heat. To account for this, peppermint oil may be added to the batter before baking. The pie will then taste as good as it looks and smells.

short pastry crust
½ cup (35 g) minced fresh peppermint (leaves only)
3 large eggs, separated
1 cup (250 ml) organic yogurt
½ cup (125 g) superfine sugar
8 drops peppermint oil (optional)

Preheat the oven to 350°F (175°C). Line a straight-sided 9½- to 10-inch (23.5- to 25-cm) tart pan with short pastry crust. Cover the bottom with the minced peppermint. Beat the the egg yolks until lemon colored, then add the yogurt, sugar, and peppermint oil (if desired). Beat the egg whites until they form stiff peaks, then fold into the egg mixture. Fill the prepared crust and bake for 35 to 40 minutes or until set in the center and turning a golden yellow color. Cool on a rack. Best when served cold.

CUMBERLAND VALLEY CLAFTY PUDDING
(SCHNITZGLAAFDI)

As far as I can determine, this recipe first appeared in print in 1881 in The Cumberland Valley Cook and General Recipe Book *as part of the cultural revival among the Dutch then taking place." Our Glaafdi and the French clafoutis probably share a common origin, although the Pennsylfaanisch word does not derive from French but from the past participle of* laufe, *"to run or pour." A true Glaafdi is a batter pudding that comes out of the oven looking like a cake.*

YIELD: 6 TO 8 SERVINGS

2 cups (130 g) dried apple slices (*Schnitz*)
2 cups (500 ml) boiling water
cracker crumbs
1 cup (125 g) all-purpose flour
1 teaspoon baking powder
1 teaspoon ground cinnamon
1 teaspoon ground clove
4 large eggs
1 cup (250 g) vanilla sugar (see note)
1 cup (250 ml) unsulfured molasses
confectioners' sugar

Put the apple slices in a small heatproof bowl and cover with the boiling water. Infuse 1 hour or until the apples are soft. Drain and reserve the liquid and the fruit separately.

Preheat the oven to 375°F (190°C). Grease a 10½-inch (27 cm) porcelain baking dish and dust it with cracker crumbs. Sift together the flour, baking powder, cinnamon, and cloves. Combine the eggs and vanilla sugar in the bowl of an electric mixer and beat until frothy. Gradually beat in the molasses, reserved liquid from the infused apples, and the flour mixture.

Spread the apples evenly over the bottom of the baking dish and pour the batter on top. Bake for 30 to 35 minutes or until the top is golden and the center is set. Cool on a rack, then dust the top with confectioners' sugar. Serve warm or at room temperature.

Note: To make vanilla sugar, store 3 vanilla beans in a quart (liter) jar of granulated sugar for at least 1 month. Otherwise, mix 1 tablespoon (15 ml) of vanilla flavoring with 1 cup (250 g) granulated sugar and use as directed above.

HICKORY NUT CORN CAKE
(HICKERNISS-WELSCHKANNKUCHE)

YIELD: 10 TO 15 SERVINGS

3 cups (375 g) stone-ground organic white cornmeal
1½ cups (185 g) all-purpose flour
1½ tablespoons baking powder
1½ teaspoons sea salt
¾ cup (185 g) sugar
3 large eggs
2 cups (500 ml) whole milk
¼ cup (60 ml) unsalted butter, melted
1½ tablespoons (22 ml) vanilla extract
1 cup (125 g) finely chopped hickory nuts
½ cup (50 g) whole or partly broken hickory nuts
2 tablespoons (30 g) granulated sugar

Preheat the oven to 400°F (205°C). Sift together the cornmeal, flour, baking powder, salt, and sugar 3 times. Beat the eggs until lemon colored and combine with the milk, melted butter, and vanilla. Gently sift the cornmeal mixture, a little at a time, into the liquid ingredients to form a batter and then fold in the chopped nuts. Pour the batter into a greased baking pan measuring approximately 9 by 12 inches (23 by 30 cm). Scatter the whole or partly broken nuts over the batter and, with the back of a spoon, gently press them into it. Bake for 35 minutes or until set in the center. As soon as the cake comes from the oven, scatter the sugar over the top and cool on a rack. Serve at room temperature.

York County Peppermint Pie, an Easter favorite.

TASTE THE HARVEST

From the first burst of strawberries in May to the last frosty apples of November, the Pennsylvania Dutch cook engages in a mad race against abundance and the quickly changing seasons. The garden explodes in April from cold, wet clods into a waving sea of salad greens, followed by a succession of culinary riches right up to winter's first freeze.

When the rest of the world is enveloped in snow, our garden labors grace the table. We like to sort through our larders packed full of canning jars and other provisions ranged like fine old books with memories of summer sealed inside.

It was common among the Dutch to celebrate seasonal bounties with fairs, both in the spring and in the fall. The Delaware Valley Chapter of the American Institute of Wine and Food has recently revived this idea. Its "Taste the Harvest" fair held in Philadelphia each September is beginning

Above: Typical Pennsylvania Dutch garden divided into quadrants with raised beds. Right: Herb "Pappy" Lamar Bumbaugh (age 82) in his Berks County lair.

to rival the huge, lively market fairs of the eighteenth century where country growers and city cooks rubbed elbows, exchanged ideas, and went home contented that the money parted with or the produce sold was well worth the effort of the haul.

The most popular of all the harvest fairs were the cherry fairs held in late June and early July to show off the first fruits of summer. The cherry fairs at Strasburg in Lancaster County in the period between 1780 and 1825 were regionally famous.[1] In those days nearly every Dutch farmstead possessed at least one long row of cherry trees leading up the lane to the house.

If we could have followed that lane around to the back, where the summer kitchen stood cheek-by-jowl against a bakehouse, we would have come upon a whitewashed fence. This delineated the cook's inner sanctum out-of-doors, for the neatly fenced kitchen garden was an extension of the pantry inside. It was not rare to find Pennsylvania Dutch cooks running barefoot in the summer back and forth between these two crucial nerve centers of cookery. It never surprises me when a Pennsylvania Dutch cook smiles confidingly to confess that, in the rush to gather fresh rhubarb or groundcherries from the garden, a rolling pin somehow found its way among the dill.

The Pennsylvania Dutch attitude toward the kitchen garden is split between the rational or the scientific and the intuitive. On the one hand, we find the theories of theosophical agriculture, with its heavily Rosicrucian emphasis appealing to old Pennsylvania Dutch strains of Pietism and mysticism. On the other, we have figures like occult doctor Johann Georg Hohman, whose half-dozen books and pamphlets dealt with everything from gardening by the phases of the moon to spells for taking off the effects of witchcraft.

The nineteenth-century drug firm of Boerke & Tafel in Philadelphia published hundreds of titles in English and German promoting its homeopathic and Swedenborgian views. Among these was Julius Hensel's *Bread from Stones* (1894), a tract on the regeneration of farmland that was a precursor of the ideas of Rudolf Steiner. Steiner's theories on organic farming have many followers in Pennsylvania today, and it is no accident that *Organic Gardening* is now one of the most influential publications to come out of the Pennsylvania German region.

My grandfather once said to me in Pennsylfaanisch: "My garden is the doctor of my soul." I never doubted him because these words were consistent with the Virgin Sophia stories that he related to me as a child. Old paintings in Pennsylvania Dutch folk art depicted gardens as fenced-in miniatures of the Garden of Eden, reinforcing the idea that our kitchen garden was much more than rows of plants.

The typical Dutch kitchen garden was fenced in and generally divided into quadrants with paths and raised beds. Each of the quadrants was in turn subdivided, like the zodiac charts accompanying Pennsylvania Dutch almanacs to help determine the most propitious time or the most propitious part of the garden for planting, pruning, and harvesting.

In treating the kitchen garden as a symbolic if not spiritual representation of Eden, the next obvious step was to view the plants in it for their healing and sustaining powers, both moral and physical. This medieval concept is still a persistent theme in Pennsylvania German culture, tracing to two figures who typify the dichotomy of attitudes about the garden itself: the mystic Hildegard of Bingen (1098–1179) and Albertus Magnus (1193–1280), Count of Böllstadt in Swabia.

For the Pennsylvania Dutch, Hildegard's legacy comes largely in the form of dietary advice and ideas about health

that over the centuries following her death filtered down into popular culture from her great work on *Heilkunde,* the art of healing. Perhaps the greatest female medical practitioner of the Middle Ages, Hildegard advocated preventive medicine and anticipated the theories of macrobiotics, homeopathy, and even theosophical agriculture. Her mysticism and especially her ideas about wholeness and wellness remain quite appealing. Coupled with the Virgin Sophia, she has sparked renewed interest in the feminist roots of Pennsylvania German culture. Certainly the vegetarian, celibate women who became the Spiritual Virgins of Ephrata Cloister in the eighteenth century echoed the Hildegard model.

Hexefuss on a Hubbard squash, said to mark the curse of a witch.

It is not rare to find Hildegard's hand guiding the quills that wrote down old home remedies. But evidence of Hildegard's influence is even more direct than that. For example, she specifically recommended spelt as a health food because of its easy digestibility—a happy fact only recently discovered by patients suffering from the effects of AIDS. On this point Hildegard's advice is well worth reinvestigation by the scientific community. A collection of spelt simples published in the Sauer family's *Der Hoch-Deutsche Americanische Calender* for 1822 paraphrased Hildegard's advice regarding spelt, especially those that applied to common illnesses:

Toasted spelt bread with milk or chicken broth is both good to eat and a remedy for upset stomach.

On the supernatural side of the garden fence, Albertus Magnus is a very real but hidden presence in the literature and practice of powwowing, or *Braucherei.* A blend of witchcraft and faith healing, *Braucherei* is still quite prevalent in the Pennsylvania Dutch countryside, especially among the Amish.

Powwowing often overlaps with the work of herb grannies, but it does not deal directly with cookery unless, for example, a witch has *verhext* (put a spell on) the bread or has caused abnormal things to happen in the kitchen with the object of instigating injury or fatality. Then powwowing takes over to counter the mischief. Our popular witchcraft manuals, like Johann Georg Hohman's *Der lange Verborgene Freund (The Long Lost Friend)* or Albertus Magnus's *Egyptian Secrets for Man and Beast,* are crammed with bits of information about specific garden herbs and their occult uses. Albertus Magnus was not the real author of the guide bearing his name; it is likely that few powwowers realize that the historical person was both a German and a Catholic saint. Yet Albertus Magnus is part of a rich lore that is in no threat of extinction. After all, as one *Brauchmeeschter* pointed out to me, powwowing is a lot less expensive than health insurance—and it pays off sooner.

St. Hildegard's best intentions have been transformed into practice by Sarah Morgan, who lives in the Bieberdaal (Beaver Valley) near Pine Grove in Schuylkill County. She is a saver and trader of seeds, the happy mistress of a kitchen garden overflowing with rare, old-fashioned varieties of flowers and vegetables.

I had suspected as much when I first saw the foundation ruins of her old summer kitchen by the road, for they were encrusted with *Hauswachs* (in English, called hen-and-chicks). Meaning "house guard" in Pennsylfaanisch, they had been planted on those foundations as good luck to protect the property from lightning. Country people have a healthy respect for the *Blitz.*

Among the unusual plants that Sarah grows are pink—or rose-skinned—Jerusalem artichokes with distinctive brown stripes; a small blue potato about the size of a walnut grown in the Beaver Valley for at least one hundred years; and a mysterious annual called Mrs. Schmitt's Flower, an exotic pink-flowering plant with a bamboo-like stem. A woman Sarah knew only as Fraa Schmitt gave her seeds many years ago, and since the plant had no name, she dubbed it Mrs. Schmitt's Flower.

Sarah and her husband have also planted a fine stand of chinquapin chestnuts. American chinquapins are sweet and often go into *Seimawe* and turkey stuffings. They are cooked with dried corn, sometimes with a little chocolate added to create a delightful and unusual flavor. They are even dried and ground into flour, as the Swedish scholar Peter Kalm noted during his travels through Pennsylvania in the 1750s. Chestnut flour is a very old ingredient among the Pennsylvania Germans, both for bread and for pastries.

Usually when I head into the countryside to interview sources like Sarah Morgan, the focus of my visit is one particular dish or recipe. I had heard about Sarah's Sauerkraut-and-Porter Cake, and that is what drew me into the Beaver Valley. Sarah, however, disclosed other surprises, like her Pregnancy Pickles. "They keep for nine month," she jotted at the bottom of the recipe, "Or you can eat them in a week, if you get to feeling that way."

As the Sarah Morgans are becoming rarer and rarer in our countryside, so too are the garden plants and vegetables they raise. The Landis Valley Museum in Lancaster County has begun to gather and propagate historic Pennsylvania German garden plants for its Heirloom Seed Project. The project has found many enthusiastic supporters, and the museum now issues an annual catalog of seeds for sale. Many of the project's beans and vegetables are illustrated in this book, and ordering information may be found in the Cook's Guide to Regional Shopping (p. 184).

Vegetarianism and other radical dietary systems were practiced among the Pennsylvania Germans from the earliest period of settlement, beginning in the 1690s with the mystic Johannes Kelpius and his millennialist community of hermits on the Wissahickon near Philadelphia. They were followed by groups and individuals attracted to Pennsylvania because of its religious tolerance. Foremost among the German community were the followers of Conrad Beissel, who established Ephrata Cloister during the 1730s in Lancaster County and later Snow Hill in Franklin County.

Druggist and book printer Christoph Sauer (1693–1758) of Germantown, who printed many books and tracts for the Ephrata Pietists, composed one of the first American herbals,

Sarah Morgan grows pink-skinned Aerdebbel (Jerusalem artichoke) in her garden near Pine Grove.

called the *Kurtzgefasstes Kräuterbuch* (*The Concise Herbal*). Sauer's son, Christoph Jr., issued the herbal in yearly installments between 1762 and 1778 in *Der Hoch-Deutsche Americanische Calender*. Printed so that the installments could be bound together as a book and written from a Pennsylvania German point of view, the almanacs provide an extraordinary insight into the huge array of plants, herbs, and spices then in use for both medical and culinary purposes.

Chinquapin chestnuts (top), dumpling squash, and Jerusalem artichokes from the Beaver Valley.

and *Bodegeschmack*, food that tastes of local soils.

Hufeland's theories on macrobiotics planted the seeds for the homeopathic movement, championed in the United States by Constantine Hering (1800–1880). In 1835 he founded the North American Academy of the Homeopathic Healing Art in Allentown, Pennsylvania. Eventually the academy moved to Philadelphia, where it became Hahnemann Hospital.

Hering's translation of Jahr's *Manual of Homeopathic Medicine* (Allentown, Penn., 1836) did much to promote homeopathic ideas within the American medical community. Homeopathy's use of botanical medicines already agreed with many of the medical practices in Pennsylvania Dutch folk culture, providing a scientific pedigree for home remedies and powwow cures.

An important sidelight of this movement, aside from widespread experimentation with homeopathic cookery, was the explosion of interest in viticulture as a healthful alternative to the excesses of whiskey. Viticulture received quite a boost after 1835 by virtue of its medical associations.

Hering and his homeopathic colleagues, Johannes Helffrich of Weisenburg (author of a homeopathic veterinary book) and J. G. Woesselheft of Bath, Pennsylvania, established a twenty-acre vineyard in Berks County in 1837. Their activities were directly connected to similar wine experiments in Hermann, Missouri, which Helffrich visited in 1847 to observe a Rhineland-style wine fest. The Missouri connection remained strong throughout the pre–Civil War period, and in 1857, Georg Husmann of Hermann published his treatise *Weinbau in Amerika* (*Viticulture in America*) at Allentown through Mohr and Troxel, owners and editors of the *Bauern-Journal*.

A long-standing desire among the Pennsylvania Germans to retain wine drinking as an integral part of their food habits also promoted the hand of the vineyardist. Vineyards were common throughout the region during the eighteenth and nineteenth centuries, and red wine drinking was a central feature of the Pennsylvania German table, at least until the end of the eighteenth century.[2] Government excise taxes in the 1790s on red wines from Spain and Portugal effectively removed them from the working man's diet, leaving in their stead domestic whiskey as an alternative beverage. Pennsylvania German farmers spent the next fifty years trying to

During the eighteenth and nineteenth centuries, Pennsylvania German printers issued a steady flow of books and pamphlets dealing with their deep interest in botanical subjects, from tracts on "Indian" remedies (cures attributed to Native American sources) to extracts from Christoph Wilhelm Hufeland's treatise on macrobiotics first issued in 1797. His work was popular, for his concepts intermeshed with the old Dutch notions of seasonality—sowing and harvesting, even cooking, by the phases of the moon—

develop a native viticulture that would fill the void, and many books were written by local wine growers with this object in mind.

A treatise written in 1849 by Swiss-born Johann Auer (1788–1858) of the Schweizer Halle vineyards near Bethel in Berks County, Pennsylvania, was probably the most influential. Although his wine experiments were cut short by his death in 1858, Auer was a great believer in the future of "blue burgundies," a grape varietal known in France and the United States as pinot noir. Since the climate of south-eastern Pennsylvania is very similar to that of Burgundy, the pinot grape has again in the 1990s interested vintners in our region. A hybrid with similar characteristics called chambourcin is proving even more promising.

J. B. Garber's article on "Sweet Wine versus Sour Wine" in the March 1870 Lancaster Farmer observed that the Pennsylvania Dutch did not favor the sweet, fruity wines that were being promoted at that time in the United States. The Dutch retained their preference for dry, light wines, both white and red. The persistence of this taste preference made it difficult to sell sweet wines on the Pennsylvania German market, for they did not match well with the cookery, except as dessert or "funeral" wines, sweet wines served with cake to mourners.

Garber's remarks were eventually turned upside down by temperance and industrialization. Temperance rooted out wine drinking as a food habit among large portions of the Pennsylvania Dutch community. Industrialization replaced that habit with another "addiction" called sugar. With the increase of sugar in the 1880s, recipes became more and more incompatible with wine.

The canning revolution further contributed to sugar consumption up and down the Pennsylvania Dutch menu, since the perfection of vacuum sealing meant that salt and vinegar could be decreased in favor of sugar. Pottsville Pickle (p.120) is an example of this increased sweetness. Pickles that had hitherto served more or less as garnishes gradually evolved into the role of salads or important side dishes.

The first wave of canning jars to advance upon the Pennsylvania Dutch kitchen were the patented self-sealing fruit jars manufactured by Arthur, Burnham & Gilroy of Philadelphia between 1855 and the Civil War. The novelty of glass jars proved popular, and many publications, like the Allentown Bauern-Journal, not only promoted the Arthur jars through illustrated articles but also provided detailed recipes in German.[3] Aside from the convenience, several factors combined to hasten acceptance, most of which were related to health. Canned fruits and vegetables also appealed to vegetarians who wanted "noncarnal" food the year around, and this played into the hands of radical diet reformers of the time.

The most famous Pennsylvania Dutch vegetarian cook was Clara Landis, M.D., of the Philadelphia Electro-Hygienic Institute, who featured, among other "New Inventions," her Improved Compound Electro-Magnetic Hot Air Baths, as well as Dr. Scott's Electric Corsets. In 1864, Dr. Landis published The Improved Hygienic Cook-Book, which served as a blueprint for her dietary theories advocating the American Hygienic Movement. Her ideas mingled diet and health principles based on homeopathy, phrenology, temperance, vegetarianism, and radical Christianity. The Hygienic Movement gained widespread popularity among the Pennsylvania Dutch following the Civil War. By drawing on scriptural arguments for support, Dr. Landis contributed to a decline in the use of herbs and spices in our cookery, as well as a rejection of many traditional foods and dishes.

Some of the Hygienic ideas have a strikingly modern ring to them, such as advocating tomato sauce in place of meat-based sauces, using eggplant as a meat substitute, and frying on soapstone griddles because they do not require greasing with fat. But perhaps most appealing was the call for what Dr. Landis termed first-hand food, fresh food eaten in its natural state.

On the other hand, when reading through her cookbook, it is easy to see where the Victorian slide into blandness found inspiration. "Condiments I do not mention," wrote Dr. Landis, "If you wish good health, rosy cheeks, elastic muscles, strong bones, and calm nerves, you must live upon plain food, plainly and simply prepared." To make her point, she continued: "All condiments or seasonings are used at the expense of life power, drying up the secretions, causing false appetites."[4] And this, in her mind, ran counter to a Christian diet. Herbs and spices, any kind of high flavoring, were viewed as an adulteration, an attack on the moral wellness of the soul.

Considering the central role that herbs and spices played in traditional Pennsylvania German cookery, along with the direct association they had with the occult, it is clear why Hygienic Christianity drew the line where it did. It has been argued that the evangelical conversion process was not only a religious act but a form of de-ethnification and Americanization. The resulting homogeneity affected many Pennsylvania Dutch, at least in culinary terms.

M. S. Weber's *Magazine of Human Culture,* published at Farmersville in Lancaster County during the 1880s, echoed Clara Landis's sentiments. "Pork, pastry, pepper, spice, coffee, tea, grease, concentrated and fermented foods feed the fleshy lusts, and befoul our bodies with disease," wrote the editor. "We ought to have a Hygienic Institute in every church."[5] To imagine that these ideas are purely historical is to overlook the fact that today, especially among certain segments of the Mennonite community, there is an openly antagonistic attitude toward all forms of "gourmet" cookery and an active search for a cuisine that meets the requirements of Christian morality.

Despite the influence of the Hygienic Movement and other religious groups, the Pennsylvania Dutch did not abandon their taste for strongly contrasting flavors and spices. Sweet-sour flavors, for example, play a consistent role in our cookery, especially in our pickles and our salads, both hot and cold. The use of green (unripe) seeds to flavor pickle and preserve recipes, enhancing the sweet-sour opposition, is one of the distinctive features of Pennsylvania Dutch cookery and, unfortunately, one of the first to be altered when our recipes are printed in mainstream publications. The classic sweet-sour dressing used with salads consisted of one-third part oil (commonly olive oil or rapeseed oil), one-third part mild honey, and one-third part vinegar made from pear or apple cider. In practice, these proportions varied with the range of sweetness in the honey and acidity in the vinegar, especially homemade vinegar, which the Dutch still take pride in.

James Stuart, a Scot traveling through Pennsylvania in 1783, noted in his travel journal that inns throughout the region served hot sweet-sour dressings on their salads, but "this was not relished."[6] Several members of his party, not liking Pennsylvania German cookery, declined the olive oil in favor of strong ham stock. Without the oil, Mr. Stuart's hot salad would not feel "slick" when eaten, a texture that some colonial Americans found repulsive, even from harmless vinaigrettes. Since many of our hot salads are little different in texture from stir-fried vegetables, we may be grateful that American taste has become somewhat more adventuresome since the eighteenth century.

Above: Sgraffito terrapin plate (1990) by Jeff White, Lebanon, Pennsylvania.
Right: Premium wines from the Dutch region.

BEVERAGES FROM FIELD AND GARDEN

BLUE MOUNTAIN TEA
(BLOOBARRIER TEE)

Blue Mountain Tea, both the name of the plant and the drink, is brewed with fresh or dried leaves of sweet or anise-scented goldenrod (Solidago odora). In former times, farmhands would gather and dry the leaves in summer, then peddle the tea from farm to farm during the winter — once a very lucrative cottage industry. Today it is mostly older Mennonite women who gather the wild herb to sell in farm markets. The only way to find the tea, aside from hunting for it in the wild, is to go into a market and ask around. The farm market at Kutztown is a good place to start, since several of the herb and tea dealers stock it from time to time.

YIELD: 4 TO 6 SERVINGS

1 pint berry box (15 g) dried leaves of anise-scented goldenrod
1 quart (1 liter) boiling spring water
sugar or honey to sweeten

Heat a large teapot by rinsing it in hot water. Wipe the outside dry. Add the leaves and boiling spring water. Cover and steep 4 to 5 minutes, then strain and serve plain or sweetened with sugar or honey. The tea may also be served cold.

Advisory: People who have goldenrod allergies should not be affected by this tea, since it is the pollen, not the leaves, that causes an allergic reaction. The only precaution needed when using anise-scented goldenrod or any other plant from the wild is to make certain that it has not been sprayed by a road crew.

CHERRY BOUNCE
(BAUNZ)

This perky Christmas drink from the 1848 Die Geschickte Hausfrau is easy to make, a perfect project for a cherry fair. Even though the initial outlay may seem expensive, the quantity made here should last for several years.

YIELD: APPROXIMATELY 3 ½ GALLONS (14 LITERS)

12 pounds (6 kg) stemmed fresh sweet cherries, preferably a mix of half morello cherries and half black oxheart cherries
9 cups (1.53 kg) brown sugar
2 gallons (8 liters) rye whiskey

Wash and drain the cherries. Put them in a tub or fruit press and mash. Be certain to break a large number of pits, since they give the bounce more flavor. Pour the mash, juice, and pits into a 10-gallon (40-liter) glass jar or bottle, such as an old bottle from a water dispenser. Add the sugar and whiskey. Cork and shake to dissolve the sugar. Put the bottle in a cool place away from direct sunlight and allow to age for 9 months. The mash will settle to the bottom. Siphon off the clear bounce and filter the rest.

Store the bounce in clean wine bottles and cork tightly. Although the bounce is ready to drink after 9 months, aging greatly improves it by taking off the rawness. For the first 2 years, the bounce retains a deep ruby color. After 5 years, it oxidizes and turns to a rich sherry color.

"FORTY-NINE BEANS"
(NEIN-UN-VAZICH BUHNE)

Back in the 1930s, during the process of moving graves from a private burial ground along Rockvale Road in Lancaster County to a plot at Longenecker's Meeting not far away, the men at work uncovered an old wine bottle. Its cork was rotten and inside was a scummy-looking liquid that contained forty-nine coffee beans — they counted them. According to the late Reuben Harnish, who witnessed it, the men were "spooked," thinking their discovery to be a relic of local witchcraft. What they had found were the dregs of a Pennsylvania Dutch cordial of eighteenth-century origin often mentioned in old books but rarely explained in recipe detail. It was Forty-Nine Beans.

I am grateful to Jacob Weisenstein of Horschbach in the Pfalz for sharing with me the simple mysteries of making Forty-Nine Beans.[7] This is his recipe, and it makes a delightful after-dinner digestive.

YIELD: 3 CUPS (750 ML)

49 roasted coffee beans
rind of 1 orange
¼ cup (60 g) superfine sugar
3 cups (750 ml) Laird's Old Apple Brandy or calvados (see note)

Put the coffee beans in a clean 750-ml wine bottle. Remove the bitter pith (white part) from the orange rind, then cut the rind into thin strips or shreds. Put them into the wine bottle with the beans and add the sugar and apple brandy. Cork and shake the bottle until the sugar dissolves. Set away in a closet to infuse for 6 months. Strain and reserve the beans. Put the beans in a clean wine bottle, add the strained cordial, and cork tightly. Serve in shot glasses.

N o t e : Laird's Old Apple Brandy is aged 7½ years. It is the same as "Jersey Lightning" and the equivalent of old-style Pennsylvania Dutch applejack, which is no longer manufactured.

WHEATLAND HARVEST TEA
(WEEZEDAALER AERNDETEE)

This recipe is said to come from Anna Landis, wife of John Weaver (1750–1833). A Mennonite, John was opposed to the practice of serving whiskey to field hands during breaks. He served this tea instead. It is a fairly close approximation of Blue Mountain Tea and will therefore serve as a substitute when Blue Mountain Tea is unavailable.

YIELD: 1 GALLON (4 LITERS)

2 pint berry boxes (140 g) fresh bergamot leaves (*Monarda didyma*)
2 pint berry boxes (140 g) fresh spearmint leaves
2 pint berry boxes (140 g) fresh lemon balm leaves
2 or 3 large bushy sprigs fresh tarragon
1 gallon (4 liters) boiling spring water
sugar or honey to taste

Put the herbs in a large heatproof bowl and pour the boiling spring water over them. Cover and infuse 20 to 30 minutes or until the tea turns bright yellow. Strain out the herbs and discard. Sweeten the tea to taste with sugar or honey. Serve hot or cold.

Above: Peach and Tomato Slump with Sage.
Right: Green Gage plums from my Pennsylvania garden.

PEACH AND TOMATO SLUMP WITH SAGE
(PASCHING UN TOMATTS SCHLUPPER MIT SALWEI)

This old-style slump defies precise definition. It can serve as a one-pot vegetarian meal or as a side dish with fried chicken, veal, or white sausage, or it can be eaten alone as a dessert.

YIELD: 6 TO 8 SERVINGS

5½ cups (725 g) sliced peaches
4 cups (500 g) plum tomatoes, seeded and cut into strips
¼ cup (30 g) slivered almonds
½ cup (65 g) coarsely chopped prunes
shredded zest of 1/2 lemon
½ cup (125 g) Picoso Sugar (p. 129)
¼ cup (60 g) white sugar
2½ tablespoons (25 g) potato starch or tapioca starch
¼ cup (60 ml) lime juice
2 tablespoons (5 g) minced fresh sage
1 recipe Slump Crust (p. 39)
2 teaspoons sugar

Preheat the oven to 375°F (190°C). Grease the interior of a large earthenware baking dish. Combine the peaches, tomatoes, almonds, prunes, and lemon zest in a deep bowl. Mix the Picoso Sugar, white sugar, and potato starch together, then stir into the fruit. Add the lime juice and sage. Fill the baking dish with the fruit mixture and pat it down. Cover with slump dough as directed on page 39, and bake for 40 to 45 minutes. Remove from the oven and scatter sugar over the crust. Serve hot or at room temperature.

PLUM FRITTERS
(BLAUME-FLITTER)

One of the immediate by-products of the eruption of Mt. Tambora in 1815 and the summerless year that followed was a spate of handbooks to help farmers deal with natural disasters. Johann Fürst (1785–1846) wrote the most popular of these guides, Der Verständige Bauer (The Prudent Farmer), *which appeared in 1817. It was a hit in Europe and widely read among the Pennsylvania Dutch. This is one of Fürst's recipes.*

Volcanoes aside, Pennsylvania plums always seem to come all at once during the hottest weeks of August. These light and crispy fritters are a delicious and practical way to dispose of overabundance — and to feed all those neighbors who show up to pick the fruit, transforming work into a picnic.

YIELD: 6 TO 8 SERVINGS

1 cup (125 g) all-purpose flour
¼ teaspoon sea salt
2 large eggs, separated
⅓ cup (80 ml) water
⅓ cup (80 ml) kirsch or brandy
cooking oil for deep frying
10 ripe plums, halved and pitted
1 cup (90 g) confectioners' sugar
½ cup (125 g) superfine sugar
1 teaspoon ground cinnamon

Sift the flour and salt together twice in a deep bowl. Beat the egg yolks until lemon colored and combine them with the water and kirsch. Add the sifted flour to the egg mixture to form a light batter. Set the batter aside to mellow for 2 hours.

Preheat cooking oil in a deep fryer to 375°F (190°C). Beat the egg whites until they form stiff peaks, then fold them into the batter. Roll the fruit in confectioners' sugar, then dip it into the batter to coat each piece evenly. Fry until golden brown, then drain on absorbent paper and dust with a mixture of superfine sugar and cinnamon. Serve immediately.

QUINCE CHUTNEY
(GWITTE TSCHUTNI)

This chutney is best the day it is made; otherwise it will discolor.

YIELD: 4 TO 6 SERVINGS

½ cup (125 ml) Sage Vinegar (p. 129)
¼ cup (60 ml) sugar
½ cup (125 ml) honey
1 medium onion (100 g), sliced
2 cloves garlic, sliced
2 cups (300 g) peeled and diced quince
2 tablespoons (5 g) minced fresh sage
¼ cup (25 g) chopped hickory nuts

Combine the vinegar, sugar, and honey in a preserving pan and bring to a hard boil. Add the onion and garlic, and cook over high heat until the onions are transparent (about 5 minutes). While the onions are cooking, combine the quince, sage, and hickory nuts in a clean bowl. When the onions are done, add the quince mixture and stir to coat the fruit thoroughly. Cover and reduce the heat to a low simmer. Continue cooking the chutney 3 to 4 minutes, but only until the quince is hot. Set aside to cool, then serve as soon as possible.

PICKLES

In the Lady's Annual Register (Boston 1837) there is a recipe for "Yellow Pickle, or Axe-jar."[8] It is one of the root recipes from which several later American pickles derive, among them corn relish and chow-chow. The etymological clue lies in the term Axe-jar, which points in the direction of India as the ultimate origin for this dish, since capsicum peppers are called ahcar there.

In the manuscript cookbook of Sarah S. Wagonhorst, wife of Kutztown printer Isaac F. Christ (1840–1904), there is an 1870s recipe for Kutztown Jar-Jar that exhibits two important Pennsylvania Dutch features: its mild sweet-sour flavor and its reliance on green fennel seeds to create a contrasting taste.

Howard German tomatoes and Lancaster County pawpaws.

KUTZTOWN JAR-JAR
(KUTZESCHTEDDLER TSCHAR-TSCHAR)

YIELD: 12 PINTS (6 LITERS)

2 cups (250 g) yellow string beans, cut diagonally into 1-inch (2-cm) lengths
4 quarts (2.3 kg) diced green tomato
2 cups (250 g) sliced celery
2 cups (300 g) chopped red bell pepper
1½ cups (225 g) chopped green bell pepper
3 cups (420 g) sliced onion
2 cups (350 g) fresh lima beans
1 cup (135 g) sliced small sprigs of cauliflower
1 tablespoon ground cassia
1½ tablespoons green (unripe) fennel seed
1½ teaspoons green (unripe) coriander seed
1½ quarts (1.5 liters) white vinegar
6 tablespoons (90 g) sea salt
2¼ cups (560 g) sugar

Blanch the string beans in boiling salted water for 4 minutes, then drain and rinse in cold water. Mix the beans, tomatoes, celery, bell peppers, onion, lima beans, cauliflower, cassia, fennel seed, and coriander seed in a large nonreactive kettle.

In another nonreactive kettle, combine the vinegar, salt, and sugar. Bring to a hard boil over high heat and continue to boil 3 minutes, then pour over the vegetables. Place the vegetables over medium heat and cook for 15 minutes, measuring from the time the hot brine was added. Stir occasionally so that the vegetables on the bottom do not cook softer than those on the top. The tomatoes and peppers should change color at the end of 15 minutes, signaling that the pickle is ready for the next step.

Pack the vegetables into hot sterilized canning jars and fill each jar with enough brine to cover the vegetables. Be certain that the brine comes to within 1 inch (2 cm) of the jar rim. Seal the jars and place in a 20-minute water bath. After the jars have cooled, store in a cool, dry place away from direct light. Allow the chow-chow to mature 2 to 3 weeks before using.

MRS. KRAUSE'S PEPPER HASH
(DER KRAUSIN IHR PEFFERHAESCH)

Mrs. Eugene F. Krause of Bethlehem was well known in the early part of this century for her pepper hashes. This is a delicious condiment with foods like scrapple, or it may be used as an ingredient in distinctive flavor combinations, as in the turkey recipe on page 170.

YIELD: 4 TO 4 ½ PINTS (1 TO 1.25 LITERS)

4½ cups (675 g) finely chopped green bell pepper
4½ cups (675 g) finely chopped red bell pepper
4½ cups (500 g) finely chopped onion
2 small pods cayenne pepper, seeded and finely chopped
1½ tablespoons celery seed
1½ cups (375 ml) cider vinegar
1½ cups (250 g) brown sugar
1½ teaspoons sea salt

Combine the bell peppers, onion, cayenne pepper, and celery seed in a nonreactive preserving kettle. Heat the vinegar in a nonreactive pan and dissolve the sugar and salt in it. Bring to a hard boil, then pour over the pepper mixture. Cook over medium heat 15 minutes or until the peppers begin to discolor. Pack into hot sterilized canning jars, seal, and place in a 15-minute water bath. Let the hash mature in the jars for 2 weeks before using.

PICKLED PEARL ONIONS
(G'PICKELTE PAERL-ZWIWWELE)

This recipe traces directly to Die Geschickte Hausfrau (1848), although the original text does not mention that fresh herbs were generally added. The favored herb was tarragon, although some cooks preferred lovage or a combination of tarragon and lovage.

YIELD: 6 PINTS (3 LITERS)

10 cups (1.5 kg) pearl onions, trimmed and papery outer skins removed
18 bushy sprigs fresh tarragon
2 cups (500 ml) spring water
6 cups (1.5 liters) white wine vinegar
1½ tablespoons sea salt
2¼ teaspoons ground turmeric

Put the onions in a large strainer and blanch 4 minutes in boiling salted water. Remove and drain immediately. Pack into hot sterilized 1-pint (500-ml) jars. As the onions are packed into the jars, add the sprigs of tarragon, 3 to each jar: 1 sprig on the bottom, 1 when the jar is half full, and 1 on top. Bring the water, vinegar, salt, and turmeric to a hard boil in a nonreactive kettle or pan and boil 3 minutes. Pour over the onions and seal with a 10-minute water bath.

MRS. MOTTER'S VINEGAR CHERRIES
(DER MOTTERIN IHR ESSICH-KAERRSCHE)

A friend of mine came across this recipe during a survey of old buildings in northern Dauphin County. The sour cherry season was at its height, and Mrs. Motter's kitchen was cluttered with pots and pans overflowing with cherries.

The Motters refer to this pickle as Colonial Cherries. In fact, not only is the recipe older than that — it can be found in seventeenth-century German cookbooks — but it is also an easy-to-make relic of precanning, precookstove technology, for no cooking is necessary.

YIELD: 3 PINTS (1.5 LITERS)

3 pounds (1.5 kg) pitted sour cherries
2 quarts (2 liters) cider vinegar
2 pounds (1 kg) sugar
1 3-inch (7.5-cm) cinnamon stick

Put the cherries in a deep, nonreactive container (such as a stoneware crock) with the vinegar. Cover and infuse 3 days. Drain the cherries and reserve the vinegar for salad dressings, pies, or some other use. Measure the cherries and put them in a clean nonreactive container. To each cup (165 g) of cherries, add 1 cup (250 g) of sugar. (In this recipe, the yield will be 6 cups of cherries, or 2 pounds [1 kg] by weight, for they will lose about 1 pound [500 g] of water weight during the infusion process.) Cover and let the cherry mixture stand 3 days, stirring from time to time until the sugar is dissolved. Pack in sterilized jars, adding a 1-inch (2-cm) piece of cinnamon stick to each jar. Seal and store in a cool place until needed. No cooking or further processing is required.

PICKLED BEET SCHNITTELS
(ROTRIEWE-SCHNIDDLE)

My great-great-grandmother Barbara Rees Weaver (1838–1903) was well known in Lancaster for this recipe. Barbara was an astute cook whose experiments with new flavor combinations often took her into unusual byways of Pennsylvania Dutch cookery. In this case, two traditional elements (raspberry vinegar and beets) are united to create a slightly fruity, slightly sour condiment.

YIELD: 4 PINTS (2 LITERS)

2½ pounds (1.25 kg) red beets
3 cups (750 ml) Raspberry Vinegar (p. 128)
1 cup (170 g) brown sugar
1½ teaspoons sea salt
½ teaspoon whole cassia (optional)

Cover the beets with water and cook until tender. Reserve 1 cup (250 ml) of the cooking liquid, provided the beets do not have a strong earthy taste. Otherwise use 1 cup (250 ml) spring water. The rest of the beet water may be reserved for making soup.

Put the beets under cold water and remove the skins. Slice into thin strips (*Schniddle*). Put the strips into hot sterilized 1-pint (500-ml) jars. Combine the raspberry vinegar, beet water, sugar, and salt in a nonreactive pan and bring to a boil. Boil hard 3 minutes, then pour over the beets. Add 2 to 3 cassia buds to each jar. Seal with a 10-minute water bath. Store in a cool place out of direct sunlight.

Alternative: Instead of sealing the pickles in jars, pour them over hard-cooked eggs in a large glass container. Cover and marinate in the refrigerator 5 days. Use the pickled eggs as garnish for salads.

Pickled Beet Schnittels (top), Mrs. Krause's Pepper Hash (center), and Sadye's Dills.

POTTSVILLE PICKLE
(POTTSWILL G'PICKELTES)

This pickle takes its name from a turn-of-the century Pottsville cookbook containing an early version of the recipe. This particular recipe, however, did not come from a cookbook but from Schuylkill County's Mahantongo Valley via the late Ora Yoder. She faithfully made these pickles at the end of each summer for more than 50 years.

YIELD: 6 PINTS (3 LITERS)

3 cups (500 g) diced ripe tomato
3 cups (450 g) diced green tomato
3 cups (255 g) shredded cabbage (pack tightly when measuring)
3 cups (450 g) chopped onion
3 cups (375 g) chopped celery
1½ cups (225 g) finely chopped red bell pepper
¼ cup (60 g) sea salt
½ cup (50 g) grated horseradish
¼ cup (50 g) white mustard seed
3 cups (750 g) sugar
3 cups (750 ml) white vinegar
½ teaspoon ground clove
½ teaspoon ground cinnamon

Combine the ripe and green tomatoes, cabbage, onion, celery, and peppers in a nonreactive bowl or glass container. Scatter the salt over the top and then let the vegetables drain overnight. The next day, press out all excess liquid, but do not rinse. Add the horseradish and mustard seed, and put the vegetable mixture into a large preserving kettle. Dissolve the sugar and vinegar in a nonreactive saucepan and bring to a hard boil. Pour over the vegetables and cook the pickle for 25 minutes over medium heat. Just before removing from the heat, add the clove and cinnamon. Pack into hot sterilized canning jars and seal with a 15-minute water bath.

SADYE'S DILLS
(DER SEEDI IHR DILLS)

The forerunner of this recipe was an old-style crock pickle known throughout the Pennsylvania Dutch region simply as Sadye's Dills. The secret is in the brine, the proportion of spring water to salt and vinegar. The rest is variable, meaning that just about any equivalent quantity of raw vegetables can be substituted for tomatoes.

YIELD: 5 PINTS (2.5 LITERS)

1 large bunch fresh dill
10 cloves garlic, sliced into thin flakes
½ red bell pepper, cut into thin strips
2 pounds (1 kg) small green cherry or plum tomatoes, cut in half lengthwise
2½ teaspoons red peppercorns
5 3-inch (7.5-cm) slices peeled fresh horseradish
1¼ quarts (1.25 liters) spring water
¾ cup (180 ml) white vinegar
¼ cup (60 g) sea salt

Put several sprigs of fresh dill on the bottom of 5 sterilized 1-pint (500-ml) canning jars. Then add to each jar 2 flakes of garlic and 1 or 2 strips of red pepper. Fill the jars half full with raw tomatoes, then add to each jar ½ teaspoon of red peppercorns, a few strips of red pepper, and a slice of horseradish. Fill the jars with the remaining tomatoes and add to the top of each a few more sprigs of dill and 2 slices of garlic. Be generous with the dill.

Heat the spring water, vinegar, and salt in a nonreactive pan and boil hard for 4 minutes. Pour over the tomatoes and seal the jars with a 20-minute water bath. Store in a cool place out of direct light. Allow the pickle to mature 3 weeks before using.

SWEET-AND-SOUR SEEDLESS GRAPES
(SUMELOS DRAUWE, SIESS-SAUR G'PICKELT)

Perhaps the most accomplished of all our pickle cooks, in recent times at least, was Catherine Emig Plagemann (1905–1976). A descendant of the old York County Emigs, she wrote a small masterpiece called Fine Preserving in 1967. The late M.F.K. Fisher was so taken with Mrs. Plagemann's book that she edited a new edition in 1986. Unfortunately, in modernizing some of the recipes, she eliminated their Pennsylvania German characteristics, such as green coriander seed, which I have restored to this recipe. It is the special combination of green coriander seed and garlicky Catawissa onion that makes this recipe so authentically Pennsylvania Dutch and so utterly delicious.

YIELD: 6 PINTS (3 LITERS)

2 pounds (1 kg) seedless green grapes, stemmed and washed

2 pounds (1 kg) seedless red grapes, stemmed and washed

6 3-inch (7.5-cm) cinnamon sticks

6 cloves garlic, sliced in half lengthwise (or 6 large Catawissa onions, sliced in half lengthwise)

3 tablespoons (30 g) green (unripe) coriander seed

6 cups (1.5 kg) sugar

2 tablespoons (30 g) sea salt

4 cups (1 liter) white wine vinegar

Cut the grapes in half and pack into hot sterilized canning jars. After filling the jars halfway, add to each 1 stick of cinnamon, 2 slices of garlic, and 1 teaspoon of coriander seeds. Add the remaining grapes, then scatter coriander over the top layer, allowing ½ teaspoon per jar.

Dissolve the sugar and salt in the vinegar in a nonreactive preserving pan and bring to a hard boil over high heat. Boil 3 minutes, then pour over the grapes. Seal the jars and store in a cool place out of direct light. No further processing is necessary. Allow the pickle to mature at least 1 week before serving.

BRANDIED QUINCE IN HONEY
(HUNNICHGWITTE)

Serve brandied quince as an accompaniment to meat dishes, especially boiled beef and veal.

YIELD: 3 PINTS (1.5 LITERS)

2 to 2½ pounds (1 to 1.25 kg) peeled and cored ripe quince

3/4 cup (180 ml) honey

1½ cups (375 g) sugar

2½ tablespoons (40 ml) white wine vinegar

1½ cups (375 ml) spring water

¼ cup (60 ml) cognac

Cut the fruit into thin, neat slices. Put the honey, sugar, vinegar, and water in a nonreactive preserving kettle and stir once. Bring the mixture to a hard boil over high heat and boil 3 minutes. Remove any scum that forms. Reduce the temperature to medium and add the fruit. Cover and simmer 20 to 30 minutes or until the fruit is tender but not soft. (This will depend on the degree of ripeness.) Remove the fruit and pack into hot sterilized jars. Reduce the remaining liquid to a thick syrup by boiling it over high heat, then set aside to cool. When lukewarm (98°F/37°C), add the cognac and pour over the fruit. Seal and refrigerate. Use within 2 weeks.

Green (unripe) coriander seeds impart a mysterious coriander taste different from that of the fresh leaves or dried seeds.

Apple Butter with Fennel
(Lattwaerrick mit Fenchel)

Granted, apple butter with fennel is rarely encountered among the Dutch today, yet at one time it was common. The rustic, aniselike flavor makes this apple butter ideal as a spread on homemade rye bread or as a filling in fritters or layered cakes. It is the preferred ingredient for Apple Butter Pie (p. 92).

Yield: 7 to 7 1/2 pints (3 to 3.75 liters)

10 pounds (5 kg) tart apples (about 26 large apples)
1 gallon (4 liters) apple cider
1 pound (500 g) brown sugar
½ teaspoon ground clove
1 teaspoon ground mace
1½ tablespoons ground fennel seed

Pare, core, and chop the apples. Combine the apples, cider, and brown sugar in a heavy 3- to 4-gallon (12- to 16-liter) nonreactive preserving pan. Bring the apple mixture to a boil over high heat. Skim off the foam, then reduce the temperature to low and cook steadily, uncovered, for 5 hours. Stir at regular intervals in a figure 8 pattern to reduce the apples to a puréed consistency. The more constant the stirring, the quicker the apple butter will thicken.

At the end of 5 hours, add the clove, mace, and fennel. Continue cooking for about 30 minutes or until thick. Pour into hot sterilized jars and seal with a 20-minute water bath.

Green Tomato Mandram
(Griene Tomatts Mandram)

Spicy raw vegetable relishes based on West Indian models are now very popular with our experimentally minded regional cooks. This recipe is intended to go with smoked pork chops, smoked goose or capon, scrapple, sausage, fried tripe, or even fried oysters.

Caution: Wear rubber gloves when chopping the habañero peppers.

Yield: 8 to 12 servings

2 cups (350 g) diced green tomato
2 cups (350 g) poached fresh yellow corn kernels
2 green habañero peppers, seeded and finely chopped
2 tablespoons finely chopped red bell pepper
1 medium onion, finely chopped
¼ cup (50 g) chopped dried apricots
¼ cup (60 ml) safflower or virgin olive oil
3 tablespoons (45 ml) Horseradish Vinegar (p. 129)
½ teaspoon sea salt
1½ teaspoons dried summer savory, coarsely crumbled

Combine the tomatoes, corn, peppers, onion, apricots, oil, vinegar, salt, and savory in a mixing bowl. Cover and marinate 2 to 3 hours in a cool place. Serve cold as a condiment or relish.

Right: Catawissa onions, the "shallots" of Pennsylvania Dutch cookery.
Far right: Early Pennsylvania apples from the orchard of the 1739 Peter Yordy House, Lancaster County.

LAMB'S LETTUCE SALAD WITH SMOKED CAPON AND NUTS

(RITSCHERLI SELAAT MIT VERENNERT HAAHNE UN NISSE)

As botanist William Barton remarked about lamb's lettuce (Valeriana radiata) in the eighteenth century, "It is cultivated in great abundance in all the kitchen gardens near the city [Philadelphia] and is to be found plentifully in our markets, during nearly the whole year. Often met with in the fields west of the Schuylkill." Lamb's lettuce is also known as corn salad. It was at one time the most important Pennsylvania German salad green after lettuce. Today it is generally sold under its French name, mâche.

YIELD: 4 TO 6 SERVINGS

2 1-quart boxes (100 g) loosely packed lamb's lettuce
2 heads Boston lettuce
1 cup (15 g) salad burnet, hard stems removed (see note)
⅓ cup (75 g) diced slab bacon
1 cup (45 g) diced bread, preferably Spelt Bread (p. 84) or whole-wheat bread
¼ cup (60 ml) Catawissa Vinegar (p. 128) or shallot vinegar
2 tablespoons (30 ml) walnut oil
⅓ cup (50 g) toasted hickory nuts
⅓ cup (50 g) unsalted peanuts, toasted
⅓ cup (75 g) chopped smoked capon
2 tablespoons (5 g) minced fresh chervil

Rinse the lamb's lettuce, Boston lettuce, and burnet separately. Drain off excess water, then put the Boston lettuce in a large bowl. Brown the bacon in a skillet over medium heat. Remove with a slotted spoon and reserve. Brown the bread in the bacon drippings, then remove with a slotted spoon and reserve. Deglaze the skillet with the vinegar. Let the vinegar boil for 1 minute, then remove from the heat. Add the walnut oil and pour the dressing over the Boston lettuce.

Stir in the lamb's lettuce, reserved bacon, diced bread, hickory nuts, peanuts, and capon. Scatter the burnet and chervil over the top and serve immediately.

Note: Burnet *(Sanguisorba officinalis)* is best in the early spring when the young leaves are most tender. As the plant matures, the stems harden and should not be used in salad. Young burnet has a pleasant flavor similar to cucumber.

Note: To toast hickory nuts, spread on a cookie sheet and bake for 8 minutes at 350°F (175°C).

Above: Lamb's Lettuce Salad with Smoked Capon and Nuts.
Right: Ritscherli (lamb's lettuce) and Ringelrose (calendulas), two traditional ingredients.

SNIPPLED BEANS
(BUHNE-SCHNIPPLE)

Snippled Beans is sauerkraut made with string beans. It is a practical idea not only because it disposes of end-of-summer abundance in a useful way but also because the "beankraut" is pleasantly mild.

This recipe was kindly given to me by Mrs. Vernon Haas of Woodville, Ohio. In the nineteenth century, crank-turned shredders were developed specifically for Buhne-Schnipple, and in Mrs. Haas's section of Ohio they were called snipplers. Mrs. Haas still prepares her beans with such a device.

YIELD: 8 QUARTS (8 LITERS) OR APPROXIMATELY 24 SERVINGS

10 pounds (5 kg) fresh string beans
1 cup (250 g) sea salt
spring water (only if necessary)
16 teaspoons (80 g) sea salt

Trim and string the beans. Cut them on the diagonal with a sharp knife to make long, paper-thin shreds, or cut them with the shredding disc of a food processor. Mix the shredded beans with 1 cup (250 g) salt, stirring to distribute the salt evenly. Fill 8 sterilized 1-quart (1-liter) canning jars with the bean and salt mixture. Pack the beans down as tightly as possible with a wooden fruit or potato masher, until liquid begins to rise above the beans. Cap each jar with a temporary lid that is kept loose so that air can escape.

Set the jars on a tray or platter to catch the overflow when the beans begin to ferment. Put the tray in a pantry or cupboard away from direct light. If the beans have not produced enough liquid to cover themselves by the next day, add only enough spring water to cover the surface of the beans. Then scatter 2 teaspoons of salt over the bean mixture in each jar. Cover again with temporary lids and store as directed for 3 weeks. At the end of each week, skim off any scum that may rise to the surface of the beans. After 3 weeks, seal each jar with a sterilized lid and store in a cool place, or seal with a 15-minute water bath.

To cook snippled beans, rinse thoroughly in cold water, then put the beans in a saucepan with enough water to cover. Cook over medium heat 20 to 25 minutes or until tender. Drain and serve hot or cold with an herb vinegar and freshly grated pepper.

Advisory: As a precaution against mold, wipe the inside rims of the jars with a clean cloth dipped in vinegar after they are filled with beans. Of course, any food that becomes moldy should be discarded.

SAFFRON-FLAVORED SPELT SALAD WITH CORN
(DINKELSELAAT MIT SAFFERICH UN WELSCHKANN)

YIELD: 4 TO 6 SERVINGS

2 cups (385 g) spelt groats (whole berries)
3 cups (750 ml) water
2½ teaspoons sea salt
½ teaspoon ground saffron (contents of 10-grain vial)
4 cups (600 g) fresh yellow corn kernels (for frozen corn, see note)
1 cup (180 g) chopped scallion
3 tablespoons (30 g) finely chopped shallot
1 cup (125 g) chopped red bell pepper
2 teaspoons ground cumin
6 tablespoons (90 ml) Garlic Vinegar (p. 128)
⅔ cup (160 ml) salad oil, preferably sunflower oil
¼ teaspoon freshly grated pepper
2 teaspoons minced fresh parsley or lovage

Rinse the spelt groats and let drain in a sieve or colander. Put 2 cups (500 ml) of water and ½ teaspoon of sea salt in a saucepan and bring to a boil. Add the spelt and boil 2 minutes, uncovered. Do not stir. Cover and remove from the heat. Cool and refrigerate 4 to 6 hours or overnight.

The next day, put the spelt in a clean saucepan with any unabsorbed water. Add 1 cup (250 ml) boiling water and the saffron. Cover and simmer 40 minutes. Do not stir or remove the lid. At the end of 40 minutes, uncover, add the corn, and cook until the corn is hot and all the liquid has evaporated. Set aside to cool.

To assemble the salad, put the spelt and corn mixture in a deep bowl. Add the scallion, shallot, bell pepper, and cumin. Stir to distribute the ingredients evenly, then make a well in the center of the mixture. Put 2 teaspoons of sea salt and the vinegar in a small bowl and whisk until the salt is dissolved. Add the oil and pepper, whisk lightly until combined, and pour into the well. Stir the salad up from the bottom and serve immediately with a garnish of parsley or lovage. This salad will keep in the refrigerator 3 to 5 days.

Note: Frozen corn may be used but should not be cooked. Simply uncover the spelt at the end of the 40-minute cooking time and cook out the excess liquid. Add the thawed corn, stir, and reserve.

DILL VINEGAR
(DILL-ESSICH)

In this recipe it is important to make the dill flavor as strong as possible, and so a large bunch of fresh dill is required. Discard the stems and use only the leafy fronds.

YIELD: 2½ CUPS (625 ML)

1 large bunch fresh dill
2½ cups (625 ml) white wine vinegar

Pack as many sprigs of fresh dill as will fit into a sterilized 750-ml wine bottle, then fill the bottle with vinegar. Cork and infuse out of direct sunlight for 2 weeks. Use as needed.

Saffron-Flavored Spelt Salad with Corn in a slip-decorated serving plate by Jeff White.

CATAWISSA VINEGAR
(CATAWISSA-ESSICH)

The flavor of this vinegar resembles a mixture of shallots and garlic.

YIELD: 2 1/2 CUPS (625 ML)

1½ cups (175 g) Catawissa onions broken into individual bulbs
2½ cups (625 ml) white wine vinegar

Remove the skin from each bulb. Put the bulbs in a sterilized 1-quart (1-liter) bottle with the vinegar. Cork tightly and infuse out of direct sunlight for 2 weeks before using. The vinegar should acquire a slightly pink color.

GARLIC OIL
(GNOWWLICH-OLICH)

YIELD: 2 1/2 CUPS (625 ML)

1 cup (150 g) crushed garlic cloves
2½ cups (625 ml) safflower oil

Put the garlic in a sterilized 1-quart (1-liter) bottle and cover with the safflower oil. Cork tightly and infuse 2 weeks in a cool place out of direct sunlight. Strain and put the flavored oil in a clean bottle. Cork and use as needed.

GARLIC VINEGAR
(GNOWWLICH-ESSICH)

YIELD: 2 1/2 CUPS (625 ML)

1½ cups (175 g) small cloves garlic
2½ cups (625 ml) white wine vinegar

Peel the skins from the garlic and nip off the base ends with a sharp knife. Put the garlic in a sterilized 1-quart (1-liter) bottle with the vinegar. Cork tightly and infuse out of direct sunlight for 2 weeks before using. As the vinegar is used, replenish it from time to time with additional garlic and fresh vinegar.

RASPBERRY VINEGAR
(HIMBIERE-ESSICH)

YIELD: 2 2/3 CUPS (680 ML)

1 cup (125 g) fresh red raspberries
2½ cups (625 ml) red wine vinegar

Put the fresh raspberries in a sterilized 750-ml wine bottle. Add the vinegar. Cork and store in a cool place away from direct sunlight. After 3 months, strain off the berries and put the vinegar in a clean bottle. Cork tightly and use as needed.

Catawissa Vinegar.

SAGE VINEGAR
(SALWEI-ESSICH)

YIELD: 2 ½ CUPS (625 ML)

1 large bunch fresh sage (leaves only)
2½ cups (625 ml) white wine vinegar

Fill a sterilized 750-ml wine bottle half full of sage, then cover with vinegar. Infuse out of direct sunlight for 2 weeks, then use as needed.

HORSERADISH VINEGAR
(MEERREDDICH-ESSICH)

To quote the 1874 Lancaster cookbook from which this recipe is taken: "Horseradish is in the highest perfection in November." Readers with gardens know this already; those without a garden should buy fresh locally grown horseradish a week or two after a heavy frost. This precaution takes advantage of a chemical change that occurs in horseradish after the leafy tops are dead.

YIELD: 2 QUARTS (2 LITERS)

1 6-ounce (186-g) piece fresh horseradish
½ cup (65 g) sliced Catawissa onion or shallot
2 small pods dried cayenne pepper
2 quarts (2 liters) white wine vinegar

Wash and scrape the horseradish, then cut it into small pieces. Put the horseradish in a sterilized 1-gallon (4-liter) bottle or jar. Add the onion, then split the peppers and add them as well. Cover with the vinegar and cork tightly. Let the vinegar mixture infuse 1 week in a cool place away from direct sunlight. Filter the vinegar through a fine sieve or large coffee filter, discarding the horseradish, onion, and peppers. Put the vinegar in sterilized small bottles, cork tightly, and store in a cool, dark place until needed.

PEPPER VINEGAR
(PEFFER-ESSICH)

This classic condiment, which is served with everything from oyster fritters to sauerkraut, entered Pennsylvania Dutch cookery from the Caribbean during the early 1800s. The basic recipe here comes from Die Geschickte Hausfrau (1848).

YIELD: 2 QUARTS (2 LITERS)

3 pounds (1.5 kg) red bell peppers, stemmed and seeded
5 cups (1.25 liters) white vinegar
2 cups (500 ml) Garlic Vinegar (opposite page)
1 cup (250 g) sugar
2 tablespoons (30 g) sea salt

Chop the peppers and put them in a food processor with 3 cups (750 ml) of white vinegar. Process the peppers until puréed, the smoother the better. Pour the purée into a large preserving pan and add the remaining white and garlic vinegar, the sugar, and the salt. Boil vigorously over medium-high heat until the mixture is reduced to 8 cups (2 liters), stirring almost constantly. If the purée does not cook down to a thick, creamy texture, reprocess while hot, then reboil for 5 minutes. Put the vinegar in sterilized jars or bottles and seal. Use like catsup.

PICOSO SUGAR
(SCHARFZUCKER)

YIELD: APPROXIMATELY ²/₃ CUP (155 G)

9 tablespoons (135 g) granulated sugar
1 tablespoon hot chili powder
12 drops oil of cassia

Mix all the ingredients in a small bowl, then store in a tightly sealed jar and use as required. This will keep for about 1 year.

THE PIG AND
HIS PARTS

"Whenever you see hog-sties built in front of dwelling-houses, you may rely upon it, you are in the state of Pennsylvania."[1] Despite the hearty greeting to the nose, the frontyard pig was indeed king of the Pennsylvania Dutch farm. Though the porker by the door is no longer a common symbol of our culture, pork has not retreated from its role as the primary meat of our cookery. Beef and venison are still the "noble" meats eaten seasonally or on special occasions. The pig, however, is the farmer's larder, and every inch of the animal has its use.

Now that home butchering is almost a thing of the past, Pennsylvania Dutch cooks rely on a limited number of country butchers for traditional meats and sausages. Typical of the butchers who still produce traditional meats of exceptional quality are the Dietrichs of Krumsville in Berks County. Verna Dietrich operates the business with her two sons and their wives and provides a

Clockwise from top left: Smoked beef ribs, Bloswarscht, *smoked pork links, smoked pheasant, and slab bacon. On the table: Pig's foot, Lebanon bologna, smoked beef tongue, and a ham.*

Berks County butcher Verna Dietrich, an authority on old-style Pennsylvania Dutch meats and sausages.

full range of traditional products, from smoked goat and lamb to fresh rabbits, beef, and pork. While it is possible to buy most of the pork products associated with traditional butchering from firms like the Dietrichs', home cooks must rely on a little creativity when it comes to such old-style dishes as Butchering Day Stew (p. 139), especially if they cannot begin with a pig.

The Pennsylvania Dutch refer to November as *Schlachtmunet* (butchering month), for this was the season when farmers prepared their meats and sausage for the winter. Today one is likely to see the word *Schlachtmunet* only in old almanacs because butchering proceeds all year long and is no longer the neighborhood event it used to be. Few families celebrate the old *Metzelsupp* with all its trappings. The verb *metzle* ("MEH-tsleh") means "to butcher," and the classic *Metzelsupp* is three things simultaneously. It is a rich sausage stew shared as a communal meal with friends and neighbors to celebrate the success of a day's

butchering. It is a gift of meat and sausage sent home with those who participated in butchering. And it is any basket of food given as a gift at Christmas, regardless of whether there is meat in the basket.

The *Metzelsupp* was a common form of Christmas giving—to those who assisted in the butchering and to special persons or families in the neighborhood, such as an impoverished widow, a preacher, or cousins who sent a quarter of beef last year. The *Metzelsupp* was a convenient way to settle the tally of old social debts. Depicted on an 1871 woodcut from a Christmas gift book (p. 153), a little girl, *Metzelsupp* basket in hand, is on her way to visit an elderly shut-in. Many tales abound from the Victorian period about children exercising such charity while battling the elements or fending off thieves or evildoers.

Aside from the exchange of food gifts, other old practices persist in connection with hog butchering, some of them extremely ancient and carrying meanings now lost. Among these are drinking a toast of warm blood from a freshly killed pig and setting a pig's head on a tall pole so that it faces the morning moon. My grandfather, when a small boy, stepped on a nail and got an infected foot as a result. The nail that caused the infection was stuck into lard, then pounded into a "moon stake" that had held one of those pigs' heads. His infection went away.

Whether or not these "moon stakes" worked, the morning moon was indeed a familiar sight, considering how early in the day traditional butchering usually commenced. In a December butchering in Somerset County in 1918, six hogs and a steer were killed at 4 A.M., and by 8 P.M. that same day, all the meats had been dressed and all the sausages made.[2]

Quite often large butcherings took place at country churches or inns following a pig shoot, and the whole community was invited as a form of fundraising. The pork-and-oyster suppers in Upper Bucks County are holdovers of this older custom, although no butchering now takes place.

Christian Germershausen outlined the following scenario for making Butchering Day Stew in 1782: A hog was butchered, and the entire household, plus a large contingent of neighbors, pitched in to help. After the pig was cut up into his various parts, the "pudding meat" (waste meat) and excess bones were placed in a large kettle and boiled to make a broth called the *Weisse Brieh* (white stock).[3] Basic

Pork Stock (p. 68) serves as a substitute for *Weisse Brieh*, even to the white color.

Most of the meat strained from the *Weisse Brieh* was chopped to form a paste for *Pottwarscht* (potpudding), a baked dish best characterized as a coarse pâté. The remaining chopped meat and herbs and the pork livers were returned to the white stock and cooked, thus transforming the *Weisse Brieh* into the *Gleene Brieh* or *Sippli*.[4] *Gleene Brieh* does not translate as "little soup" but as "humble soup," the meal given to house servants and farmhands as a reward for helping with the butchering. The cooked livers were removed from the *Brieh*, broken up, and served to anyone who wanted a piece, the only condiment being salt.

In the Old World the owners of the farm and invited guests sat down to *Metzelsupp* (described above), which was a more substantial version of the *Gleene Brieh* that included a sampling of the sausages just made. The stew might be thickened slightly with roux made from spelt flour and lard, but if the stew was meaty, roux was not absolutely necessary.

Germershausen also outlined the pecking order regarding what form of Butchering Day Stew should be served to whom, and I can imagine that there must have been grumbling over it.[5] In my family, as I believe was the case in many Pennsylvania Dutch households, relatives, guests, and servants all sat together at the same table and ate the same fare—a pragmatic way to avoid class ritual from the old country and petty discords in the new.

The *Weisse Brieh* is one of the building blocks for a family of dishes that are the by-products of butchering, including potpuddings, scrapples, and souses, which are still very popular. Specific recipes vary greatly, reflecting individual tastes or regionalized preferences, such as the liberal use of ground coriander in Berks County.

With the decline of home butchering since the nineteenth century, pork livers have not generally been kept separate as hors d'oeuvres but now serve as a primary ingredient in potpuddings and better grades of scrapple. The Dietrichs use pork livers to thicken and flavor potpudding and as a stuffing in liver sausage. Their potpudding is baked in earthenware crocks. When the pudding cools, it jells and is then sealed with a layer of rendered fat. Many cooks place sprigs of fresh rosemary in the fat to further flavor the pudding. In former times, crocks of jelled potpudding were stacked in a cool place with boards between the crocks.

Rabbit season at the Saw Mill Hunt Club, Lancaster County, 1908.

Above: Wrought iron flesh fork (1780–1810).
Right: Restored hearth at the Hans Herr House, Lancaster County.

When needed, the pudding was heated in a pan until it fell apart. It was then eaten as a hash or gravy during cold weather, usually served over potatoes, bread, or noodles.

An alternate procedure was to make liver sausage, which, being perishable, had to be eaten immediately. In this case, the ground-up meats and pork livers were stuffed into a beef or hog bung (large intestine), called *Grossdarrem*, and boiled in the *Weisse Brieh* until firm. This was served hot as the main course of a meal or eaten cold like lunch meat.

The Dietrichs refer in English to their *Weisse Brieh* as "scrapple broth," and indeed this is the basic white stock upon which most scrapple recipes are based. To make their scrapple, which the *New York Times* has singled out as one of the best in Pennsylvania, the Dietrichs create a *Gleene Brieh* rich in ground-up meats and liver, thickened with cornmeal and buckwheat. Poured into pans, it is allowed to set. The scrapple is then sliced and fried in a skillet until brown on both sides.

There are hundreds of Pennsylvania Dutch variations on the basic concept of thickening meat stocks with grains or flours to create dishes similar to scrapple. Every family seems to have its favorite heirloom recipe. Among these is the Sausage Mush recipe on page 142, which makes a delicious light luncheon food and even works well as a party snack.

Another popular dish similar in concept to *Lewwerwarscht* (liver sausage) is *Schwartemawe* (literally, "pig stomach stuffed with bits of skin"). The German equivalent is *Presswurst* (head cheese). The Dietrichs' version of *Schwartemawe* (p. 8) is made by filling a beef bung with pieces of chopped meat (tongue is most evident), then boiling it in *Weisse Brieh*. After cooling and jelling under a weight, the sausage is lightly smoked. The Dietrichs' recipe contains cayenne pepper, which gives the dish its red color. This *Schwartemawe* is sliced or diced as a cold hors d'oeuvre.

The one part of the pig that is esteemed as a culinary symbol of our culture is the stomach. The cultural position of *Seimawe* among the Pennsylvania Dutch can be traced back to Europe and the Celto-Roman cookery of the Rhineland. Like the boar's head, the stomach held symbolic meaning in religious ritual of that period. Some of this was carried over into the cookery of the Middle Ages and preserved to the present time. The stuffed *Seimawe* is also one of the pork dishes lowest in meat and fat, being mostly potatoes and breadcrumbs. It is just an overly large sausage. Salem Church at Rough-and-Ready, Pennsylvania, is famous for its stuffed pig stomach dinners.

The pig itself is divided into various cuts of meat that serve as ingredients for a number of traditional Pennsylvania Dutch dishes. There are two basic categories: fresh meats, which come generally from the fore part of the animal, and smoked meats, which come from the hinder parts.

Traditional fresh pork is butchered to make cuts of meat not generally available outside Pennsylvania German areas.

The diagram below shows a pig butchered for traditional cuts. Such a pig does not yield pork chops and has very small shoulder cuts. The largest cut is the *Rickmeesel,* or back piece, made by cutting down both sides of the backbone along parallel lines four to six inches from the center (depending on the size and sex of the pig). The *Rickmeesel* is cut into small sections and used primarily for stewing with sauerkraut or for sour braising if it is meaty enough.

Because the *Rickmeesel* cuts through the ribs that form chops, it leaves on the underside two long strips of meat, one large and one small, called the *Fischschtick* (fish cut) or *Fischfleesch* (fish meat). The name derives from the shape; the English equivalent would be eye of the round or tenderloin. Some Dutch also call this the *Siessefleesch* (sweet meat) because it is considered the tenderest of all the cuts of pork. The *Rickmeesel* stops between the shoulder blades at the *Jutt* or *Seitnick.* This cut includes the back of the neck and butt. Because it is cut from under the shoulders, pigs butchered in this manner yield very small shoulder cuts. The *Jutt* or *Seitnick* is considered the best cut to use for sour braising.

Meats were traditionally smoked in the *Rauchkammer,* a small chamber or closet in the attic, lathed and plastered on the inside to fireproof it from sparks.[6] One end of the *Rauchkammer* was built up against the fireplace chimney, which had a hole cut into it so that smoke from the cooking hearth below could escape and circulate before rising out of

A. Rickmeesel
B. Jutt *or* Seitnick

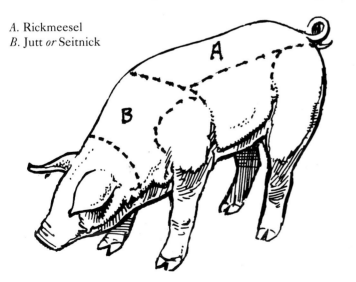

Summer sausage prepared in the shape of a football.

the house. Placed at such a distance from the heat, meats were essentially cold smoked. Since the smoke rolled in the flue many times before reaching the smoke closet, most of the unhealthful tars and other carcinogenic substances precipitated out before coming in contact with the meat.

Originally, meats were smoked to sterilize them for keeping purposes. The *Rauchkammer* accomplished this and produced hams equal in flavor to the famous Westphalian hams of Germany. In fact, the *Rauchkammer* was an essential feature of the old Westphalian method. Many Pennsylvania Germans still have *Rauchkammer* in their attics, although very few are still in use.

Once the Dutch switched to coal-burning stoves in the nineteenth century, the *Rauchkammer* could no longer be used for smoking meats, since coal smoke is poisonous. The smoke chamber was then moved out-of-doors as a separate structure, and smoking was done over wood chips. This represented a shift to hot-smoking techniques used by other Americans.

The Pennsylvania Dutch made two types of pork sausage: "fresh" (raw) and smoked. In concept, fresh sausage is the same as ground sausage elsewhere in the United States but flavored differently and often combined with other meats.

The blend of fresh pork and smoked pheasant in the recipe for Pheasant Sausage (p. 139) is only one example of this. There are even recipes for fresh white sausage made with ground pork, veal, and oysters, as well as with rabbit.

Next in line after pork is beef, which is used by the Dutch to make a variety of meat and sausage products assimilated from early American cookery. Foremost among these is mincemeat, which in former times served our farmers as winter's beef counterpart to pork potpudding. Both mincemeat and potpudding were stored in the same type of earthenware pots. And both could be stored in the same unheated areas of the house during cold weather.

Beef is also the primary ingredient for *Summerwarscht*, or summer sausage, one of the few meat products formerly eaten during hot weather—hence the name. Summer sausage is generally marketed as Lebanon bologna, of which there are two types, one sweet (containing honey or brown sugar) and one "plain" or sour, usually flavored with vinegar. Recipes vary greatly, as does opinion among butchers as to what subtle features differentiate the types of Lebanon bolognas. Most can be traced to English recipes used in southeastern Pennsylvania during the eighteenth century, although over time the bolognas have acquired a

peculiarly regional character, especially in flavoring and in the way they are smoked. Sweet Lebanon made as a *Bloswarscht*, or bladder sausage, is not likely to appear on meat counters outside the Pennsylvania Dutch area; nor are the sweet Lebanons made in the form of footballs, a modern counterpart to the same idea.

Not much research has been carried out among our butchers on specifically Pennsylvania Dutch cuts of beef. My impression is that our beef butchering practices "went English" quite early, with the result that very few peculiarly Dutch cuts of beef are even known—let alone sold—by butchers today. The only old-style cut mentioned consistently is the wedge rump, or *Dreieckichbrode* (three-cornered roast), which seems to have been popular in the eighteenth-century for sour braising.

Historically, the most popular form of fresh meat was the sour braised roast because nearly any large secondary cut of meat could be used. The roast was either marinated and then steam baked in part of the marinade, or simply steam baked in a sour-based sauce. I have included traditional recipes for beef, pork, ham, and rabbit. In addition to this, I have provided directions for marinating a venison ham that does not require cooking.

Winter butchering scene at the Deibler farm, Mahantongo Valley, 1920.

PORK-AND-POTATO GUMBIS WITH WILD MUSHROOMS
(SEIFLEESCH-UN-GRUMBIERE GUMBIS MIT MORCHELE)

I cannot accurately date this classic Gumbis recipe, but it has all the stylistic components of the late eighteenth century — the introduction of potatoes, for instance. More importantly, cumin is a key flavoring ingredient, and the Thick-Milk Sauce pulls it all together in an unusual yet tasty way.

When the Pennsylvania Dutch said wild mushrooms, they meant morels, which appear in the woods of our region in great abundance toward the end of April. Where morels are not available, substitute any sort of brown mushrooms — edible, of course.

YIELD: 6 TO 8 SERVINGS

10 cups (850 g) finely shredded savoy cabbage (most of 1 large head)

3 cups (350 g) chopped red onion

1½ pounds (750 g) cooked pork, sliced and cut into small pieces

3 cups (750 g) peeled and diced potatoes

4 tablespoons (10 g) chopped parsley

3 cups (375 g) chopped wild mushrooms (preferably morels)

1 teaspoon cumin seed

2 cups (500 ml) Basic Pork Stock (p. 68)

Thick-Milk Sauce (recipe follows)

Preheat the oven to 350°F (175°C). Make a layer of cabbage on the bottom of a deep porcelainized kettle or Dutch oven, then add a layer of onion, a layer of meat, a layer of potatoes, 2 tablespoons (5 g) of parsley, half of the mushrooms, and ½ teaspoon of cumin, in this order. Repeat with another layer of ingredients in the same order, covering the top with a layer of cabbage. Add the stock, cover, and bake 1 hour. When done, stir the *Gumbis* to mix the ingredients and serve with hot Thick-Milk Sauce.

Note: The stock for this recipe can be made with leftover bones and pan drippings from roast pork. Mix the pan drippings and bones with 1½ quarts (1.5 liters) of water. Boil gently 1 hour and skim off the fat. Strain the stock, return it to the pan, and boil rapidly over high heat until reduced to 2 cups (500 ml). The stock should be dark brown and full-flavored, like bouillon.

THICK-MILK SAUCE
(DICKEMILLICH SOSSE)

Thick milk, or clabber, is raw milk that is allowed to sour and thicken to a junket-like consistency. Pennsylvania Dutch cooks now generally use yogurt as a substitute, but sour cream will also work. Do not skimp on the dill vinegar; it is essential.

YIELD: 8 SERVINGS

1 cup 250 ml) plain whole-milk yogurt or sour cream

⅔ cup (160 ml) whole milk

1 teaspoon sea salt

3 tablespoons (45 ml) Dill Vinegar (p. 127)

Combine the yogurt, milk, salt, and vinegar with a whisk. Beat until perfectly smooth, then warm in a saucepan over medium heat until hot. Do not boil. Pour into a warm sauceboat and serve immediately.

Note: If the sauce is not hot enough, it will curdle when poured over the *Gumbis*.

BUTCHERING DAY STEW
(METZELSUPP)

This is a recipe that should rightly begin with the words "First catch a pig." I have not completely eliminated the pig, but I have consolidated the process of butchering and cooking it into about 25 minutes.

YIELD: 8 TO 10 SERVINGS

3 quarts (3 liters) Basic Pork Stock (p. 68)
6 ounces (180 g) liver sausage, skinned and chopped
1 teaspoon ground summer savory
1 teaspoon ground sage
4 ounces (125 g) coriander-flavored smoked sausage, sliced
4 ounces (125 g) white sausage, sliced lengthwise, then cut in diagonal pieces
4 ounces (125 g) blood sausage, diced

Put the stock, liver sausage, savory, and sage in a deep saucepan and cook gently until the sausage falls apart (about 20 minutes). Stir from time to time to break up the meat. Skim off any scum that may form as the sausage cooks.

While the liver sausage is cooking, mix the coriander-flavored and white sausages in a skillet and fry until the pieces begin to brown. Lift out with a slotted spoon and reserve. Discard the excess fat.

Once the stock is heated and the liver sausage is blended into the soup, add the fried sausages and the diced blood sausage. Cook 5 minutes, then serve immediately. This is an excellent soup as a first course or as a cold-weather main dish.

PHEASANT SAUSAGE
(FASANEWARSCHT)

This Palatine recipe has descended in the Haldeman family of Lancaster County. It takes two seeming opposites (pork and pheasant) to create a delicious lean sausage.

YIELD: 24 2-OUNCE (60-G) PATTIES (12 SERVINGS)

12 ounces (375 g) lean pork
8 ounces (250 g) fatty pork
1¼ pounds (625 g) meat from 1 smoked pheasant (meat from a 2- to 2½-pound/1- to 1.25-kg bird)
1 tablespoon sea salt
2 teaspoons grated nutmeg
2 teaspoons white pepper
1 cup (250 ml) dry white wine
1 sausage casing (optional)

Mix the lean and fatty pork with the pheasant meat. Save the carcass to make soup stock. Grind the meat in a sausage grinder or food processor, then add the salt, nutmeg, and pepper. Work the seasonings into the sausage with the hands, then add the wine. Mold into 2-ounce (60-g) patties or stuff into prepared sausage casing. Fry until brown on both sides or freeze for later use.

Note: A prepared sausage casing is not necessary but can be purchased from any local butcher. Natural casings should be used within two or three days of stuffing unless the sausage is frozen.

Purslane Fritters, or Faux Sausage
(Seibatselkuche, odder blinde Warscht)

A prototype for this recipe may be found in Das Branden-burgische Koch-Buch (Potsdam, 1732). The idea of making faux meat dishes for Lent or other times of abstinence is not at all new to Pennsylvania Dutch cookery. Anyone who is concerned about fat intake will welcome this high-baroque, low-cholesterol version of the ubiquitous breakfast sausage.

Yield: 15 sausage patties (6 to 8 servings)

1 cup (75 g) minced purslane or watercress
1 cup (100 g) plus 2 tablespoons (5 g) breadcrumbs
2 tablespoons zanté currants
1 tablespoon ground ginger
½ teaspoon freshly grated pepper
½ teaspoon sea salt
3 large eggs
vegetable oil (for frying)

Combine the minced purslane, breadcrumbs, currants, ginger, pepper, and salt. Beat the eggs until lemon colored and stir into the crumb mixture to form a thick paste. Using a tablespoon for a measure, mold 15 cakes. Flatten them to form sausage patties. Fry in hot vegetable oil until golden brown on both sides and serve immediately.

Left: Butchering Day Stew (Metzelsupp) consists of white stock (Weisse Brieh) and various sausages. Potpudding (back left) and Scrapple (cut in triangles to show texture) are two traditional by-products of butchering.
Right: With a tart and lemony flavor, weedy purslane (Portulaca oleracea) can be transformed into meatless sausage or used in salads and summer soups.

SAUSAGE MUSH
(WARSCHTBREI)

The natural marriage between cheese and cornmeal is high-lighted with coriander sausage and lightly fried peanuts. If the mush is sliced and cut into small strips, it can be fried and served as a party snack. Vegetarians can eliminate the sausage and fry the peanuts in sunflower or vegetable oil.

YIELD: 8 TO 12 SERVINGS

2½ teaspoons sea salt
1½ cups (210 g) organic yellow cornmeal
1½ cups (225 g) chopped smoked pork sausage
½ cup (75 g) unsalted roasted peanuts
1½ cups (185 g) grated Swiss cheese
1 teaspoon ground coriander
½ teaspoon white pepper
1½ teaspoons dried thyme

Add the salt to 1 quart (1 liter) of water in a saucepan and bring to a gentle boil over medium heat. Whisk the cornmeal into 2 cups (500 ml) of cold water until smooth, then pour into the boiling water. Stir to prevent lumps. Cook gently for approximately 25 to 30 minutes, adding more boiling water if necessary.

While the cornmeal is cooking, brown the pork sausage in a skillet, drain, and reserve. Do not discard the excess fat. Use it to fry the peanuts lightly, no more than 3 to 4 minutes. Drain the peanuts and reserve.

After the cornmeal has cooked 20 minutes, add the grated cheese. Stir with a wooden spoon or batter stick to keep the consistency of the mush as smooth and creamy as possible. Once the mush is cooked, add the reserved sausage and peanuts, the coriander, white pepper, and thyme.

Pour the mixture into a greased bread pan and allow it to set overnight. In the morning, turn out the mush and slice. Fry the slices slowly in a little butter in a skillet until they develop a rich, crisp crust. Serve immediately.

STUFFED PIG'S STOMACH, OR "DUTCH GOOSE"
(SEIMAWE GENANNT "DEITSCHER GANS")

When Pennsylvania Dutch cooks choose to show their mettle, this is the test of accomplishment. The best indication of failure is that, when pierced with a knife, Seimawe deflates and burps its filling all over the plate. Keep in mind that Seimawe is a species of sausage meant to be cut in slices. The secret is in the way it is sewn up so that no

Seimawe (Stuffed Pig's Stomach) served with Snippled Beans cooked with pickled red beans and limas. In the right corner are rivels with diced carrots.

leakage occurs during boiling; otherwise, the filling will be runny. A large needle and strong thread are mandatory. The right texture is not difficult to accomplish, and it can be studied in the detailed picture (opposite page) by those cooks who find they have problems with firmness.

My recipe is easier and better than most of those I have tasted in Alsace and not nearly as fatty too.

YIELD: 10 TO 12 SERVINGS

1 cleaned pig's stomach
1½ cups (8 ounces/250 g) diced lean slab bacon
3 cups (350 g) chopped onion
1⅓ cups (12 ounces/375 g) ground beef, pork, or venison
1½ teaspoons coarsely grated pepper
¼ teaspoon ground cayenne
1 tablespoon ground marjoram
½ teaspoon ground cardamom
1 teaspoon dried savory
2 teaspoons sea salt
½ cup (50 g) rye breadcrumbs or spelt breadcrumbs
3 large eggs
6 cups (2½ pounds/1.5 kg) diced cooked red potatoes, peeled or unpeeled
clarified butter

Soak the pig's stomach 2 to 5 hours in salted water, then rinse and drain. Put the slab bacon in a large skillet and fry over medium heat until it begins to brown. Remove the bacon with a slotted spoon and pour off the fat. Do not clean the skillet. Put the skillet back on the stove and add the onion. Fry over medium heat until soft, then add the ground meat. Cook until the meat changes color, then transfer the meat and onion mixture to a deep mixing bowl. Add the reserved bacon, pepper, cayenne, marjoram, cardamom, savory, salt, and breadcrumbs. Beat the eggs until lemon colored, then add to the meat mixture. Fold in the cooked potatoes.

Salem Church in Rough-and-Ready, Pennsylvania, is well known for its suppers featuring traditional recipes.

Turn the stomach inside out. Using a needle and thread, sew up the 2 smallest holes in the stomach so that they are absolutely tight and will not leak. Turn the stomach right side out and fill it with the stuffing until it is tightly packed and there is no room for air pockets. Sew up the large opening as tightly as possible, leaving only a small space inside for the expansion of the filling.

Bring 2 gallons (8 liters) of salted water to a hard boil. Reduce the heat and add the stomach. Simmer, uncovered, for 3 hours. At the end of 3 hours, preheat the oven to 375°F (190°C). Remove the stomach from the water and set it in a baking dish, seam side down. Bake for 20 to 25 minutes, basting often with clarified butter only until the surface of the *Seimawe* achieves a deep golden brown color. Serve immediately on a hot platter.

SCRAPPLE
(PANHAAS)

Much commercial Panhaas *is fatty because of what is thrown into it.* Homemade Panhaas *does not need to have any fat in it at all, even though a small amount does help give it its distinctive texture and flavor.*

The recipe here is based on my great-great-grandfather's, but most of the fat has been eliminated. Best of all, the recipe can easily be made at home, without starting with a whole pig.

YIELD: 9 6-INCH (15-CM) LOAVES (APPROXIMATELY 72 SERVINGS)

1 pork heart (approximately 8 ounces/250 g)
1 pound (500 g) meaty pork ribs (mix of fatty and lean)
2 pounds (1 kg) pork liver
2 cups (250 g) organic yellow cornmeal
1½ cups (210 g) organic buckwheat flour
2½ tablespoons (30 g) sea salt
1½ tablespoons freshly grated pepper
2½ tablespoons (25 g) ground sage
½ teaspoon ground clove

Trim the fat from around the top of the heart and remove the so-called deef ears, or sinews. Cut the heart into 4 pieces and put it in a heavy stewing kettle with the pork ribs and liver. Add 3 quarts (3 liters) of water, cover, and simmer gently for 3 hours or until the meat is falling from the bones.

Strain the broth into a clean pan. Pick the meat and fat from the ribs. Discard the bones and run the meat through a meat grinder or food processor. The texture should be somewhat coarse. Then grind the heart and liver as fine as possible. Mix the 2 textures of ground meat together and stir into the strained broth. Bring to a simmer over medium heat.

Sift together the cornmeal, buckwheat flour, salt, pepper, sage, and clove. Gradually add to the simmering meat mixture, stirring to eliminate lumps. Cook for 30 minutes, stirring almost constantly to prevent scorching on the bottom. Add extra hot water if the batter becomes too dry. After 30 minutes, the scrapple should acquire a thick, mashed-potato-like consistency. It is now ready to pour into pans.

Lightly grease 9 bread pans 6 by 3½ inches (15 by 8.5 cm) and fill with the batter. Set the pans on racks to cool. When cool, cover with plastic wrap and set in the refrigerator overnight. The next day, turn the scrapple loaves out onto a clean surface and cut each loaf into 8 slices. Use immediately or wrap individually with plastic wrap. Put the wrapped slices in freezer bags and store in the freezer for later use.

Slip-decorated redware pan for Westphalian Pannas *(scrapple) from Kamperbrück near Crefeld, Germany. Dated 1729.*

To fry fresh scrapple, dust each slice with flour. Lightly grease a skillet and get it very hot over high heat. Lower the heat to medium and add the slices. When they develop a thick crust on the bottom, turn them over and brown the other side. Serve very hot with a choice of typical Pennsylvania Dutch condiments: Pepper Hash (p. 117), Pepper Vinegar (p. 129), or molasses. I do not like molasses on *Panhaas*, but the Dutch of Lehigh County won't eat it any other way.

Note: Freezing causes scrapple to become loose and crumbly; therefore frozen scrapple should never be fried. So much the better for those who want to eliminate fried foods from their diet. Preheat the oven to 375°F (190°C). Lay the thawed scrapple slices on an ungreased cookie sheet and bake for 45 minutes. Turn each piece at least once so that it browns evenly on both sides. Serve immediately.

SOUR BRAISED BEEF
(SAUERBRODE)

Sauerbrode has long been a feature of Pennsylvania Dutch cookery, one of those special-occasion dishes reserved for Sunday dinners or festive events.[7]

Different from the usual sauerbraten preparation, the meat is not marinated before it is cooked; sourness is controlled by adding vinegar at the end, which results in a greater contrast between the flavors of the meat and its sauce.

Serve with plain Egg Pasta (p. 51), Buwweschpitzle (p. 173), or spelt boiled and served like rice.

2½ cups (270 g) coarsely chopped scallion
1½ teaspoons caraway seed
⅔ cup (160 ml) Black Vinegar Sauce (p. 146)
3½ to 4 pounds (1.75 to 2 kg) beef roast, preferably shoulder cut
4 small cloves garlic, sliced in half lengthwise
2 large sprigs lovage or flat-leaf parsley
¼ cup (60 ml) Raspberry Vinegar (p. 128)
coarsely grated black pepper

Preheat the oven to 300°F (150°C). Cover the bottom of a heavy porcelainized Dutch oven with the chopped scallion. Scatter caraway seed on top, then add the black vinegar sauce and 1⅓ cups (330 ml) of water. Place a rack or trivet in the Dutch oven that is just high enough to keep the meat above the liquid. Set the meat on the rack and spread the garlic and lovage leaves over the top. Cover tightly and bake for 2 hours or until the meat is tender.

Remove the meat, slice it into individual portions, and arrange on a hot serving platter. Drain the scallion and caraway, reserving the liquid, and spread around the meat. Set the platter in the oven for a few minutes to keep it warm while making the sauce.

To prepare the sauce, boil the reserved liquid in a saucepan over high heat until reduced by half. Add the raspberry vinegar, taste, and adjust the seasonings, then spoon the sauce over the meat and serve immediately with coarsely grated pepper.

SOUR BRAISED HAM WITH BLACK VINEGAR SAUCE
(SCHUNKEBRODE MIT SCHWATZE ESSICH SOSSE)

Black Vinegar Sauce was often used like barbecue sauce, brushed over grilled fish or dabbed on spit-roasted fowl such as goose or duck. It was also brushed over the exterior of sausages and hams as they were smoked. Here it is used to impart flavor to steam-baked ham in the style of the old sour pot roasts.

YIELD: 8 TO 10 SERVINGS

1 country smoked ham (5½ to 6 pounds/2.75 to 3 kg)
4 medium onions (14 ounces/400 g), cut in quarters
1½ cups (375 ml) Black Vinegar Sauce (recipe follows)
6 fresh bay leaves
1 tablespoon fennel seed

Preheat the oven to 300°F (150°C). Put a rack in the bottom of a Dutch oven and set the ham on it. Place the quartered onions around the ham and pour the vinegar sauce over it. Pour ½ cup (125 ml) of water over the onions, then tuck the bay leaves down among the onions. Scatter the fennel seed over the ham. Cover and bake for 2 hours or until the ham is tender. Baste the ham from time to time with the liquid from the pan.

Serve the ham hot from the oven with a sauceboat of Black Vinegar Sauce on the side, or prepare a gravy from the pan liquid.

To prepare a gravy, strain the pan liquid and discard the onions and herbs. Put the liquid in a saucepan and bring it to a hard boil over high heat. Boil until reduced to 1¾ cups (430 ml), then add ¼ cup (60 ml) of Raspberry Vinegar (p. 128) and ½ teaspoon ground cayenne.

Sour baked ham is a summer dish often served with stewed fresh yellow peaches and Cottage Cheese *Spätzle* (p. 50). It may also be served cold.

BLACK VINEGAR SAUCE
(SCHWATZE-ESSICH SOSSE)

Black vinegar has the color of molasses. The last time I saw the real thing was in a cask belonging to an elderly cousin of mine; her mother had made it in 1927. Cousin Mary used that vintage vinegar like a precious elixir in mincemeats and sour fricassees, as well as multitudes of sweet-and-sour dressings during the hot months of the year. Once very much a part of our historical cookery, black vinegar has now more or less disappeared, even though excellent old recipes for it abound. It is nearly the same as Italian balsamic vinegar, which may be used as a substitute.

Black Vinegar Sauce, which is a syrup made from old vinegar, was used in the past mostly in summer cookery as a substitute for sharp molasses, which it closely resembles. Some Pennsylvania Dutch even put it on vanilla ice cream.

YIELD: 2 ½ CUPS (625 ML)

6 cups (1½ liters) balsamic vinegar
1½ cups (135 g) brown sugar
1 cup (200 g) muscat raisins or pitted dried sweet cherries

Combine the vinegar, sugar, and raisins in a heavy saucepan. Bring to a hard boil over high heat and boil until reduced to 2½ cups (625 ml), about 20 minutes. Strain out the raisins and discard or save for pies. Cool the syrup and store in a jar in the refrigerator until needed.

SOUR BRAISED PORK WITH VINEGAR CHERRIES
(SAUER SEIFLEESCHBRODE MIT ESSICH-KAERRSCHE)

This sweet-and-sour dish takes advantage of the Motter recipe for Vinegar Cherries. If Cherry Bounce is not available, use plain rye whiskey as a substitute.

YIELD: 8 TO 10 SERVINGS

2 cups (400 g) Mrs. Motter's Vinegar Cherries (p. 119)
1 cup (150 g) chopped onion
⅔ cup (160 ml) liquid from Vinegar Cherries
⅓ cup (80 ml) Cherry Bounce (p. 112)
5½ to 6 pounds (2.75 to 3 kg) center-cut pork loin
¼ cup (30 g) grated sapsago cheese

Above: Sour Braised Pork is coated with a layer of sapsago cheese.
Far right: Sour Braised Pork with Vinegar Cherries served here with peas and saffron noodles with shredded dandelion greens and peppers.

Preheat the oven to 300°F (150°C). Spread the cherries and onion over the bottom of a large roasting pan that has a tight-fitting lid. Add the liquid from the cherries, 1 cup (250 ml) of water, and the cherry bounce. Place a trivet or small rack in the cherry mixture so that the meat will rest just above the level of the liquid. Lay the meat on the trivet, bone side down, and sprinkle the cheese over the top.

Cover and bake for 2½ hours, then remove the lid. Bake an additional 20 minutes or until the cheese crust is a golden color. Carve the meat into individual portions and serve on a hot platter surrounded by the cherries. Strain the liquid and serve separately as a sauce.

Haasepeffer *(Sour Braised Rabbit)* with poached morels.

SOUR BRAISED RABBIT
(HAASEPEFFER)

The basic outline for this recipe appeared in the January 9, 1894, issue of the Berks County Hamburger Schnellpost. The most popular local wines used at that time were produced at the wineries of William H. Kalbach near Hamburg and at the Reininger Wine Cellars near Reading. For this recipe I suggest a chambourcin as a modern substitute or even one of the robust pinot noirs from York County.

YIELD: 4 TO 6 SERVINGS

1 rabbit (3 to 3½ pounds/1.5 to 2 kg)
1 cup (185 g) diced streaky slab bacon
2 medium onions, sliced
1½ cups (375 ml) dry red wine
4 small fresh bay leaves
2 cloves garlic, crushed
4 small carrots, quartered lengthwise
6 dried morels, each about 2 inches (5 cm) long
1 cup (250 ml) clabbered raw milk or plain whole-milk
    yogurt
2 tablespoons (30 ml) Raspberry Vinegar (p. 128)
salt and freshly grated pepper to taste
minced fresh marjoram

Preheat the oven to 375°F (190°C). Cut the rabbit into small pieces. Put the bacon in a large heavy skillet and brown the rabbit over medium heat for about 10 minutes. Using a slotted spoon, transfer the meat and bacon to a deep, heavy baking dish, preferably earthenware. Pour off all but 1 tablespoon of fat from the skillet, add the onions, and fry until soft. Ladle the onions over the meat, then deglaze the skillet with 1 cup (250 ml) of wine. Pour this over the rabbit and add the remaining wine, 1 cup (250 ml) of water, the bay leaves, garlic, carrots, and morels. Be certain to press the morels down between pieces of meat so that they will absorb moisture during baking. Cover and bake for 1 hour 20 minutes.

Remove from the oven and lift out the rabbit with a slotted spoon. Keep the rabbit hot in a shallow serving dish while preparing the sauce.

To prepare the sauce, discard the bay leaves and set aside the cooked morels. Purée the remaining bacon, vegetables, and pan juices in a food processor. Add the milk or yogurt and the raspberry vinegar. Adjust the seasonings and pour over the rabbit. Return the rabbit to the oven for 10 to 15 minutes or until the sauce is heated but not boiling. (Boiling will curdle it.) Slice the morels in half lengthwise and garnish the rabbit with them. Scatter minced marjoram over the top and serve immediately.

Note: Poprobins (p. 53) are usually served with this dish. In the picture above, they have been mixed with boiled spelt and cooked dried cherries.

MARINATED VENISON HAM

(SAUER HAERSCH-SCHUNKE)

Similar to prosciutto di Parma in flavor, Venison Ham is like corned beef in texture and color. If care is taken to trim away the fat, it is possible to create an exceptional hors d'oeuvre very low in cholesterol.

YIELD: APPROXIMATELY 30 SERVINGS

2½ pounds (1.5 kg) venison ham (weight after trimming)
½ cup (45 g) coriander seed
3 cloves garlic, sliced thin
1 medium onion, sliced
2 tablespoons (10 g) cracked peppercorns
20 juniper berries
4 fresh bay leaves, bruised
10 tablespoons (150 ml) sherry vinegar
2 cups (500 ml) virgin olive oil

Trim the smoky outer skin off the ham and remove any fat. Cut the meat into 4 equal pieces, each 2 to 3 inches (5 to 7.5 cm) thick. Put them in a deep glass or porcelainized container large enough so that the pieces of meat fill the bottom but do not overlap. Add the coriander seed, garlic, onion, peppercorns, juniper berries, and bay leaves. Stir to distribute them evenly, then mix the vinegar and oil together and pour over the meat. Cover and set in a refrigerator at least 3 days, preferably 6 to 8 days, before serving. Turn the meat from time to time, and be certain that it is kept covered by the marinade.

To serve. dry the meat with a paper towel and slice or shave it as thin as possible. Brush a small amount of the marinade over the surface of the serving dish, then cover it with sliced meat in the manner of a *carpaccio*. Like smoked goose and capon, it can also be cut into shreds and served in salads.

Note: Game laws in many states do not permit the sale of venison unless it is farm raised and inspected. Many country butchers like the Dietrichs specialize in preparing venison for customers who bring them the hams. The processing fee is based on the weight of the meat and any dressing that may be required. During hunting season it is usually possible to find hunters who are willing to sell or barter part of their take.

Above: Marinated Venison Ham sliced paper-thin with freshly grated pepper. Overleaf: A Pennsylvania Dutch Christmas with cakes, clear toy candies, a Moravian doll from Christiansbrunn Cloister, and a Grischdaagsmoije *of mountain laurel.*

THE MASKS OF MIDWINTER
Foods for Holiday Feasting

The Moravian towns of Bethlehem, Nazareth, and Lititz in Pennsylvania are transformed each Christmas into virtual fairylands of candlelight, star lanterns, and evergreens. For the Moravians, Christmas is extremely elaborate, with highly ornamented pyramids of fruit and evergreens and entire miniature villages of *Putz* (carved figures) built under the Christmas tree or across one wall of the main room in the house. Since the Pennsylvania Dutch consist of so many diverse religious groups, it is difficult to make generalizations about the way Christmas is celebrated. However, against this rich tapestry of Christmas feasting—from the Moravians, who prepare for it months in advance, to the Amish, who observe Christmas only as a religious holiday, without Christmas trees, gifts, or even special holiday foods—there are certain customs that do characterize the Pennsylvania Dutch majority.

Er schloft, er schloft! do lit er, wie ne Grof!
Du lieben Engel, was i bitt,
By Leib und Lebe verwach mer nit,
Gott gits de Sünen im Schlof!

Dessiné par B. Zix   Gravé à Strasbourg, par F. Simon

Above: Grischdaagsmoije *hanging from the ceiling of the master bedroom.*
Right: Switches for bad children were left under the Christmas tree.

Foremost among these is the idea of erecting some type of tree decorated with foods and ornaments. This custom is associated with the fact that December 24 was observed as Adam and Eve Day, which focused on the Tree of Life. Most European historians of Christmas recognize this custom as a Christian reshaping of pre-Christian midwinter observances that brought greenery into the house.

The oldest forms of the Pennsylvania Dutch Christmas "tree" were not actually trees but branches. The *Grischdaags-zweeg* or *Zuckerbaam* was usually a large branch of wild cherry brought into the house on St. Barbara's Day (December 4) so that it would bloom by Christmas. It was hung with cookies and candies, the main gifts children received. A variant of the *Grischdaagszweeg* was the *Grischdaagsmoije*, an evergreen bush, usually mountain laurel or juniper, set up on a table or hung from the ceiling. On page 150, I have re-created a *Grischdaagsmoije* of mountain laurel based on a woodcut printed in Philadelphia in 1845. This was the most

ing nuts and candy at the shrieking mob. Being spooked by the *Belschnickel* is one of the great childhood games the Pennsylvania Dutch reminisce about most when the subject of old Christmas customs comes up. The *Belschnickel* still appears now and then but has been replaced for the most part by the benign and portly Santa Claus.

An extension of the *Belschnickel* tradition was the custom of belschnickling, which took place on Second Christmas (December 26), in former times a great market day throughout the Dutch Country. The belschnicklers were usually teenagers dressed in costumes who "mummed" from house

common type of Pennsylvania Dutch Christmas tree before the Civil War.

On Christmas Eve it was customary in some households to leave empty plates on a table near the tree, one for each child in the family, so that they could be filled with cookies and candies by the *Grischtkindel* (Christ Child) during the wee hours of darkness. Bad children were left switches like the ones pictured on page 152.

Aside from the *Grischtkindel*, the other major gift bringer was the *Belschnickel*, the Pennsylvania Dutch counterpart to Santa Claus. An adult member of the family would don furs and a frightening mask, and on Christmas Eve, when all the children were assembled, this fierce-looking creature would burst into the house ringing bells, snapping whips, and toss-

Left: A Christmas Metzelsupp *based on the 1871 woodcut shown above.*

Moravian Zuckerbecker *(sugar toy maker) Charles Regennas filling candy molds for Christmas.*

to house amid the din of noisemakers demanding refreshments. Mifflinburg Rose Soup (p. 171) and *Niss-Schtengle* (p. 163) evolved almost exclusively as foods for belschnicklers.

In homes where alcoholic drinks were served, Cherry Bounce (p. 112) or Forty-Nine Beans (p. 113) might also make its way to the table. The drunken rowdiness of the belschnicklers caused many municipalities to outlaw the custom with the rise of temperance in the late nineteenth century. The trick-or-treaters of today's Halloween now imitate the belschnickling tradition, but it is the Mummers'

Parade on New Year's Day in Philadelphia that is the most direct descendant of this custom.

Christmas day itself was a time for unabashed celebrating, or "schmausing," a time to relish the labors of weeks of preparation, be it butchering and sausage-making or the seemingly endless baking of cookies and cakes. The Society of Pennsylvania German Gastronomes issued a pamphlet in 1928 on classic Pennsylvania Dutch feasting under the pen of Bland Johaneson. It extolled the kind of old-style schmausing for which towns like Womelsdorf had once been famous. There was a time when *Schmaus* was considered a vulgar way of saying banquet in Pennsylfaanisch, and only the word *Fescht* would do. But today the very quaintness of *Schmaus* with its rustic "chow-down" connotations evokes pleasant images of lusty feasting under backyard grape arbors or, in cold and snowy weather, at a vast table spread with culinary booty within full view of the Christmas tree.

St. Martin's Day (November 11) initiated the unofficial beginning of holiday feasting. Historically this was the day when rents were collected from tenant farmers and others who had agreed to use one's land for a fee.[1] For rich farmers with large incomes falling due, *Mordidaag* was a day for celebration, a time to feel generous yet also a time to think ahead toward Christmas and all the *Metzelsupp* debts that demanded repaying. The farmer who was both rich peasant and poor nobleman was our true Father Christmas, for it was in his best interest to keep the festive traditions alive.

Goose cookery is one of those traditions that remains very much alive. If the pig may be called the king of Pennsylvania Dutch meats, then the goose is the king of fowl. From feather beds to *Zidderli* (goose aspic), the goose provides the household with a vast array of useful products. Necks are stuffed and served like sausage, and the eggs are a springtime delicacy, often decorated and brought out at Christmas as an exotic *Putz* (decoration) for the tree. Eggs of all kinds were used as Christmas tree decorations, a custom now transferred to the egg trees of Easter.[2]

Hundreds of Pennsylvania Dutch recipes are devoted to goose, including goose and spelt dumplings, goose liver and wild chestnut terrine, goose liver scrapple, goose potpie with venison, and roast goose in many variations. The centerpiece of this cookery, however, is the goose liver pie made for Christmas. Julius F. Sachse waxed eloquent in his *German Sectarians* on the subject of goose liver pie.[3] The *Genslewwerboi* he described with such relish was none other than a country cousin of the famous Strasbourg goose liver pâté. There are numerous recipes for our old-style goose liver pies, but perhaps the most luxurious is the one that appeared in *Der alte Germantown Calender* for 1863. It included truffles, but I am sure very few Pennsylvania Dutch cooks used them, even though it is possible to find truffles in our woods.

One of the most lasting contributions of the goose to our Christmas feasting is the marriage of roast fowl and sauerkraut. The Old World combination was invariably sauerkraut and goose. Among the Pennsylvania Dutch this custom was transformed into sauerkraut and turkey and remains a central feature of our Christmas cookery west of the Susquehanna River and into northern Maryland. For this reason I have included a roast turkey recipe, a perfect match with the Brendle family's Gingerkraut (p. 174).

The Christmas table was spread with as much variety as possible, with goose and duck taking their place beside turkey and any of the potroast recipes in the previous chapter. Some of the sour braised meats were given special touches for the season, such as gingerbread crumbled over sour braised pork, or duck baked in goat's milk.

Also popular were wine noodles—a molded pudding called *Nudelkuche* in Pennsylfaanisch, which consisted of boiled noodles, dried fruit, nuts, and butter. Baked in a deep earthenware dish, it was turned out on a platter and served with wine sauce. The *Neuer Gemeinnütziger Pennsylvanischer Calender* for 1909 printed a recipe with the remark that a bowl of soup, a glass of wine, and *Nudelkuche* constituted a perfect menu for a light evening meal. The belschnicklers would certainly have agreed, and so would have the Pennsylvania-German Jews, who made this same dish under the name of *kugel*.

The oldest food consistently connected with the Pennsylvania Dutch Christmas, and one that appeared on nearly every table regardless of religious affiliation, was *Hutzelbrod* ("HOOT-sel-brote").[4] Sourdough bread was sweetened with honey and filled with dried fruit infused in rum or wine and then rolled up into a large cigar-shaped *Feschtleeb* and baked. The Milk Bread recipe (p. 83) is ideal for *Hutzelbrod*.

Another Christmas specialty was Dutch cake, like *Hutzelbrod* a form of sweetened bread. It often contained raisins or zanté currants and was generally baked in a Bundt mold. The Moravians sometimes baked the cake in the form of a Baby Jesus, either by using specially shaped earthenware molds or by shaping the dough by hand. The most medieval Dutch cake recipe in this book is the hand-shaped gingerbread *Mummeli* ("mummers") on page 159. This same dough can be used to make *Wickelkindkuche* (Baby Jesus Gingerbread), although the dough for the Weaverland Wedding Bread is best for elaborate molds because it takes patterns well and bakes a rich, golden yellow.

Twelfth Night, or Epiphany, was another important feast day, for it was on this day that the Christmas trees were shaken and the children were allowed to dive for the fallen goodies.[5] King cakes were baked with beans buried inside, and lucky was the individual who found the bean in his or her portion. All of this took place amid considerable merrymaking, dancing, and card playing. The Pennsylvania Dutch have their own card game called *Gaigel*, which shares the same deck of cards with pinochle but otherwise bears no similarity. *Gaigel* cards were often used as decoration on Twelfth Night cakes to symbolize luck and good fortune.

Winter feasting comes to a halt with *Fastnacht* (Shrove Tuesday), the final gulp of schmausing that signals the beginning of Lent. *Fastnacht* is an important day for the Dutch, and there is considerable lore surrounding both the observation and the doughnuts made to celebrate it. *Fastnacht* cakes are made throughout midwinter feasting, even at Christmas, as evidenced in many articles in old Pennsylvania German newspapers extolling the virtues of Christmas fat cakes and their partner dish, *Coffeebrockle*.

Coffeebrockle, or "coffee soup," is a breakfast dish made by breaking up doughnuts and dropping the pieces into a hot cup of coffee. I have never given it high marks for elegance, but as a wake-up call to the brain, it certainly clears the head of vapors from too much schmausing. And for a Pennsylvania Dutch cook with a busy agenda, it is a most appropriate toast to good fortune in the coming year.

Right: Gaigel, *a popular card game among the Pennsylvania Dutch. The deck shown here dates from 1883 and was printed at Williamsport, Pennsylvania.*

CARL HEINITSCH'S GINGERBREAD COOKIES
(DEM CARL HEINITSCH SEI LEBKUCHE)

Heinitsch's drugstore, founded at Lancaster in 1782, is still selling medicines, but what the family is probably best known for is its spicy gingerbread. Carl Heinitsch (d. 1803) came to this country from Lutzen, Saxony, in 1772 and brought with him this heirloom recipe for Lebkuche (honey cake). It is prepared in two very different ways, one as a Christmas tree decoration, the other as a crunchy nut-filled cookie. Lewis Miller, a nineteenth-century York County folk artist, illustrated a Christmas tree hung with Heinitsch gingerbreads in one of his drawings.[6] I have provided directions for the tree decoration and the nut cookies, since both make delightful eating.

YIELD: 3 DOZEN CHRISTMAS TREE DECORATIONS OR 5 DOZEN NUT COOKIES

8 ounces (250 g) lightly salted butter
1 cup (250 ml) unsulfured molasses
1 cup (250 ml) honey
1 cup (250 g) brown sugar
5¾ cups (805 g) spelt flour
1 teaspoon ground allspice
¾ teaspoon ground clove
1½ teaspoons ground ginger
1½ teaspoons ground cinnamon
grated zest of 1 lemon
whole blanched almonds
zanté currants

Melt the butter in a saucepan with the molasses, honey, and sugar over low heat, just enough to warm the mixture. Do not boil. Sift together the flour and spices, then add the lemon zest. Make a well in the middle of the flour mixture and add the warm liquid. Stir and work into a stiff paste. Cover and set in the refrigerator to ripen 4 days.

When ready to bake, preheat the oven to 375°F (190°C). To make the Christmas tree decorations, roll out the dough ¼ inch (6 mm) thick and cut into rectangles measuring 2½ by 3½ inches (6.5 by 8.5 cm). Set these on greased baking sheets and press an almond into the center of each. Press a currant into each corner, then bake for 10 to 12 minutes or until the cookies begin to brown around the edges. Remove from the oven and let cool 3 minutes before lifting the cookies from the baking sheet. Then transfer them to racks. As the cookies are cooling, pierce each one with a skewer to make a hole for the ribbon that will be used to tie it to the tree. When the cookies are cool, loop ribbons through the holes and tie the cookies to the Christmas tree.

To make the nut cookies, roll out the dough as prepared above and knead into it 8 ounces (250 g) sliced almonds. Fold the dough over and roll out to ½ inch (1 cm) thick. Cut into rectangles measuring 2 by 3 inches (5 by 7.5 cm) and set these on greased baking sheets. Bake for 15 minutes. Cool on racks and store in airtight containers.

The flavor of both cookies improves with age. They are best when 2 to 3 weeks old.

Carl Heinitsch's Gingerbread Cookies with a gingerbread cutter.

Christmas Gingerbread Men, or "Mummeli"
(Grischdaags Mennli, odder Mummeli)

This is one of the earliest types of gingerbread that I have come across in Pennsylvania Dutch cookery. The basic recipe was brought to America in the eighteenth century by immigrants from Hessia. Mummeli are still baked in the New Berlin area of Union County and other parts of central Pennsylvania.

Traditionally, Mummeli are made with spelt and barley flours, which create a distinct texture and flavor; the mix was once believed to impart certain magical properties to the little men. If spelt and barley flours are unavailable, substitute whole-wheat flour.

YIELD: 4 MUMMELI, 9 TO 10 INCHES (22.5 TO 25 CM) TALL

½ ounce (14 g) active dry yeast

2 cups (500 ml) lukewarm milk

5½ cups (770 g) organic spelt flour

5 cups (700 g) organic barley flour

½ cup (125 g) unsalted butter

¾ cup (180 ml) honey

4 large eggs

1 tablespoon grated nutmeg

1 teaspoon sea salt

2 tablespoons (30 ml) unsulfured molasses

2 tablespoons (30 ml) saffron water (see note)

Proof the yeast in the lukewarm milk mixed with 1 cup (250 ml) warm water. Sift together the spelt and barley flours and put 3 cups (420 g) in a deep bowl. Make a well in the center of the flour and stir in the yeast to form a thick slurry. Cover and set in a warm place until the slurry has risen and is completely covered with bubbles, then stir it down.

Cream the butter and honey. Beat the eggs until lemon colored and blend with the butter mixture. Add this mixture to

Grischdaags "Mummeli." *Turn the page upside down and they change into pig masks.*

the slurry. Sift together the remaining flour mixture, the nutmeg, and the salt, and gradually stir into the slurry. Add only enough flour so that the dough is not sticky when handled. (In humid weather, an additional ½ cup/ 70 g of spelt flour may be necessary.)

Knead the dough for 15 minutes on a clean work surface, then mold into 4 equal-sized balls. Break off a small piece from each dough ball, and roll out to form 20-inch (50-cm) ropes of equal length. Form the large balls into *Mummeli* figures like the ones illustrated above. Lay them on greased baking sheets. Decorate the figures with the ropes of dough by tying them around the necks and across the chests. Set the *Mummeli* aside to recover in a warm place for 20 minutes. While they are rising, preheat the oven to 375°F (190°C). Once the *Mummeli* are fully risen, bake them for 30 minutes. Remove them from the oven and glaze with a mixture of molasses and saffron water. Return to the oven and bake an additional 15 minutes. Cool on racks.

Note: To make saffron water, dissolve ½ teaspoon of powdered saffron (the contents of a 10-grain vial) in 2 tablespoons (30 ml) of water. To make the saffron-molasses glaze, mix the saffron water with the molasses in the recipe above.

AUNT SARAH'S APEAS CAKES
(DER AENDI SARAH IHR EEPIESKUCHE)

Aunt Sarah's Apeas were traditionally baked in 6- or 7-inch (15- or 17.5-cm) earthenware saucers, which give the best results, so use small pie plates when making this recipe. During the 1880s and 1890s these popular Apeas were sold at the 1762 Red Lion Inn, now the Sumneytown Hotel, which happily is still in business. For Epiphany (January 6) each cake contained a bean, but since Apeas are now eaten mostly as a breakfast cake with coffee, the customary bean is no longer present.

YIELD: 3 7-INCH (17.5-CM) CAKES OR 6 TO 8 SERVINGS

3 cups (420 g) pastry flour
1 cup (200 g) dark brown sugar
1 teaspoon baking soda
1 teaspoon cream of tartar
1 teaspoon sea salt
1 tablespoon ground cinnamon
½ teaspoon ground clove
grated zest of 1 lemon
6 tablespoons (90 g) butter
2 large eggs
½ cup (125 ml) whole milk
1 tablespoon aniseed
2 tablespoons granulated sugar
½ teaspoon grated nutmeg

Preheat the oven to 375°F (190°C). Sift together the flour, brown sugar, baking soda, cream of tartar, salt, cinnamon, and clove twice, then add the lemon zest. Using a sieve or pastry blender, work the butter into the flour mixture to form a fine crumb. Beat the eggs until lemon colored, then combine with the milk. Make a well in the center of the crumb mixture and pour the eggs into it. Stir to form a thick batter.

Scatter the aniseed on the bottom of 3 greased 7-inch (17.5-cm) pie pans, then fill them with the batter. Mix the granulated sugar and nutmeg and sprinkle half of the mixture over

the surface of the cakes. Bake for 30 minutes. As the cakes come from the oven, scatter the remaining nutmeg sugar over the tops, then cool on racks.

HONEY JUMBLES
(HUNNICH KRENZLIN)

This versatile recipe comes from Ohio. If a little more flour is kneaded into the dough, it will become stiff enough to shape into pretzels, which are used as decorations on the traditional Pennsylvania Dutch Christmas tree.

YIELD: APPROXIMATELY 5 DOZEN

4 cups (500 g) pastry flour
½ teaspoon sea salt
2¼ teaspoons baking soda
1½ tablespoons unsalted butter
1 cup (250 ml) honey
¼ cup (60 ml) unsulfured molasses
¼ cup (60 ml) dark rum
¾ teaspoon vanilla extract

Sift together the flour, salt, and baking soda three times in a deep bowl to distribute the soda evenly (see note). Make a well in the center of the flour.

Melt the butter in a saucepan over medium heat, then add the honey and molasses. Warm the mixture but do not let it boil. Pour into the well in the flour. Add the rum and vanilla, and stir together to form a soft dough. Cover and set in the refrigerator to ripen at least 2 hours before baking.

To make the jumbles, preheat the oven to 350°F (175°C). Roll out the dough to 4 ropes ½ inch (1 cm) in diameter. Cut the ropes into 4-inch (10-cm) strips. Join the ends to form rings and set these on greased baking sheets. Bake 13 minutes, then cool on racks. Store in airtight containers.

N o t e : If the soda is not evenly distributed throughout the flour, it may show up on the surface of the cookies as pits or flecks of discoloration when they are baked.

12/25/93 - I recall my Mother, Florence Kern Mohr, making an "Apiece Cookie" from a handwritten recipe. Anise was one of the flavors among others. - Evelyn Mohr Sawyer

*From top to bottom: Kutztown Jumbles and Nut Sticks, Honey Jumbles
(golden rings), "Mice" Cookies, Cinnamon Stars, Springerle Cookies (center),
also shaped into orange-and-white* Rauwekuche *("caterpiller" cookies), and
Carl Heinitsch's Gingerbread Cookies (bottom).*

KUTZTOWN JUMBLES
(KUTZESCHTEDDLER KRENZLIN)

This delicate jumble recipe was published on a rare German-language broadside (one-page handout) issued by bookseller Isaac Christ of Kutztown in about 1870.

YIELD: 4 TO 5 DOZEN

3 large eggs
2 cups (500 g) superfine sugar
1 cup (250 ml) sour cream
5 cups (700 g) pastry flour
1 teaspoon baking soda
½ teaspoon ground mace
1½ teaspoons ground cinnamon
1½ teaspoons grated nutmeg
confectioners' (10-X) sugar
aniseed

Beat the eggs until lemon colored, then gradually add the sugar. Beat until light and the sugar is dissolved, then add the sour cream. Sift together the flour, baking soda, mace, cinnamon, and nutmeg twice, then fold into the egg mixture to form a soft dough with the consistency of peanut butter. Cover and set aside to ripen overnight in the refrigerator.

Preheat the oven to 325°F (165°C). Dust a clean work surface liberally with confectioners' sugar. Using the hands, roll large scoops of dough in the sugar to form long ropes about ½ inch (1 cm) in diameter. Cut these into 4-inch (10-cm) lengths and join at the ends to form rings. Scatter aniseed on greased baking sheets and lay the rings on the seeds. Bake 18 to 20 minutes or until the cookies are golden brown on the bottom. Cool on racks and store in airtight containers.

Note: The confectioners' sugar allows the dough to be handled, but too much handling rubs off the sugar. It is the generous coating of sugar that gives these jumbles their characteristic "crinkly snow" appearance.

Kutztown Jumbles.

"MICE"
(MEISLI)

Kids of all ages love edible creatures, and Wilbur Zimmerman, my friend from central Pennsylvania, is one of them. This old-fashioned Christmas shortbread, an heirloom recipe from his wife's family, was a favorite among Pennsylvania Dutch children a century ago. Fitted out with currant eyes and little paper ears and tails, the cookies actually resemble — well, what else — real mice!

YIELD: ABOUT 30 MICE

¾ cup (185 g) unsalted butter
2 tablespoons confectioners' (10-X) sugar
1 tablespoon (15 ml) rosewater or rum
1 cup (75 g) finely ground hickory nuts or hazelnuts (see note)
2 cups (280 g) all-purpose flour
confectioners' (10-X) sugar

Preheat the oven to 325°F (170°C). Cream the butter and sugar, then work in the rosewater. Add the hickory nuts, then gradually beat in the flour until a stiff dough is formed. Mix the dough with the fingers and knead it until smooth. Break off pieces of dough and mold into 2-inch (5-cm) mouse "bodies." Remember, mice are thicker at the back than at the head. Pinch the face a bit to create a long nose. Refer to the cookies shown on page 161 for general shape and appearance.

Put the mice on greased baking sheets and bake for 20 to 24 minutes or until light brown on the bottom. Remove from the oven and roll the hot cookies in liberal amounts of confectioners' sugar. Set on racks to cool.

To make the cookies look more realistic, stick little pieces of currants into the faces where the eyes go, and cut out paper ears and tails. If stiff paper is used, it is possible to cut points on the bases of the ears and tails so that they will stick into the baked dough. Store in airtight containers.

Note: The nuts, regardless of type, must be ground to an even, fluffy, sawdust consistency—the texture and weight are crucial. This is easy to accomplish with a Swedish nut mill (*mandelkvarn*) or a coffee grinder but not with a food processor. Food processors will only reduce nuts to a fine, gritty consistency before turning them into a paste.

NUT STICKS
(NISS-SCHTENGLE)

Traditionally served to belschnicklers with rose soup, this cookie first appeared in the Neuer Gemeinnütziger Pennsylvanischer Calender for 1909. In the Pfalz, as in Alsace, they are known as Nuss-Spritzen and are formed by forcing the dough through a pastry gun. This allows for some of the fanciful shapes our German brethren create for Christmas. The Pennsylvania Dutch, however, hand-roll the dough into fat almond-shaped sticks; hence the term Schtengle.

YIELD: 4 TO 5 DOZEN

½ cup (125 g) unsalted butter
½ cup (125 g) superfine sugar
1 extra-large egg
3¼ cups (8 ounces/250 g) finely ground hazelnuts or hickory nuts
¼ cup (60 ml) rosewater
2 cups (250 g) pastry flour
1 teaspoon ground cinnamon
1 teaspoon ground allspice
3 tablespoons (90 g) rosehip jam
⅓ cup (60 g) confectioners' sugar

Cream the butter and sugar. Beat the egg until lemon colored and work into the butter mixture. Fold in the nuts and rosewater to form a batter. Sift the flour and spices together twice, then add to the batter. Stir to form a soft dough. Cover and refrigerate for 5 hours.

Preheat the oven to 350°F (175°C). Form the dough into fat almond-shaped sticks 2 inches (5 cm) long, and set on greased baking sheets. Bake for 15 minutes or until golden brown on the bottom, then cool on racks.

While the cookies are cooling, combine the rosehip jam with the confectioners' sugar in a small bowl. Pack this into an icing decorator with a small tip and make a zigzag of icing down the center of each cookie. Serve as an accompaniment to Mifflinburg Rose Soup (p. 171).

St. Martin's Horns (Mordihanner).

St. Martin's Horns
(Mordihanner)

There are a great many apocryphal stories about the "invention" of Vienna rolls, croissants, and similar horn-shaped breads. In truth, the crescent shape is ancient, and in western European culture, it has some long-forgotten connections with the "horns" of the moon.[7]

This particular recipe spread from the Schwenkfelder sect of Montgomery County to other groups in Pennsylvania. It may also be found in the Neues Allgemeines Schlesisches Kochbuch (The New, General Silesian Cookbook, Breslau, 1835).

YIELD: 24 HORNS

1 tablespoon sugar
¼ teaspoon ground saffron (see note)
1 cup (250 ml) lukewarm whole milk
½ ounce (14 g) active dry yeast
5½ cups (685 g) all-purpose flour
2 teaspoons sea salt
½ cup (100 g) superfine sugar
14 tablespoons (210 g) unsalted butter
3 large eggs
½ cup (60 g) slivered almonds
1 cup (140 g) zanté currants
1 teaspoon ground allspice
2 tablespoons (30 g) brown sugar
48 small currants
1 tablespoon unsulfured molasses
1 tablespoon rosewater

Dissolve the sugar and ground saffron in the milk, then proof the yeast in it. While the yeast is proofing, sift together the flour, salt, and sugar twice. Then work the butter into the flour mixture using a sieve or a food processor until fine, soft crumbs are formed. Beat the eggs until lemon colored and combine them with the yeast mixture. Make a well in the center of the flour mixture and pour the liquid mixture into it. Form this into a dough, adding more flour if necessary to keep it from sticking to the fingers. Knead at least 5 minutes or until soft and spongy, like bread dough. Cover and set in a warm place until doubled in bulk.

Roll out the dough as thin as possible, preferably ⅛ inch to ¼ inch (3 to 6 mm) thick, then cut it into uneven triangles measuring 6 by 6 by 5 inches (15 by 15 by 13 cm). Arrange the triangles so that the short side of each is facing the edge of the worktable. Mix the almonds, 1 cup (140 g) of currants, the allspice, and brown sugar, and spread evenly on all of the triangles.

Starting at the bottom edge of each triangle, roll the dough up into a tube so that the tip of the triangle ends up on the bottom exactly under the middle of each roll. Turn the ends to form a crescent. At this point, the horns should resemble unbaked croissants.

Arrange the horns on greased baking sheets, cover, and let rise in a warm place (allow 25 minutes). Preheat the oven to 375° F (190°C). Stick each horn with a skewer or knife to make a pair of "eyes." Gently press a small currant into each hole, then bake the horns for 20 minutes.

Dissolve the molasses in the rosewater. Remove the horns from the oven and brush each liberally with the molasses glaze. Return to the oven and bake 5 minutes. Cool on racks. Serve at room temperature.

Note: The saffron must be ground to a fine powder or there will be yellow streaks in the dough. The easiest way to powder saffron is to grind it in a wooden mortar. When buying saffron, remember that 10 grains of whole dried saffron stamens will yield roughly ½ teaspoon of ground saffron.

SPRINGERLE COOKIES
(SCHPRINGERKUCHE)

To make proper Springerle Cookies, one must have Springerle molds. The most enthusiastic Springerle lover I know is Caroline Kallas, who imports and sells a full range of exquisite reproduction molds in her shop in River Forest, Illinois. For ordering details, see page 185.

YIELD: APPROXIMATELY 5 DOZEN

3 large eggs
1⅓ cups (250 g) confectioners' sugar
2 cups (250 g) pastry flour
½ teaspoon baking powder
grated zest of 1 lemon
1 tablespoon aniseed

In a deep bowl, beat the eggs until lemon colored, then fold in the sugar and beat until light. Sift the flour and baking powder together twice. Add the lemon zest to the batter, then fold in the flour mixture. Form the dough into a ball and cover. Set in the refrigerator to ripen for 10 hours.

To use a springerle mold, first chill it in the refrigerator. Brush it lightly with olive oil, then wipe with a dry cloth. If the mold has an elaborate design, dust it lightly with flour. These precautions will prevent the mold from sticking to the dough.

To make the cookies, roll out the dough ½ inch (1 cm) thick on a clean work surface. Press the chilled mold into the dough and gently pull away. Cut out the cookies along the borders of the designs, and set them on clean baking sheets to dry in a warm place overnight or at least 12 hours. The drying process prevents the cookie pictures from cracking as they bake.

Preheat the oven to 300°F (150°C). Scatter the aniseed on lightly greased baking sheets and set the cookies on top. Bake approximately 30 minutes, depending on the size of the cookies, or until golden brown on the bottom. Cool on racks and further decorate with colored icings if desired.

WHITE PEPPERNUTS
(WEISSE PEFFERNISS)

Recipes for white peppernuts or even white gingerbread are relatively scarce, yet they are greatly treasured by our cooks. One of the best recipes appeared in the Neuer Gemeinnütziger Pennsylvanischer Calender issued at Lancaster in 1895, and it is given here as it appeared in the original, rewritten to make better sense of the old-style measurements and ingredients, particularly the pastry flour, which is crucial.

YIELD: 9 DOZEN

3¼ cups (400 g) organic whole-wheat pastry flour
1¾ cups (400 g) superfine sugar
2 teaspoons baking powder
1 tablespoon grated nutmeg
1 tablespoon ground cinnamon
1 teaspoon ground clove
grated zest of 1 lemon
½ cup (95 g) minced citron
4 large eggs
5 tablespoons (75 ml) sour cream
1 cup (125 g) all-purpose flour
confectioners' sugar (optional)

Sift the pastry flour, sugar, baking powder, nutmeg, cinnamon, and clove together three times in a large bowl. Add the lemon zest and citron. Beat the eggs until lemon colored and combine with the sour cream. Make a well in the center of the dry ingredients and pour the egg mixture into it. Stir to form a sticky dough. Then knead in the all-purpose flour until the dough no longer sticks to the hands. Form the dough into a ball, cover, and set in the refrigerator to ripen for 2 days.

To bake, preheat the oven to 325°F (170°C). Break off pieces of dough and roll into balls the size of large cherries. Set them on greased baking sheets, allowing ample space for puffing. Bake 12 minutes, then cool on racks. Roll in confectioners' sugar if desired. Store in airtight containers at least 2 weeks before serving. The flavor of these cookies improves with age.

PREACHER'S FARTS
(PAFFEFATZLE)

Ministers, ever the butt of endless jokes, were not given a reprieve at Christmas. Children love these delicious little fritters, which are still served during the holidays in a broad region stretching from Lebanon to Allentown. What outsiders won't find are many Pennsylvania Dutch bold enough to explain what the dish is called. Now no one will have to ask.

YIELD: 8 TO 10 SERVINGS

oil or fat for deep frying
1½ cups (185 g) all-purpose flour
¼ teaspoon sea salt
1 tablespoon sugar
1 teaspoon baking powder
1 cup (250 ml) whole milk
3 tablespoons (45 g) unsalted butter
3 large egg yolks
¼ cup (60 g) sugar mixed with 1 teaspoon ground cassia or cinnamon

In a deep pan or fryer, heat the oil or fat until it reaches a temperature of 375°F (190°C). While the oil is heating, combine the flour, salt, 1 tablespoon of sugar, and baking powder. Heat the milk and melt the butter in it. Pour this hot over the flour mixture—this technique is known as *Brand-Deeg* in Pennsylfaanisch—and beat well. When the batter cools, cream the egg yolks and stir into the batter. At this point the batter should become thick and ropey.

Once the oil is heated and is beginning to smoke, dip a small batter stick or spatula into the batter. Push the batter off the end so that it slides in irregular "splatter" shapes into the hot fat, allowing about 1 tablespoon of batter per fritter. Make only 5 or 6 fritters at a time, frying them until golden brown on both sides. Drain on absorbent paper and dust with a mixture of sugar and cassia or cinnamon. Serve warm or at room temperature.

MAHANTONGO DIAMOND DOUGHNUTS
(MACHADUNKI FETTKUCHE)

This recipe comes from Emma L. Yoder (1873–1961) of Hegins, in the Mahantongo Valley. It came to her from her grandmother, but it is probably much older, since the diamond shape for All Saints cakes can be traced to the ninth century. This same recipe is also used for Fastnachts (p. 168).

YIELD: 26 3-INCH (7.5-CM) CAKES

3½ cups (435 g) all-purpose flour
½ teaspoon baking soda
¼ teaspoon cream of tartar
½ cup (125 g) superfine sugar
1 large egg
1½ cups (375 ml) sour cream or plain whole-milk yogurt
cooking oil
confectioners' (10-X) sugar or Picoso Sugar (p. 129)

Sift the flour, baking soda, cream of tartar, and sugar together twice. Beat the egg until lemon colored and combine with the sour cream. Sift the flour mixture into the sour cream and stir to form a soft dough. Roll out ½ inch (1 cm) thick on a clean work surface dusted with flour. Cut into 3-inch (7.5-cm) diamonds or parallelograms. Make a 2-inch (5-cm) slit in each, cutting all the way through so that the cakes can be spread apart to form a hole in the center. Set the cakes aside to dry for a few minutes. While they are drying, heat oil in a deep fryer to 375°F (190°C). Once it begins to smoke, add the cakes 4 or 5 at a time, keeping them spread apart as they drop into the hot fat. The cakes will puff and float as they fry.

Fry until dark golden brown on one side, then roll them over with a slotted spoon and fry until brown on the other. Lift them out with a slotted spoon or strainer and drain on absorbent paper. Continue in this manner until all the cakes are fried. Dust with confectioners' sugar or picoso sugar.

Mahantongo Diamond Doughnuts.

BROTHER JOHANNES'S FLAXSEED FASTNACHTS
(DEM BRUDER HANNES SEI FLAXSUME-FETTKUCHE)

Brother Johannes is a member of the Christiansbrunn Brotherhood, a religious community in the Mahantongo Valley. The brotherhood maintains a mystic lifestyle patterned after eighteenth-century Pennsylvania Moravians. Just as one tool served many functions in the spartan living conditions of two hundred years ago, so too does this recipe fulfill many demands. Brother Johannes's recipe not only makes delicious Fastnachts, but the same dough can be used to make muffins, cupcakes, bread, and Dutch Cake, our form of Christmas Stollen.

YIELD: 48 FASTNACHTS

3 mealy potatoes (1 pound/500 g), peeled
1 tablespoon sugar
6 tablespoons (90 ml) safflower oil
¼ ounce (7 g) active dry yeast
1 large egg
1 cup (250 ml) goat's milk
¾ cup (180 ml) unsulfured molasses
2 teaspoons sea salt
3 cups (420 g) organic spelt flour
1 cup (140 g) organic rye flour
½ cup (70 g) organic buckwheat flour
1 cup (140 g) roasted yellow cornmeal
1 teaspoon ground clove
1½ teaspoons grated nutmeg
1½ teaspoons ground cinnamon
1½ teaspoons ground allspice
¼ cup (1 ounce/15 g) flaxseed
2½ to 3 cups (310 to 375 g) unbleached all-purpose flour
oil or fat for frying

Cook the potatoes in 4 cups (1 liter) of water until soft. Measure out 3 cups (750 ml) of the potato water and dissolve the sugar in it. Put the potatoes in a mixing bowl and mash to a smooth consistency with the oil. When the potato water is lukewarm, proof the yeast in it.

Beat the egg until lemon colored, then add the goat's milk, molasses, and salt. Beat this mixture into the mashed potatoes to form a smooth batter. Once the yeast has formed a strong head, add it to the batter.

Sift together the spelt flour, rye flour, buckwheat flour, cornmeal, clove, nutmeg, cinnamon, and allspice. Stir in the flaxseed. Add the flour mixture to the potato batter and stir to form a thick slurry. Cover and set aside until doubled in bulk.

Once the sponge has risen, stir it down. Scatter 1 cup (125 g) of all-purpose flour on a clean work surface or dough trough. Knead the all-purpose flour into the slurry, 1 cup at a time, until the dough is no longer sticky to the touch.

To make *Fastnachts*, roll out the dough ½ inch (1 cm) thick and cut into 2-inch (5-cm) squares. Set these on cookie sheets. Using a knife or the blade of a sharp spatula, press an X from corner to corner into each *Fastnacht*, then let them recover for approximately 20 minutes.

While the *Fastnachts* are rising, heat oil or fat in a deep fryer to 375°F (190°C). With a skewer or knife, make a hole in the center of each raised *Fastnacht* where the X intersects. Fry 3 or 4 cakes at a time in the hot oil until they turn dark brown on the bottom, then roll them over and fry on the other side. Test one of the cakes for doneness in the center if it is not clear how long they should fry. Lift out with a slotted spoon and drain on absorbent paper. Repeat until all the cakes are fried. Serve the *Fastnachts* with a bowl of honey or unsulfured molasses for dipping.

Brother Johannes in his kitchen at Christiansbrunn Cloister in the Mahantongo Valley.

Roast Turkey with Pepper Hash and Rye Whiskey

(Welschhinkelbrode mit Pefferhaesch un Kanndramm)

This unusual recipe combines tradition with inventiveness. My friend Fritz Blank suggested the idea of stuffing pepper hash under the skin. He uses the technique for duck, but it works just as well with chicken or goose. This recipe does not call for stuffing because it is keyed to the recipes for Gingerkraut (p. 174) and Buwweschpitzle (p. 173), which should be served with it. Where hickory nuts are not available, substitute pecans.

YIELD: 10 TO 12 SERVINGS

1 12-pound (6-kg) roasting turkey
2 cups (450 g) Mrs. Krause's Pepper Hash (p. 117)
¾ cup (180 ml) liquid pressed from Mrs. Krause's Pepper Hash
7 tablespoons (105 ml) walnut oil
¼ cup (75 g) tomato paste
1 cup (250 ml) rye whiskey

1½ teaspoons sea salt
1 teaspoon coarsely grated pepper
2 onions, quartered
1 tablespoon superfine sugar

Preheat the oven to 450°F (235°C). Rinse the turkey, wipe it dry, and lay it on its back. With a small, sharp paring knife, starting at the *neck end*, gently work the skin loose from the breast. Once the membrane between the skin and meat begins to pull away, force one hand under the skin and push along the surface of the meat until all the skin covering the breast is loose. Work gently to avoid tearing the skin.

Place a large strainer over a bowl and pour the pepper hash into it. Press out the liquid and reserve it. Measure the hash and liquid separately to yield the quantities specified.

Combine the pepper hash with 3 tablespoons (45 ml) of the walnut oil, the tomato paste, and ¼ cup (60 ml) of the rye whiskey. Season with 1 teaspoon of the salt and the pepper.

Using a large spoon (or a pastry bag without a small tip), fill the space between the skin and breast with the pepper hash mixture. Truss the legs and wings, and set the turkey, breast side up, on a rack in a large roasting pan.

Pour the reserved liquid from the pepper hash into the cavity and insert the onions. Mix the remaining 4 tablespoons (60 ml) of walnut oil and ½ cup (125 ml) of rye whisky and set aside as a basting mixture. Pour 3 cups (750 ml) of water in the roasting pan and set the turkey in the oven. Close the door and immediately reduce the heat to 350°F (175°C). Baste the turkey every 30 minutes with the basting mixture and drippings from the pan. Bake 3 to 3 ½ hours, or until the temperature at the center of the meat tests 185°F (85°C).

Once the turkey tests done, transfer it to a hot platter and let it cool for 10 minutes. While the turkey is cooling, prepare a sauce by straining ¾ cup (180 ml) of the pan drippings and skimming off the fat. While still hot, combine this with the remaining ¼ cup (60 ml) of rye whiskey, ½ teaspoon salt, and the sugar. Serve in a hot sauceboat.

To serve the turkey, ornament the platter around the bird with little heaps of Gingerkraut and *Buwweschpitzle* with toasted hickory nuts. As the turkey is carved for individual portions, peel back the skin and give each serving a spoonful of the cooked pepper hash.

Whiskey bottle, circa 1885.

MIFFLINBURG ROSE SOUP
(MIFFLINBARRIER ROSESUPP)

Popular in the Buffalo Valley area of Union County into the early part of this century, this old-fashioned soup was made only at Christmas. It served not as a starter course for Christmas dinner but as a refreshment for the belschnicklers who went from house to house begging for treats. Many cooks accompanied it with almond or hazelnut cookies decorated with an icing made from rose hip jam (p. 163).

YIELD: 6 TO 8 SERVINGS

4 large red potatoes (2 pounds/1 kg), peeled
1 cup (150 g) chopped carrots
1 cup (250 g) chopped onion
2 tablespoons (30 g) unsalted butter
3 tablespoons (45 g) sugar
1½ teaspoons sea salt
1 cup (250 ml) whole milk
1 cup (250 ml) cream
1 tablespoon (15 ml) rosewater
unsprayed rose petals (red or pink)

Put the potatoes in a small saucepan, cover with water, and cook until soft. Drain and discard the potato water or save for making Sourdough Liquid Yeast (p. 79).

While the potatoes are cooking, put the carrots and onions in a separate saucepan with 2 cups (500 ml) of water. Cover and cook until soft. Reserve both vegetables and cooking liquid.

Put the cooked potatoes, carrots, onions, and cooking liquid in a food processor and add the butter, sugar, salt, and milk. Process until puréed, then add the cream. Pour the soup into a clean saucepan and warm it gradually over a low heat. When the soup is hot but not boiling, add the rosewater. Serve immediately in cups garnished with minced rose petals.

MRS. WEISSENBURG'S "DUTCH MARBLE" GOOSE EGGS
(DER FRAA WEISSENBURG IHRE GANSOIER FUN "DEITSCHER MARMOR")

Mrs. Weissenburg was a sprightly old Moravian lady who lived in Fountain Hill near Bethlehem, Pennsylvania. My friend Jonas Slonaker interviewed her in 1976, a few years before her death, and recorded her technique for coloring eggs in this traditional manner. Jonas also discovered an easier way using aluminum foil. Goose eggs are not absolutely necessary; chicken eggs will do just as well. Simply allow three chicken eggs for each large goose egg.

"Dutch marble," or in dialect, Deitscher Marmor, is the old Pennsylvania expression for faux marbre. The term applies to painted columns in churches as well as to eggs.

YIELD: 4 GOOSE EGGS OR 12 CHICKEN EGGS

4 large goose eggs or 1 dozen white chicken eggs
36 large pieces yellow onion skins (papery outer skins)
string or aluminum foil
1 cup (40 g) broken yellow onion skins
1 white chicken egg

Wash and dry the eggs. Be certain they are at room temperature or they may crack during the boiling process. Put the large onion skins in a bowl and pour cold water over them. Infuse 1 to 2 minutes, just long enough to make the skins pliant but not soft. Pour off the water and wrap each egg in the skins as tightly as possible. Be certain to use several pieces of skin on each egg, making about 3 layers, so that the skin patterns go in different directions. Then tie each egg with string in a netlike pattern to hold the skins in place (Mrs. Weissenburg's method). Or, instead of string, wrap the eggs as tightly as possible with aluminum foil (Jonas Slonaker's method).

Put the wrapped eggs in a deep nonreactive saucepan and cover with water. Add 1 unwrapped chicken egg as a control. Then add the broken onion skins and bring the water to a boil. Reduce the heat and simmer for 20 to 25 minutes. When the control egg is dark brown, the wrapped eggs are ready.

Remove the pan from the heat and set aside. Let the eggs stand in the onion liquid for 5 minutes, then remove the skins and rinse the eggs. Set them on a rack to dry. To display the marbleized eggs, arrange in a small basket out of direct sunlight. If they are not broken, the eggs will dry out and can be kept from year to year.

N o t e : If the eggs are boiled in a cast-iron pot to which ¼ cup (60 ml) of vinegar has been added, the eggs will dye a rich olive green.

Left: Mrs. Weissenburg's "Dutch Marble" Goose Eggs. Opposite: Twisted Buwweschpitzle fried with hickory nuts, a festive side dish for Christmas.

"Boys' Bits" with Toasted Hickory Nuts
(Buwweschpitzle mit Gereeschte Hickerniss)

Buwweschpitzle, *little potato dumplings about 1 1/2 inches (3 cm) long and pointed at both ends, are made from the same dough as* Nocken *(gnocchi). The* Schpitzle *must be cooked twice, first boiled, then fried. The fanciest* Schpitzle *are the twisted ones pictured here.*

Buwweschpitzle *are mostly served as a side dish or as a garnish, usually in connection with some special-occasion menu, as each* Schpitzle *must be made by hand. The yield given here is appropriate for a* Christmas *dinner. Half of this quantity will suffice for lesser occasions.*

Yield: 8 to 12 servings (about 290 "bits")

1½ cups (150 g) boiled mealy potatoes, riced or mashed
2 cups (280 g) whole-spelt flour or whole-wheat flour
1 teaspoon sea salt
2 large eggs
¼ cup (60 ml) walnut oil
2 cups (200 g) toasted hickory nuts (see p. 124, note)
sea salt

Put the potatoes in a deep bowl. Sift 1 cup (140 g) of flour mixed with 1 teaspoon of salt over the potatoes. Make a well in the center. Beat the eggs until lemon colored, then pour them into the well. Using a large spoon or fork, combine the eggs and dry ingredients into a smooth, slightly sticky dough.

Scatter ½ cup (70 g) of the remaining flour on a clean work surface. Put the dough on top and knead until all of the flour is worked in. Scatter the rest of the flour on the work surface. Break the dough into balls and, using the hands, roll in the flour to form ½-inch (1-cm) ropes.

Using a sharp knife, cut the ropes into diagonal pieces 1½ inches (3 cm) long from point to point. Set the *Schpitzle* on baking sheets to dry for about 25 minutes before cooking.

When the *Schpitzle* are ready to cook, bring 2 gallons (8 liters) of salted water to a hard boil. Reduce the heat to a simmer and add the dumplings about 20 at a time. The *Schpitzle* will sink to the bottom, then rise to the surface. Let them cook 5 minutes after they begin to float. Lift them out with a slotted spoon and set on dry baking sheets. Repeat until all the dumplings are cooked.

Heat the walnut oil in a skillet and sauté the dumplings until golden brown on all sides. Reserve and keep warm until ready to serve, or reheat in a microwave oven.

When ready to serve, combine with the toasted hickory nuts, season with salt, and pile in heaps around the roast turkey right before it is brought to the table.

GINGERKRAUT
(IMBERGRAUT)

Glenn Brendle, a solid Pennsylvania Dutch farmer from Atglen in Chester County, kindly shared this recipe with me, a Christmas specialty made in the Brendle family for several generations. I have altered Glenn's recipe slightly to complement the roast turkey, using walnut oil instead of lard and substituting toasted mustard seed for caraway or anise.

YIELD: 6 TO 8 SERVINGS

¼ cup (60 ml) walnut oil
2 tablespoons (15 g) white mustard seed
2 medium onions (300 g), sliced
2 cups (500 ml) turkey stock (see note)
2 pounds (1 kg) sauerkraut, drained of liquid (see note)
3 tablespoons (50 g) coarsely shredded fresh ginger root
15 juniper berries
3 tablespoons (15 g) chopped red bell pepper

Heat the oil in a deep nonreactive saucepan. Add the mustard seed and sizzle until they pop and begin to turn gray (about 1 minute). Add the sliced onions and cover. Let the onions sweat for 10 minutes, then add the turkey stock, sauerkraut, ginger, and juniper berries. Cover and simmer over low heat for 1 hour. Add the chopped pepper as a garnish and serve immediately.

Note: Turkey stock should be prepared in advance by boiling the liver, heart, giblets, and neck in 3 cups (750 ml) of water for 30 minutes. For a vegetarian alternative, use Spelt Stock (p. 81) or the liquid infusion reserved from soaking dried morels.

Note: Homemade sauerkraut may be salty and should be rinsed thoroughly before cooking. For packaged sauerkraut, follow the cooking instructions supplied on the label.

MRS. ETTING'S SUGARKRAUT
(DER ETTINGIN IHR ZUCKERGRAUT)

Sugarkraut was served as a festive dish at Christmas by the Pennsylvania Dutch and on the eve of Purim by the Pennsylvania-German Jews. Where the Dutch might use bacon or smoked goose, their Jewish acquaintances used smoked tongue and the requisite garnish of chopped pistachios.

The Neuer Gemeinnütziger Pennsylvanischer Calender for 1892 published an old-fashioned recipe for Sugarkraut, not too different from this one, which is said to have come from Mrs. Elijah Etting of York. The wife of a prominent Jewish merchant, Mrs. Etting was well known throughout the Pennsylvania Dutch region during the 1760s and 1770s for her fine cookery and cultivated entertaining.

YIELD: 6 TO 8 SERVINGS

¼ cup (60 ml) garlic oil or garlic-flavored olive oil
3 medium onions (500 g), sliced
3 tablespoons (45 g) brown sugar
2 pounds (1 kg) sauerkraut, drained well
2 cups (500 ml) sweet white wine
2 cups (500 ml) beef stock or stock from boiled tongue
½ cup (100 g) muscat raisins
2 cups (300 g) diced cooked smoked tongue
2 tablespoons (10 g) capers
¼ cup (60 ml) dark rum
¼ cup (35 g) chopped pistachios

Heat the oil in a heavy saucepan. Add the onions and sugar and stir to coat the mixture with oil. Cover and sweat over low heat until the onions are soft (about 8 minutes). Add the sauerkraut, wine, stock, and raisins. Cover and simmer 50 minutes. Add the tongue and capers and simmer, uncovered, for 10 minutes. Stir in the rum and serve immediately with a garnish of chopped pistachios.

Mrs. Etting's Sugarkraut.

RED CABBAGE WITH QUINCE
(ROTGRAUT MIT GWITTE)

From the Lotz family of Bethlehem, this is an ideal vegetable dish for large dinners. The red cabbage does not discolor, and best of all, it is good — perhaps even better — when reheated the next day.

YIELD: 8 TO 12 SERVINGS

2 tablespoons (65 g) packed finely chopped slab bacon
1 medium onion (100 g), chopped
3 pounds (1½ kg) red cabbage, finely shredded
1 pound (500 g) quince, peeled and shredded
½ cup (125 ml) Raspberry Vinegar (p. 128)
¼ cup (60 ml) honey
2 teaspoons sea salt
½ teaspoon cayenne pepper

Heat the bacon in a large saucepan and fry the onion in it until transparent (about 2 minutes). Add the cabbage and stir to coat with the onion mixture. Cover the pan tightly and reduce the heat to a low simmer. Steam the cabbage 30 minutes without lifting the lid, then add the quince, vinegar, honey, salt, and pepper. Cover and cook an additional 25 minutes, stirring the mixture from time to time. Serve hot as a side dish or at room temperature as a salad.

Note: Tart apples may be substituted for the quince, although it is quince that gives this dish its characteristic flavor.

It is possible to turn this recipe into a one-pot dinner by serving the cabbage with grilled white sausage or by adding chopped roast veal.

SWEET-AND-SOUR STUFFING
(SIESS-SAUERES FILLSEL)

This sweet-and-sour stuffing from Lebanon County takes advantage of the traditional combination of quince, sage, and honey that appears in the chutney recipe on page 115.

YIELD: SUFFICIENT FOR 1 GOOSE OR 2 CHICKENS (APPROXIMATELY 6 SERVINGS)

8 juniper berries
1½ cups (150 g) white breadcrumbs (*Mutschelmehl*)
2 cloves garlic
½ teaspoon sea salt
2 teaspoons ground sage
1½ tablespoons minced fresh sage
2 cups (300 g) peeled and diced quince
2 large eggs
¼ cup (60 ml) apple wine
3 tablespoons (45 g) melted butter
2 tablespoons (30 ml) honey
¼ cup (60 ml) Sage Vinegar (p. 129)

Preheat the oven to 375°F (190°C). Put the juniper berries in a blender or food processor with ½ cup (50 g) of the breadcrumbs and process until the berries are the texture of coarse pepper. Add the garlic and process until minced. Put the breadcrumb mixture in a large bowl and add the remaining breadcrumbs, the salt, ground sage, fresh sage, and quince. Mix thoroughly, so that all ingredients are evenly distributed.

Beat the eggs until lemon colored, then add the apple wine, butter, honey, and vinegar. Combine the liquid mixture with the crumbs to form a thick, doughlike batter. Grease a deep earthenware baking dish and pour the batter into it. Smooth with a spoon or spatula, then bake for 35 minutes.

Remove from the oven and break up the stuffing with a fork. Serve immediately with roast fowl or pork chops or as a vegetarian side dish.

Left: The Ringelros *as a symbol of happiness and good luck on a Pennsylvania Dutch Christmas card from the 1870s.*
Overleaf: Hearth cook, Susan Lucas, in eighteenth-century Moravian dress, waits for freshly baked Hickory Nut Corn Cake to cool in the kitchen at Newlin Mill.

GLOSSARY OF PENNSYLVANIA DUTCH FOOD TERMS

Throughout this book, I have used a standardized form of spelling for Pennsylfaanisch based on the three-volume dialect dictionary of M. Ellsworth Kyger, the most complete Pennsylvania-German dictionary to date. Pennsylfaanisch food terms are relatively easy to master once the basic sounds are understood.

As in Yiddish, there are no silent letters in Pennsylfaanisch, and there are no umlauted vowels as in German. The double *aa* sound is the same as *aw* in English, as in the word *awning*. The double *ee* sound is the same as *ay* in English, as in *May*—it takes the place of *ä* in German. The double *ww* sound is the same as *v* in English, but with a slight *f* sound to it. A single *w* is pronounced exactly like an English *v*. And lastly, a final *e*, as in *Zwiwwele* (plural form of "onion"), is pronounced as though it were *eh* in English: "TSVIH-vel-leh." A final *i*, which is our diminutive equivalent of *-chen* in German, is pronounced like a long *e* in English. It is usually preceded by an *l*, as in *Ritscherli*: "RICH-er-lee." Thus, when a soup (*Supp*) becomes a *Sippli*, or "little soup," we are discussing a broth or, more accurately, a soup that is mostly broth, a "thin" soup. For those who want to learn Pennsylfaanisch, language kits and tape cassettes are available through the mail from Pennsylvania German Enterprises, listed on page 187.

Speakers of standard German will note with repeated irritation and confusion that our case endings are often dropped and that many nouns have different genders in Pennsylfaanisch. These ambiguities provide our language with a huge reserve of puns and humorous word combinations.

Bladder Campion (Latin, *Silene latifolia*; Pennsylfaanisch, *Dauwegrepche-Selaat*). The dialect name derives from the shape of the seed pod. The plant is sometimes mistakenly called catchfly, which is similar in appearance. This perennial salad herb was long considered superior to dandelion and was once extensively cultivated. Introduced from Europe, it is naturalized throughout the eastern United States. It prefers meadows and blooms from midsummer to frost. The greens are best in the early spring and late fall.

Blind ("BLINT"). As in English, this term means "blind" in Pennsylfaanisch, but when used in a culinary context it means "false" or *faux*. For example, *Blinde Ente* (faux duck) is a type of meat loaf imitating duck meat.

Bottle Hen (*Bottelhinkel*). Used extensively for stewing, bottle hens are old hens that develop very fatty and sometimes featherless posteriors. They are popular among the Pennsylvania-German Jews, who value them for their fat.

Buckwheat (*Buchweeze*—"BOOCK-vaytsa"). A staple winter food in the Pennsylvania Dutch region. Traditionally, the grains were sun dried in October, then the husk removed. The grains were separated, hand winnowed, then ground into grits, meal, or flour at a local mill specially fitted for this purpose.

In cookery, the flour was normally extended with black spelt or whole-wheat flour, as, for example, in buckwheat dumplings or bread. Flour for buckwheat cakes was commonly extended with a soft white cornmeal similar to that used for Mexican tortillas. The variety of corn used for this purpose was called flour corn and is now extinct in southeastern Pennsylvania. It is believed to have been introduced from Jamaica in the seventeenth century.

Burnet, Salad Burnet (Latin, *Poterium sanguisorba*; Pennsylfaanisch, *Nagelgraut*). The dialect name translates as "nail herb." Used in salads or in cold drinks, it is sometimes infused in white wine to make a spring tonic. White wine flavored with burnet was often mixed with "English Champagne" (effervescent gooseberry wine) and served with sliced raw cucumbers in a punch bowl at weddings or other festive occasions. This made a drink called Cool Cup (*Kiehlkopp*).

Butter (*Butter* or *Budder*—"BOO-der"). The traditional butter used in Pennsylvania Dutch cookery was unsalted sour cream but-

Bladder campion

of ways, from dumplings to fricasees served over waffles. Very large catfish are prepared like carp.

Cheese (*Kees*). Over twenty different types of Pennsylvania Dutch cheese have been identified from historical records, most of which are no longer produced. Among these are several types of cream cheese, some with hard rinds, others resembling Brie. Still available in limited quantities are *Handkees* (hand cheese), generally sold under the misnomer "ball cheese" (it is not ball shaped); *Schmierkees* (cottage cheese) flavored with fresh chives; and a type of pineapple cheese with a soft, runny interior. This latter cheese takes its name from its shape, which is caused by the nets in which it is hung to age. Pineapple cheese is sometimes smoked. Swiss cheese, now commonly called farmer's cheese or Amish farmhouse cheese, is sometimes marinated in apple wine or white wine and herbs a few days before it is eaten.

Cheese Mallow (Latin, *Malva rotundifolia;* Pennsylfaanisch, *Keesbabble*—"CASE-bob-leh"). Naturalized from the Pfalz in the early eighteenth century, this herb produces an edible fruit that was highly prized by Pennsylvania Dutch children.

Corn, Dried. The only commercial Pennsylvania producer is the John F. Cope Company of Rheems. White sweet corn is toasted so that the sugar content carmelizes slightly to yield a yellow-brown dried product. The finished corn contains about 5 percent water, as opposed to 75 percent in fresh corn. Dried corn is reconstituted through cooking much like rice and yields four to five times its dry bulk. Old-style non-sweet dried corns are no longer sold commercially but are still made at home.

Crackling Soup (*Griewesupp*—"GREE-va-zupp"). This is a popular party dish made with pork or chicken cracklings (*Griewe*) and meat stock. It is often prepared in conjunction with pork butchering. Cooked with *Weissebrieh* as a soup, it is now considered a specialty of Perry County, although the dish is also found in Pennsylvania German settle-

ter. Black butter (*Schwatzebutter*), butter scorched in a hot skillet until dark brown or black, is still a popular "sauce" among the Amish and many Pennsylvania Dutch cooks.

Butterschmalz, or clarified butter. Used extensively in eighteenth- and nineteenth-century cookery, the term is now archaic in Pennsylfaanisch.

Butterschtrietzel. Not the same as Moravian *Schtrietzel* (Braided Dutch Cake). Among the Schwenkfelder Sect, this term of Silesian origin is applied to *Baamkuche* or

Schpiesskuche, a cake made by dripping batter onto a spit rotating slowly over hot coals. When the cake is baked, it is turned upright on one end, giving the appearance of a stack of large doughnuts. This type of cake was made only for weddings or other festive occasions. It fell out of fashion in the nineteenth century, although many local bakeries continued to make it until about World War I.

Catfish (*Katzefisch*). This is a very popular warm weather fish among the Pennsylvania Dutch and is cooked in a large number

ment areas of West Virginia and southern Ohio. The Pennsylvania-German Jews make *Griewesupp* exclusively with chicken cracklings and chicken stock.

Crayfish (*Wasserkrebse*). Chikisalunga, a creek in Lancaster County, is an Indian name meaning "place where crayfish burrow." Crayfish were considered a delicacy among the Pennsylvania Germans in the eighteenth and nineteenth centuries. *Der Amerikanische Bauer* in 1851 published a long article on techniques for catching crayfish for culinary purposes.

German Rampion (Latin, *Oenothera biennis*; Pennsylfaanisch, *Kewwich*—"KAY-vick"). Also known as evening primrose, this herb was once widely cultivated for its small, beet-like root. Historically, the boiled roots were used in soups and stews, particularly pepperpots. The young shoots in the early spring were used in salads and resemble lamb's lettuce (*Ritscherli*) when prepared this way.

Germantown Wedding Rolls (*Germantauner Hochzichsweck*). Sourdough rolls made of spelt and wheat flour are molded into a distinctive three-cornered shape; hence the alternative name *Dreieckichweckli* (Three-Cornered Rolls). The rolls were brushed with egg and scattered with aniseed before baking. The concept originated in Westphalia and was most likely brought to Pennsylvania in the late seventeenth century. The form is medieval and may have phallic implications. The rolls are now archaic and have not been made commercially since the nineteenth century.

Gravel Cake (*Graewwelkuche*—"GREH-vel-koo-keh"). Also known as *Grumbierekuche* (Potato Cake), *Schwenkfelderkuche* (Schwenkfelder Cake), *Heidelbarrier Graewwelkuche* (Heidelberg Gravel Cake), and *Allenschteddler Zuckerkuche* (Allentown Dutchcake). This yeast-raised cake, made with potatoes, eggs, and wheat flour, is baked in a round bread-loaf shape. It is covered with large buttery crumbs called grevel, a word derived from the same root as *gribble*. The cake is still available in many farm markets. It is usually eaten as a breakfast cake with coffee.

Chickweed

Gravy. Pennsylfaanisch uses the word *Sosse* ("SOH-sa") for a prepared sauce, and *Brieh* ("BREE") for a liquid expressed from meat or the natural juice of any foodstuff.

Groundnut. The Pennsylfaanisch term *Grundnuss* is variously applied to two distinct edible plants: the peanut (Latin, *Arachis hypogaea*) and the bog potato (Latin, *Apios tuberosa*). In Pennsylvania Dutch colonial records and even down to the 1860s, the peanut is referred to as *Grundniss* because of its similarity (in shape and size) to the pear-shaped tubers of the common groundnut or bog potato. *Apios tuberosa* is a pealike vine that produces a tuber once widely used in Pennsylvania Dutch cookery both raw and in any recipe where true potatoes were called for. It is still considered the very best among our native wild foods, and in terms of flavor it is far superior to the Peruvian potato.

Jerusalem Artichoke (Latin, *Helianthus tuberosa*). The Pennsylfaanisch term *Erdebbel*

("AYRD-ebbel"), meaning "ground apple," is not to be confused with Pennsylfaanisch *Grumbiere* (ground pear), the term for potato. The roots of the Jerusalem artichoke were commonly pickled for winter salads.

Johnny-Jump-Up (Latin, *Viola tricolor;* Pennsylfaanisch, *Freischamgraut*—"FRY-shom-grout"). A spring garden flower used extensively in former times as a garnish in spring salads. The leaves were used to thicken soups; hence the alternate name wild okra.

Kettlefoot or Spider (Pennsylfaanisch, *Kesselfuss*—"KESS-el-foos"). A three-legged utensil, usually a foot high or taller, on which to set large kettles used in hearth cookery and in such outdoor activities as apple butter boiling. A small version of the kettlefoot is commonly called a tripod or in Pennsylfaanisch, a *Dreifuss* ("DRY-foose").

Kohlrabi (Latin, *Brassica oleracea*; Pennsylfaanisch, *Grautriewwe*—"GROUT-ree-ve," meaning "cabbage turnip"). This is also called *Schwowweriewwe*, usually translated as "Swabian turnip," but which in common usage means "cockroach turnip." Introduced into German cookery via contact with Celto-Romans, this is one of the oldest root vegetables in the Pennsylvania Dutch culinary repertory.

Microwave. The most current Pennsylfaanisch verb is *nuke* ("NOO-keh"), past participle *g'nukt*, as in microwaved soup: *g'nukte Supp*. A microwave oven is a *Nukoffe*. The term is borrowed from American slang, to "nuke" something.

Mustard (*Senf*—"SENF"). Mustard seed, powdered mustard, and prepared mustard were among the leading export products from Pennsylvania in the eighteenth century. Some of the earliest glass factories in Pennsylvania produced black glass bottles for the mustard manufacturers. One of the first registered trademarks in colonial Pennsylvania was a mustard label incorporating the coat of arms of William Penn.

Mustard figured largely in traditional Pennsylvania Dutch cookery. The dried seeds were either fried or added without cooking to such dishes as hot slaw, potato salad, and the bacon dressings used on greens. The prepared mustards were often used as components in other recipes. For example, mustard mixed with apple butter was a popular condiment for roasted or grilled meats.

Mutschelmehl. ("MOO-tchull-male"). Dried white breadcrumbs from the interior part of Milk Bread (*Millichbrod*). Coarse matzoh meal can be used as a substitute.

Pear (*Bier*—"BEER"). The pear was one of the most highly prized of all the Pennsylvania Dutch orchard fruits. Three pears played a major role in our classic cookery: the Diller pear, developed about 1752; the butter pear (Doyenné blanc), one of the most popular for making pear butter; and the Seckel pear. Diller pears were considered the best late-summer pears for Green Pear Pie. Of these three, only the Seckel pear is available in our farm markets today.

The Seckel pear is named for the Pennsylvania German wine merchant Lorenz Seckel (1747–1823), who discovered the original tree (a natural hybrid) on his farm near Philadelphia. The Seckel pear is similar to the German Rousselet pear, but far superior. It is used extensively in fall cookery, especially with venison, pheasant, and goose.

Pot Fork (*Offegawwel*—"OFF-eh-gavel"). A long-handled two-pronged fork designed to lift and move cookpots on the raised hearth or in an oven. Surviving examples are now exceedingly rare but were once necessary tools in raised hearth cookery.

Prickly Pear Cactus (Latin, *Opuntia vulgaria*; Pennsylfaanisch, *Deifelszung*—"DYE-fels-tsoong"). The dialect name literally means "devil's tongue." This native plant was once widespread in the dry barrens above Sumneytown in Montgomery County. A common vegetable in Philadelphia markets in the eighteenth and nineteenth centuries, the dried fruit was used like figs in local

Rocket

cookery. The fruit ripens in November and tastes like pomegranate.

The pads (green part) were singed of spines and used like okra as thickeners in pepperpots and stews. Although two large patches of the cactus were known to survive near Sumneytown into the 1920s, overharvesting has now made this plant nearly extinct in its natural habitat in southeastern Pennsylvania.

Ramp (Latin, *Allium tricoccum*; Pennsylfaanisch, *Gnovlichgraut*—"NO-vlickgrout"). Known in Pennsylfaanisch as "wild garlic," this strong-tasting member of the lily family was widely used in Pennsylvania Dutch cookery until about 1900. Due to overharvesting, the vegetable is now quite rare in the Pennsylvania Dutch region.

Because of its similarity to *Sisymbrium allaria*, a plant native to Germany, ramps were one of the first native American herbs to be acculturated into Pennsylvania Dutch cookery. Although the German and American plants are unrelated botanically, the dialect name for both is the same. The Pennsylvania Dutch penchant for ramps was carried by settlers into the upper South, where the plant still enjoys considerable popularity.

Rocket, or Garden Rocket (Latin, *Hesperis matronalis*; Pennsylfaanisch, *Raget*). Now sold in many urban green groceries under its Italian dialect name *arugula*—the proper name in Italian is *rucola*. Garden rocket has been a popular salad green among the Pennsylvania Dutch since its introduction

Pot fork

into Pennsylvania in the late seventeenth century. I have found it widely naturalized in parts of Lebanon, Berks, Lancaster, Dauphin, and Schuylkill counties. The naturalized variety is much more robust in its growing habit, larger leafed, better flavored, and a deeper green than the arugula sold commercially in Philadelphia. This may be a product of natural hybridization. Some plants attain the size of oak leaf lettuce before turning bitter.

Salad (*Selaat*—"Zeh-LOT"). In the eighteenth and nineteenth centuries, this term applied only to lettuce or to lettuce-like salad greens. Today *Selaat* is used in the same broad sense as in English, so that Caesar salad becomes *Kaiserselaat*, ham salad becomes *Schunke Selaat*, and so forth.

Sapsago Cheese (from *Schabzieger*, "goat cheese for grating") is a rindless green cheese flavored with the herb blue melilot. Shaped into small cones, it was made in Pennsylvania into the nineteenth century but is now available only as an import from Switzerland. It is a key ingredient in historical Pennsylvania Dutch cookery.

Sauté. In Pennsylfaanisch, *schupfe*, the verb from which *Schupfnudle* is derived. Another commonly used verb is *schittle*. Both terms imply the act of shaking and frying over high heat.

Schnittel. A Pennsylfaanisch noun derived from the verb *schneide*, "to cut." When describing meats or root vegetables cut into thin strips, it has the same meaning as *julienne*. When describing herbs or leafy vegetables cut into thin strips, the meaning is the same as *chiffonade*.

Sorrel (Latin, *Rumex acetosa*; Pennsylfaanisch, *Sauerambel*—"SOWER-ambel"). A common Pennsylvania Dutch garden herb used as a green vegetable or as a tart fruit in cookery. It is often cooked with shad, or in pies mixed with sugar. In dried form, it is brewed into a tea as a treatment for dysentery.

Spätzle. The name derives from a plural noun signifying something small made with a spatula. The root word is *Spatel*, from Latin *spatula*, although many German dictionaries incorrectly derive *Spätzle* from *Spatz* ("sparrow").

Sweat (*schwitze*—"SHVI-tseh"). In its culinary meaning, to gently fry a food in a tightly covered skillet so that the natural essences (*Briehe*) do not escape. Onions are often cooked this way as a preliminary step before being combined with other ingredients.

Wall Rocket (Latin, *Diplotaxis tenuifolia*; Pennsylfaanisch, *Mauer Raget*). This fernyleafed salad green is now naturalized from old gardens. The flavor is similar to common garden cress. I have found it growing in numerous undisturbed meadows in the Mahantongo Valley. Livestock seem to avoid it, so it often develops into large patches.

COOK'S GUIDE TO REGIONAL SHOPPING AND LOCAL INGREDIENTS

APPLE BUTTER

Bauman's Pennsylvania Dutch Apple Butter
The Bauman Family
Sassamansville, PA 19472
phone: 215-754-7251

See also Produce (organic)/ Keefer Orchards;
Raspberry Products

APPLE JACK / APPLE BRANDY

Laird's Straight Apple Brandy
Laird's Old Apple Brandy (Premium, aged 7½ years, the original "Jersey Lightning")
Laird & Company
Larrie W. Laird
Scobeyville, NJ 07724
phone: 201-542-0312
Firm established in 1780.

BIRD TREES

Daniel G. Strawser
Traditional Folk Art Carver
2741 Buckner Road
Thompson Station, TN 37179
phone: 615-790-8789
Specializes in traditional bird trees and animal carvings.

BREWERIES

Dock Street Brewery
225 City Line Avenue
Bala Cynwyd, PA 19004
phone: 215-668-1480
Premium beers and ales.

Pennsylvania Brewing Company
Thomas V. Pastorius
800 Vinial Street
Pittsburgh, PA 15212
phone: 412-237-9400
Specializes in Pennsylvania Pilsner.

Stoudt Brewing Company
65 West Main Street
Adamstown, PA 19501
phone: 215-484-4387
Premium beers and ales.

D. G. Yuengling & Son, Inc.
5th and Mahantongo Streets
Pottsville, PA 17901
phone: 717-662-4141
Ales and dark beers. Oldest brewery in the United States, established 1829.

BUCKWHEAT (ORGANIC AND NONORGANIC)

Burkitt Mills
P.O. Box 440-A
Penn Yan, NY 14527
phone: 315-536-3311
Whole groats, flour, and roasted.

James H. Haldeman
1466 Jerry Lane, R.D. 5
Manheim, PA 17545
phone: 717-665-2339
Mail order.

BUTTER PRINT AND MOLD CARVINGS

D. D. Dillon Carvings
Don Dillon
850 Meadow Lane
Camp Hill, PA 17011
phone: 717-761-6895
Butter prints and cookie molds. Brochures available.

Old Buttermold Pattern Products
Martha Barnham and Sidney Dodson
Box 551, 722 Clay Street
Franklin, VA 23851
phone: 804-562-4925
Butter prints a specialty. Mail order.

Carl E. Roos
400 South Center Street
Pottsville, PA 17901
phone: 717-622-7747

CHEESE AND DAIRY PRODUCTS (BIODYNAMIC)

Seven Stars Farm Store
Box 550
West Seven Stars Road
Kimberton, PA 19442
phone: 215-935-1444
Premium-grade natural yogurts, farmhouse cheeses, and milk produced on a 400-acre farm according to the tenets of Rudolf Steiner.

Shenk Cheese Company
Paul S. Shenk
1980 New Danville Pike
Lancaster, PA
phone: 717-393-4240
Ball cheese, cup cheese, and farmer's cheese.

Fleur de Lait Foods, Inc.
254 South Custer Avenue
New Holland, PA 17557
phone: 717-354-4416
Premium-quality cream cheese. No additives. The only real Pennsylvania cream cheese now on the market.

CHRISTMAS SUPPLIES

Gerlachs of Lecha
P.O. Box 213
Emmaus, PA 18049
phone: 215-965-9181
Traditional ornaments, *Putz* figures, scrap pictures, paper products. Catalogs available.

The House-on-the-Hill
Caroline K. Kallas
P.O. Box 5221
River Forest, IL 60305
phone: 708-969-2588
Reproduction springerle and gingerbread molds. Catalogs available.

CLEAR TOY CANDIES (TRADITIONAL)

Charles H. Regennas
130 West Lemon Street
Lititz, PA 17543
phone: 818-626-2395
Clear toys and handmade candies. Mail order.

COOKIE CUTTERS (HANDMADE)

Charles E. Rittle
2845 E. Cumberland St.
Myerstown, PA 17067
phone: 717-866-6634
Stock and commission work.

CORN, DRIED (TRADITIONAL)

John F. Cope Company, Inc.
Tom Cope, General Manager
156 West Harrisburg Avenue
Rheems, PA 17570
phone: 717-367-5142 or 653-8075
Dried white sweet corn, schnitz butter, preserves, and jellies.

CORNMEAL

Nathaniel Newlin Grist Mill
Harold Dabbs Woodfin, Jr., Director
Newlin Mill Park
219 South Cheney Road
Glen Mills, PA 19342
phone: 215-459-2359
Specializes in stone-ground yellow cornmeal, but wheat can be ground on commission. Built in 1704, the mill was restored to working order in the late 1950s.

James H. Haldeman
1466 Jerry Lane, R.D. 5
Manheim, PA 17545
phone: 717-665-2339
Roasted and unroasted cornmeal. Mail order.

CORN SALAD (RITSCHERLI)

Lakeville Specialty Produce Company
P.O. Box 202
Washingtonville, PA 17884
phone: 717-437-3171
Marketed under its French name, *mâche*. Hydroponically grown.

COUNTRY STORE (OLD ORDER MENNONITE)

Echo Hill Country Store
Luke S. Weaver
R.D. 1, Box 1029
Fleetwood, PA 19522
phone: 215-944-7858
Bulk foods, cooking and baking supplies.

FARMLAND PRESERVATION

American Farmland Trust (National Office)
1920 N Street NW, Suite 400
Washington, DC 20036
phone: 202-659-5170

FLOUR

Arrowhead Mills, Inc.
Box 2059
Hereford, TX 79045
phone: 806-364-0730
Organic wheat, buckwheat, and rye flours; cornmeals. Available in stores and by mail order.

The Great Valley Mills
Steven Kantoor
Road 3, Box 1111
Barto, PA 19504
phone: 215-754-7800
for mail orders: 800-688-6455
Professional-grade ground flours, pastry and bread flours. Available wholesale, retail, and by mail order.

Nolt's Mill
360 Mt. Sidney Road
Witmer, PA 17585
phone: 717-393-1369
Traditional flour mill that supplies Amish
and Mennonite bakeries. In the nineteenth
century it belonged to the Quaker Gibbons
family.

Rohrer's Mill
273 Rohrer Mill Road
Ronks, PA 17572
phone: 717-687-6400
Traditional flour mill, offering wholesale and
retail flours.

For readers in the Midwest, I recommend:
Hodgson Mill Enterprises, Inc.
Gainesville, MO 65655
Stone-ground rye and cornmeals.

Elam Mills
Division of National Bakers Services, Inc.
Broadview, IL 60153-4499
Whole-wheat pastry flour and other flour
specialties.

GOAT CHEESE (FARMHOUSE)

Greystone Chèvratel
Douglas Newbold
764 Millview Road
Malvern, PA 19355
phone: 215-296-0463

Woodchoppertown Chèvre
Robert Spots
R.D. 3, Box 127
Boyertown, PA 19512
phone: 215-689-5948

HEARTH UTENSILS

Thomas and Linda Loose
Route 2, Box 2410
Leesport, PA 19533
phone: 215-926-4849
Whitesmith and blacksmith wares, metal
inlays. Commission work and mail orders.

HEIRLOOM SEEDS
(PENNSYLVANIA DUTCH)

Landis Valley Museum
2451 Kissel Hill Road
Lancaster, PA 17601
phone: 717-569-0401
Catalog available.

HERBALIST

Mountain Bummy's Herb Society
Lamar W. Bumbaugh
P.O. Box 60
Lyons Station, PA 19563-0060
phone: 215-682-1640
Herbs and wild plants, fresh and dried. Wild
nuts, walking sticks. Quantities limited.

HERBS AND SPICES

The Herb Shop
20 East Main Street
Lititz, PA
phone: 717-626-9206
Dried herbs, spices, and specialty foods.

HOMINY, LARGE

Juniata Cheese Shop
Wilbur D. Graybill
R.D. 2, Box 916
Mifflintown, PA 17059
Uncooked, unprocessed white hominy corn
and handmade butter churns.

HONEY (NATURAL)

Bacton Hill Apiaries
John Tappe, Beekeeper
184 West Valley Hill Road
Malvern, PA 19355
phone: 215-363-9485

HORSERADISH

Kelchner's Horseradish Products
Dublin, PA 18917
phone: 215-249-3439

KNIFEMAKER (TRADITIONAL)

Abram Rissler
1794 Spring Hollow Road
East Earl, PA 17519
phone: 215-445-7423
Also makes wildlife and waterfowl carvings.
Commission work.

MEATS

Stauffer Homestead Farm
Charles Miller
145 Fetterville Road
East Earl, PA 17519
phone: 215-445-6209
Organic beef, lamb, and pork.

Dietrich's Meats and Country Store
Verna Dietrich
660 Old 22
Krumsville, PA
mailing address: Lenhartsville, PA 19534
phone: 215-756-6344
Dietrich's has a market stand at Renninger's
Farmer's Market, Noble St., Kutztown,
Pennsylvania, open Friday 12 noon to 8:00
P.M. and Saturday 8:00 A.M. to 5:00 P.M. Will
ship mail order.

S. Clyde Weaver, Inc.
5253 Main Street
East Petersburg, PA 17520
phone: 717-569-0812
Traditional smoked meats, sausages, and
specialty cheeses.

Troutman Brothers
High Road
Klingerstown, PA 17941
phone: 717-425-2341
General line of beef and pork products and
traditional sausages. Retail sales on premises
and at the Lewisburg, Hometown, and Gratz
farm markets.

MORAVIAN COOKIES
(TRADITIONAL)

Mrs. Travis Hanes
Route 2, Box 431
Friedberg Road
Clemmons, NC 27012
phone: 919-764-1402
Mail order. Brochures available.

MORAVIAN DOLLS
(HANDMADE)

Christiansbrunn Brotherhood
c/o Brother Christian
R.D. 1, Box 149
Pitman, PA 17964
No telephone. Mail order only.

MUSHROOMS
(REGIONAL AND EXOTIC)

East Coast Exotics, Inc.
James P. Bertogli
P.O. Box 468
Toughkenamon, PA 19374
phone: 215-268-0771
Morels.

MUTSCHELMEHL

Bären Zeiher Echt Ulmer Mutschelmehl
Zeiher und Laible GmbH & Co.
7900 Ulm/Donau
Germany
Mutschelmehl is still sold commercially in
Germany and is available in some American
specialty food shops under this brand name.
It is sold in 200-g boxes.

PENNSYLVANIA DUTCH CULTURE

The Pennsylvania German Society
P.O. Box 397
Birdsboro, PA 19508
Individual Membership: $40.00 per year

PENNSYLVANIA DUTCH LANGUAGE KITS

Pennsylvania German Enterprises
Richard Druckenbrod
1929 West Livingston Street
Allentown, PA 18105
phone: 215-437-0567
Language kits with grammars and cassettes.
Mail order.

PENNSYLVANIA DUTCH LIVING HISTORY

Goschenhoppen Historians
Red Men's Hall
Route 29
Green Lane, PA 18054
phone: 215-234-8953
Sponsor the annual Goschenhoppen Folk
Festival in August, recommended for atten-
tion to authenticity.

Joseph Schneider Haus Museum
466 Queen Street South
Kitchener, Ontario N2G 1W7
Canada
phone: 519-742-7752

Landis Valley Museum
2451 Kissel Hill Road
Lancaster, PA 17601
phone: 717-569-0401
Closed Mondays.

The Peter Wentz Farmstead
P.O. Box 240
Worcester, PA 19490
phone: 215-584-5104

PENNSYLVANIA FOOD SPECIALTIES

Pennsylvania General Store
Reading Terminal Market
Michael and Julie Holahan
12th and Arch Streets
Philadelphia, PA 19107
phone: 215-592-0455 or 800-545-4891

PEWTER TABLEWARE
(TRADITIONAL)

Jay Thomas Stauffer
707 West Brubaker Valley Road
Lititz, PA 17543
phone: 717-626-7067
Handmade tableware, candlesticks, etc.
Commission work. Mail order.

POTTERS

Dorothy E. Long
558 Willis Lane
Wayne, PA 19087
phone: 215-688-8793
fax: 215-688-1762
Culinary and general wares. Catalogs available.

Lester Breininger
Taylor Mansion
476 South Church Street
Robesonia, PA 19551
phone: 215-693-5344
Studio and retail. Sgrafitto and slip decorated
redware pottery. Commission work.

The Foltz Pottery
Carl Ned Foltz
225 North Peartown Rd.
Reinholds, PA 17569
phone: 215-267-2676
Sgraffito and slip decorated redware pottery.

Oley Valley Redware
Gerald H. Yoder
William Thomas Logan
3818 Pricetown Road
Fleetwood, PA 19522
phone: 215-944-0227
Sgraffito and slip decorated redware pottery.
Commission work.

Turtlecreek Pottery
David T. Smith & Company
3600 Shawhan Rd.
Morrow, OH 45152
phone: 513-932-2472

Jeff White
studio: 2012 Penn St.
Lebanon, PA 17042
phone: 717-272-0806
retail: Booth #1
Black Angus Antiques Mall
Rte. 272
Adamstown, PA 19501
phone: 215-484-4385

Sgraffito and slip decorated redware pottery.
Commission work.

POULTRY

Eberly Poultry, Inc.
Levi W. Eberly & Sons
1095 Mt. Airy Road
Stevens, PA 17578
phone: 215-267-6440 or 267-4499
Philadelphia Market: 215-457-3521
Organic, natural poultry products, custom
poultry processing, wholesale and retail.
Chickens, turkeys, muscovy ducks, capons,
geese, rabbits, pheasants, partridges, quail,
guinea hens, game birds.

PRETZELS

Handmade Pennsylvania Dutch Pretzels
Alfred Milanese
101 Thompson Street #9
New York, NY 10012
phone: 212-925-9738
Distributes hand-twisted traditional hard
pretzels from Lancaster County in the New
York City area.

Schwartz's Pretzel Bakery
Janet C. Schwartz
4353 Frankford Avenue
Philadelphia, PA 19124
phone: 215-288-0918
Specialties: *Braided Soft Pretzels* (*Zoppbrezle*)
and *Trophy Pretzels* (large, ornamental).

Uncle Henry's Pretzel Bakery
Bowmansville, PA 17507
phone: 215-445-4690
Traditional hard pretzels. Recommended:
*Uncle Henry's Old Fashioned Hearth-Baked
Hand-Twisted Pretzels*, no sugar, no shorten-
ing, no preservatives, no salt.

PRODUCE (ORGANIC)

Bertoldi's Cedar Hill Gardens
Deborah Bertoldi
Freemansville Road (near Green Hills)
Reading, PA 19607
phone: 215-777-0178
Herbs, produce, fresh flowers. Retails for
several other local producers.

Carleybrook Gardens
R.D. 4, Box 4708
Hartz Road
Mohnton, PA 19540
phone: 215-856-7392
Produce and flowers.

Overbrook Herb Farm
Paul and Nancy Tsakos
2213 Bethel Road
Lansdale, PA 19446
phone: 215-699-7628
Herbs, produce.

Spring Lake Farm / Keefer Orchards
Atlee Keefer and Charlene Keefer
725 Farm View Road
York Springs, PA 17372
phone: 717-528-4475
Fruit and fruit products, including peach and
apple butters.

RASPBERRY PRODUCTS

Tait Farm
R.D. 1, Box 330
Centre Hall, PA 16828
phone: 814-466-6910
Raspberry shrub, raspberry vinegar, apple
butter. Mail order.

SAFFRON

Evelyn Groff
644 Beaver Valley Pike
Lancaster, PA 17602
phone: 717-464-2147
Home-grown. Supplies are limited and subject to variable harvest conditions.

Assouline and Ting, Inc.
Joel Assouline
314 Brown Street-Northern Liberties
Philadelphia, PA 19123
phone: 215-627-3000
Imported. Wholesale and retail.

SAUERKRAUT

Heebners Sauerkraut
Lancaster County Farmer's Market
Wayne, PA 19087
phone: 215-687-0307
Mild.

SPELT

Purity Foods, Inc.
Wilhelm Kosnopfl
2871 West Jolly Road
Okemos, MI 48864-3547
phone: 517-351-9231
Whole-grain spelt and spelt flours.
Wholesale, retail, mail order.

TINWARE (HANDMADE)

Karen Dunwoody
972 Valley Road
Quarryville, PA 17566
phone: 717-786-8247

Zimmerman's Tinsmithing
Clervin Zimmerman
R.D. 1, Box 36
Hegins, PA 17938
phone: 717-682-3645
Culinary and general household objects in tin
and copper.

TURKEYS

Bolton's Turkey Farm and Market
Charles Bolton, Jr., and Todd Bolton
Route 113
Silverdale, PA 18962
phone: 215-257-6047
Turkey and turkey products.

WINERIES (SELECTED)

Allegro Vineyards
Tim and John Crouch
Sechrist Road
Brogue, PA 17309
phone: 717-927-9148
UPS deliveries.

Brookmere Farm Vineyards
Route 655, Box 53
Belleville, PA 17004
phone: 717-935-5380

Calvaresi Winery
R.D. 3, Box 51
Bernville, PA 19506
phone: 215-488-7966

Chaddsford Winery
Eric Miller
Route 1, P.O. Box 229
Chadds Ford, PA 19317
phone: 215-388-6221
Premium varietals and table wines. UPS
deliveries.

Clover Hill Vineyards & Winery
John and Pat Skrip
R.D. 2
Breiningsville, PA 18031
phone: 215-395-2468

Conneaut Cellars Winery
Route 322, Box 5075
Conneaut Lake, PA 16315
phone: 814-382-3999

Fox Meadow Farm
1439 Clover Mill Road
Chester Springs, PA 19425
phone: 215-827-9731
Premium wines.

Mount Nittany Vineyard and Winery
Houser Road
Linden Hall, PA 16828
phone: 814-466-6373

Naylor Wine Cellars, Inc.
Richard Naylor
R.D. 3, Box 424
Ebaugh Road
Stewartstown, PA 17363
phone: 717-993-2431
UPS deliveries: 800-292-3370
Premium wines.

Presque Isle Wine Cellars
9440 Buffalo Road
North East, PA 16428
phone: 814-725-1314
Premium wines.

Sand Castle Winery
Box 177
Route 32, River Road
Erwinna, PA 18920
phone: 215-294-9181
Premium wines.

Slate Quarry Winery
Sid and Ellie Butler
460 Gower Road
Nazareth, PA 18064
phone: 215-759-0286

Twin Brook Winery
Cheryl Gaughan
5697 Strasburg Road
Route 2, Box 2376
Gap, PA 17525
phone: 717-442-4915

Vyncrest Winery
Jan Landis
R.D. 2, Box 983
Twin Ponds Road
Breinigsville, PA 18031
phone: 215-398-1720
Limited vintages. Tastings and tours by
appointment.

NOTES AND BIBLIOGRAPHY

NOTES

CHAPTER 1

1. For a study of the Amish relationship to Pennsylfaanisch, refer to Laura Jottini, *A Language and Cultural Island in Modern American Society: The Amish* (Milan, 1988).

2. Ludwig Wollenweber, *Gemälde aus dem Pennsylvanischen Volksleben* (Philadelphia and Leipzig, 1869), p. 142.

3. David Lick and Thomas Brendle, "Plant Names and Plant Lore Among the Pennsylvania Germans," *Proceedings of the Pennsylvania German Society* XXXIII (1923), p. 188.

4. Annemarie Wurmbach, "Kuchen-Fladen-Torte," *Zeitschrift für Volkskunde* LVI (1960), pp. 23 and 24.

5. Ladies of the Presbyterian Church, *Cook Book of Useful Recipes* (Wrightsville, Penn., 1883), p. 33.

6. Hans Wiswe, *Kulturgeschichte der Kochkunst* (Munich, 1970), pp. 201–202.

7. Albert Hauser, *Vom Essen und Trinken im alten Zürich* (Zurich, 1961), p. 42.

8. William Henry Perrin, *History of Stark County, Ohio* (Chicago, 1881), pp. 492–493.

9. Hugo Stopp, *Das Kochbuch der Sabina Welserin* (Heidelberg, 1980), p. 83.

10. Wurmbach, p. 21.

11. See, for example, Thaddäus Troll, *Kochen wie die Schwaben* (Munich, 1977), p. 94.

12. "It's Time to Chow Down at Sonker Festival," *Simple Pleasures* (Mount Airy, N.C.), Aug. 1990, p. 18.

13. *Vollständiges Nürnbergisches Koch-Buch* (Nuremberg, 1691), p. 578.

14. Wolfgang Kleinschmidt, "Die Einführung der Kartoffel in der Pfalz," *Rheinisch-westfälische Zeitschrift für Volkskunde* XXIV: 14 (1978), pp. 208–230.

15. "Dummes," *Pennsylvania Dutchman* IV:5 (Easter 1953), p. 4.

16. Hein Kröhler, "Gebredelde, Hoorich un Bettelmannsknepp," *Rheinpfalz*, Dec. 13, 1980.

17. See, for example, Werner Meyer's *Hirsebrei und Hellebarde* (Freiburg im Breisgau, 1985), which covers all of these basic foods.

18. For buckwheat, refer to Udelgard Körber-Grohne, *Nutzpflanzen in Deutschland* (Stuttgart, 1988), pp. 339–349. For spelt, refer to Wilhelm Abel, *Geschichte der deutschen Landwirtschaft* (Stuttgart, 1967), pp. 39–40.

19. Roland Bonnain, "The Bread of the Dead," *Food and Foodways* V:2 (1992), p. 196.

20. Johann David Schoepf, *Travels Through the Confederation, (1783–1784)* (New York, 1968), vol. I, p. 271.

21. *The Lancaster Examiner*, Sept. 30 and Nov. 25, 1830.

CHAPTER 2

1. See Johann Wilhelm, *Architectura civilis* (Nuremberg, 1668), plate 1.

2. Marcus Rumpolt, *Ein New Kochbuch* (Frankfurt, 1581), [p. 419].

3. Karl Schwinn, *Speis und Trank im Odenwald* (Mörlenbach, 1984), p. 68.

4. Sadie's breakfast dish is also known as *siesse Gribbel* (sweet gribble). See Ladies' Aid Society, *The Schwenkfelder Cook Book* (Kutztown, Penn., 1963), p. 119.

5. Inge Carius, *Gebildbrot: Brauchtum im Jahres- und Lebenslauf* (Königstein im Taunus, 1982), p. 16.

6. "German Cookery and Dutch Lunch Menu," *Cooking Club Magazine*, Dec. 1906, p. 653.

7. William Woys Weaver, *Sauerkraut Yankees* (Philadelphia, 1983), p. 96.

8. *Ibid.*, p. 86.

CHAPTER 3

1. David Lick and Thomas Brendle, "Plant Names and Plant Lore Among the Pennsylvania Germans," *Proceedings of the Pennsylvania German Society* XXXIII (1923), p. 222.

2. Edna Eby Heller, "Ryebread Lehigh County Style," *Pennsylvania Folklife* XII:1 (Spring 1961), p. 38.

3. Cuthbert W. Johnson, *The Farmer's Encyclopaedia* (Philadelphia, 1844), p. 218.

4. Walter Guyer, *Kleinjogg der Zürcher Bauer: 1716–1785* (Erlenbach and Zurich, 1972).

5. Johann Halle, *Magie, oder, die Zauberkräfte der Natur* (Berlin, 1786), vol. 4, p. 260.

6. "Gutes Brod," *Der Hoch-Deutsche Amerikanische Calender für 1831* (Germantown, Penn., 1830).

7. *The Pennsylvania Farm Journal* V (Nov. 1855), p. 16.

8. Ladies of the Cumberland Valley, *The Cumberland Valley Cook and General Recipe Book* (Topeka, Kan., 1881), p. 45.

9. *Housekeeper's Almanac for 1887* (Philadelphia, 1886). No pagination.

10. Julia Davis Chandler, "Moravian Domestic Life," *The Boston Cooking-School Magazine* X:7 (Feb. 1906), p. 315.

11. *The Philadelphia Bulletin*, Sept. 2, 1939.

12. "So hen die alde Leit Geduh," *Der Reggeboge* XV:1–2 (Jan.–April 1980), p. 16.

CHAPTER 4

1. See, for example, "Die Strasburger Kirschenfair" held Friday and Saturday, July 1–2, 1808, as advertised in *Der Americanische Staatsbothe und Lancäster Anzeigs-Nachrichten*, June 29, 1808.

2. William Woys Weaver, "Viticulture Among the Pennsylvania Germans," *The Journal of Gastronomy* VI:3 (Winter 1990/1991), pp. 113–129.

3. "Aufbewahren von Früchten," *Das Bauern-Journal* I:10 (Oct. 1857), p. 158.

4. Clara Landis, *The Improved Hygienic Cook-Book* (Philadelphia, 1864), p. 5.

5. M. S. Weber, *Magazine of Human Culture* (Farmersville, Penn.) VII:4 (Aug. 1886), pp. 61–62.

6. "Yellow Pickle, or Axe-jar," *Lady's Annual Register* (Boston, 1837), p. 61.

7. "Sweet-Sour Dressing," *The Pennsylvania Dutchman* IV:9 (Jan. 1, 1953), p. 15.

8. Interview with Jacob Weisenstein of Horschbach, Pfalz, Nov. 5, 1983.

9. Catherine Plagemann, *Fine Preserving*, edited by M.F.K. Fisher (Berkeley, Cal., 1986), p. 34.

CHAPTER 5

1. "Ramblings in Winter," *The Family Magazine* I:1 (Jan. 1836), p. 264.

2. Jerry F. Beach, "The Longest Day, 1918," *The Casselman Chronicle* IV:1/2 (Spring/Summer 1964), pp. 10–11.

3. Interview with Betty and Ben Mumper of New Germantown, Penn., May 3, 1986.

4. Interview with Frau Gisela Hermann of St. Julian, Pfalz, Nov. 5, 1983.

5. Christian Germershausen, "Das Hausschlachten," in *Die Hausmutter in allen ihren Geschäfften* (Leipzig, 1782), vol. 2, pp. 580–581.

6. Walther Klein, "Wo Rauch ist, muss auch Feuer sein," *Pälzer Feierowend* XIX:6 (Feb. 11, 1967), pp. 1–2.

7. William Woys Weaver, *Sauerkraut Yankees* (Philadelphia, 1983), pp. 32–33.

CHAPTER 6

1. G. Franz, "Der Martinstag im Volksleben der Pfalz," *Unterhaltungsbeilage zur Neuen Pfälzischen Landeszeitung* (Nov. 21, 1925), no. 272.

2. Wolfhilde von König, "Das Ei im Weihnachtskreis," in *Bayerisches Jahrbuch für Volkskunde* (Würzburg, 1978), pp. 134–145.

3. Julius F. Sachse, *The German Sectarians* (Philadelphia, 1899), vol. 2, p. 115.

4. Albert Becker, "Pfälzer Weihnachtsbräuche," *Pfälzerisches Museum/Pfälzische Heimatkunde*, Heft 5/6 (1922), pp. 149–150.

5. William Woys Weaver, *The Christmas Cook* (New York, 1990), p. 54.

6. Robert Turner, ed., *Lewis Miller: Sketches and Chronicles* (York, Penn., 1966), p. 45.

7. Ernst Burgstaller, *Österreichisches Festtagsgebäck* (Linz, 1983), p. 58.

SELECTED BIBLIOGRAPHY

Abel, Wilhelm. *Geschichte der deutschen Landwirtschaft vom frühen Mittelalter bis zum 19. Jahrhundert*. Stuttgart: Verlag Eugen Ulmer, 1967.

Auer, Johann. *Der Deutsche Weingärtner: Ein Handbuch also Richtschnurr und Gründliche Anleitung für Weinbauer*. Reading, Penn.: Gedruckt für den Verfasser, 1849.

Das Bauern-Journal (Allentown, Penn.: Mohr und Troxel, 1857–1858), I:1–II:7 (July 1858). In August 1858, this is joined into the German edition of Judd's *American Agriculturist*.

Bergner, Anna. *Pfälzer Kochbuch*. Mannheim: Verlag von Tobias Löffler, 1858.

Berliner, A. "Jüdischer Speisetafel." *Jahrbuch für Jüdische Geschichte und Literatur* XIII (1910).

Bonnain, Roland. "The Bread of the Dead or One Use of a Forgotten Cereal." *Food and Foodways* V:2 (1992), pp. 195–203.

Burgstaller, Ernst. *Österreichisches Festtagsgebäck*. Linz: Rudolf Trauner Verlag, 1983.

Carius, Inge. *Gebildbrot: Brauchtum im Jahres- und Lebenslauf*. Königstein im Taunus: Karl Robert Langewiesche Nachfolger, 1982.

Chandler, Julius Davis. "Moravian Domestic Life." *The Boston Cooking-School Magazine* X:7 (Feb. 1906), pp. 311–317.

Doerflinger, Marguerite and Georges Klein. *Toute la cuisine alsacienne*. Wettolsheim: Editions Mars et Mercure, 1978 & 1979.

Fabricant, Florence. "Fresh from the Baker, A New Staff of Life." *New York Times*, Nov. 11, 1992, pp. C-1 and C-6.

Frauen Verein Gesellcaft. *Cook Book. Frauen Verein Society, Trinity Lutheran Church*. Pottsville, Penn.: Privately printed, c. 1914.

Frysinger, Henry. *Valuable Recipes for Family Use*. Lewistown, Penn.: True Democrat Print, 1875.

Fürst, Anna (Marianne Strüf, pseud.). *Vollständiges Kochbuch für alle Stände*. Stuttgart: P. Balz'sche Buchhandlung, 1842.

Fürst, Johann Evangelist. *Der Verständige Bauer Simon Strüf*. Passau/Bränn: bey J. G. Gastl, c. 1824.

Geiger, Karl Theodor. "Rund um die pälzer Metzelsupp." *Pälzer Feierowend* II:41 (Oct. 14, 1950), pp. 1–2.

Germershausen, Christian Friedrich. *Die Hausmutter in allen ihren Geschäfften*. Leipzig: bey Johann Friedrich Junius, 1782.

Gibbons, Phebe Earle. *"Pennsylvania Dutch" and Other Essays*. Philadelphia: J.B. Lippincott & Co., 1872.

Girardey, George. *Höchst nützliches Handbuch über Kochkunst*. Cincinnati: Stereotypirt von F. U. James, 1841.

Günther, Friederich August. *Homöopathischer Thierarzt*. Weisenburg, Penn.: John Helffrich, 1849.

Guyer, Walter. *Kleinjogg der Zürcher Bauer: 1716–1785*. Erlenbach and Zürich: Eugen Rentsch, 1972.

Halle, Johann Samuel. *Magie, oder, die Zauberkräfte der Natur*. 4 vols. Berlin: bey Joachim Pauli, 1786.

Hark, Ann, and Preston A. Barba. *Pennsylvania German Cookery: A Regional Cookbook*. Allentown, Penn.: Schlechter's, 1950.

Hartenfels, Hjalmas. *Pfälzer Schlemmer-Brevier*. Neustadt: Verlag D. Meininger, 1983.

Hauser, Albert. *Vom Essen und Trinken im alten Zürich*. Zurich: Verlag Berichthaus, 1961.

Heller, Edna Eby. "Ryebread Lehigh County Style." *Pennsylvania Folklife* XII:1 (Spring 1961), pp. 38–39.

[Hensel, Julius.] *Bread from Stones: A New and Rationalized System of Land Fertilization and Physical Regeneration*. Philadelphia: A. J. Tafel, 1894.

Hildegard of Bingen. *Heilkunde. Das Buch von dem Grund und Wesen und der Heilung der Krankheiten*. Edited by Heinrich Schipperges. Salzburg: Otto Müller Verlag, 1957.

Hohman, Johann Georg. *Der lange Verborgene Freund*. Reading, Penn.: Gedruckt [bey Carl Augustus Bruckman], 1820.

Huffines, Lois, and John Moyer. "A Family Butchering in the Schwaben Creek Valley." *Historic Schaefferstown Record* XX:2 (April 1986), pp. 15–43.

Hufeland, Christoph Wilhelm. *Makrobiotik, oder die Kunst das menschliche Leben*. Reutlingen: bey Fleischhauer und Bohm, 1817.

Husmann, Georg. *Weinbau in Amerika. Im Speziellen: Die Cultur der Rebe in Missouri*. Allentown, Penn.: Verlag von Mohr und Troxel, 1857.

"It's Time to Chow Down at Sonker Festival." *Simple Pleasures* (Mount Airy, N.C.: Mount Airy News), Aug. 1990, p. 18.

Jahr, G.H.G. *Manual of Homeopathic Medicine*. Edited by Constantine Hering. Allentown, Penn.: In Commission by J.G. Wesselhoeft, 1836.

Johnson, Cuthbert W. *The Farmer's Encyclopaedia, and Dictionary of Rural Affairs*. Philadelphia: Carey and Hart, 1844.

Jottini, Laura. *A Language and Cultural Island in Modern American Society: The Amish*. Milan: Dott. A. Giuffre Editore/Universitá degli Studi di Cagliari, 1988.

Kaiser, Hermann. "Kochen in Dunst und Qualm: Herdfeuer und Herdgerät im Rauchhaus." *Volkskunst* X (Nov. 1987), pp. 5–10.

Keller, Mrs. J. A. *The Pennsylvania German Cook Book*. Alliance, Ohio: Privately printed, 1904.

Klein, Walther. "Wo Rauch ist, muss auch Feuer sein: Romantisches Räuchern in Rauchküchen, Rauchkammern und Rauchfängen." *Pälzer Feierowend* XIX:6 (Feb. 11, 1967), pp. 1–2.

Kleinschmidt, Wolfgang. "Die Einführung der Kartoffel in der Pfalz und die Verbreitung von Kartoffelspeisen in der Westpfalz und in den angrenzenden Gebieten der ehemaligen Rheinprovinz." *Rheinisch-westfälische Zeitschrift für Volkskunde* XXIV:14 (1978), pp. 208–230.

Kolb, Aegidius, und Leonhard Lidel. *D'schwäbisch' Küche*. Kempten: Allgäuer Zeitungsverlag, 1984.

Körber-Grohne, Udelgard. *Nutzpflanzen in Deutschland: Kulturgeschichte und Biologie.* Stuttgart: Konrad Theiss Verlag, 1988.

Kröhler, Hein. "Gebredelde, Hoorich un Bettelmannsknepp." *Rheinpfalz,* Dec. 13, 1980.

Kyger, M. Ellsworth. *An English-Pennsylvania German Dictionary.* 3 vols. Birdsboro, Penn.: The Pennsylvania German Society, 1986.

Ladies' Aid Society of Hetzel's Church. *Ladies' Aid Society Cook Book.* Pottsville, Penn.: Fertig Printing, 1924.

Ladies' Aid Society of St. Paul's United Evangelical Church of Mifflinburg. *Benefit Cook Book Containing Best Home Tried Recipes.* Lancaster, Penn.: The Merit Publishing Company, c. 1912.

Ladies' Aid Society of the Schwenkfelder Church. *The Schwenkfelder Cook Book.* Kutztown, Penn.: Kutztown Publishing Co., 1963.

Ladies of Bethlehem. *The Bethlehem Cook Book.* Bethlehem, Penn.: Times Publishing Company, 1900.

Ladies of the Cumberland Valley. *The Cumberland Valley Cook and General Recipe Book.* Topeka, Kan.: Kansas Publishing House, 1881.

Ladies of the Presbyterian Church. *Cook Book of Useful Recipes.* Wrightsville, Penn.: W. W. Moore, Printer, 1883.

Landis, Clara S. *The Improved Hygienic Cook-Book, and Domestic Economizer.* Philadelphia: Ringwalt & Brown, 1864.

Levan, J. *Pennsylvania Dutch Cook Book of Fine Old Recipes.* Reading, Penn.: Privately printed, 1934.

Lick, David E., and Thomas R. Brendle. "Plant Names and Plant Lore Among the Pennsylvania Germans." *Proceedings of the Pennsylvania German Society* XXXIII (1923).

Löffler, Friederike. *Oekonomisches Handbuch für Frauenzimmer.* Stuttgart: Johann Friedrich Steinkopf, 1795.

[Löffler, Friederike.] *Vollständiges Kochbuch für die Deutsch-Amerikanische Küche.* Philadelphia: Loes & Sebald, [1856].

Meyer, Werner. *Hirsebrei und Hellebarde. Auf den Spuren des mittelalterlichen Lebens in der Schweiz.* Olten/Freiburg im Breisgau: Walter-Verlag, 1985.

Noth- und Hülfs-Büchlein, oder lehrreiche Freuden- und Trauer-Geschichte der Einwohner zu Mildheim. 14th ed. Gotha: in der Expedition der Deutschen Zeitung, 1793.

Perrin, William Henry. *History of Stark County, Ohio.* Chicago: Baskin & Battey, 1881.

[Peters, Gustav Sigismund.] *Die Geschickte Hausfrau.* Harrisburg, Penn.: Lutz & Scheffer, 1851.

Plagemann, Catherine Emig. *Fine Preserving.* Edited by M.F.K. Fisher. Berkeley, Cal.: Aris Books, 1986.

Pollack, Herman. *Jewish Folkways in Germanic Lands (1648–1806).* Cambridge, Mass.: The M.I.T. Press, 1971.

Reinhart, Brother Peter. *Brother Juniper's Bread Book.* Reading, Mass.: Addison-Wesley Publishing Co., 1991.

Rösch, Herbert. *Schwäbisches Maultaschenbüchle.* Stuttgart: Hugo Matthaes Druckerei und Verlag, 1985.

Rumpolt, Marcus. *Ein New Kochbuch.* Frankfurt: Sigmund Feyerabendt, 1581.

Sachse, Julius F. *The German Sectarians of Pennsylvania.* Philadelphia: Privately printed, 1899.

Sauer, Christoph. *Kurtzgefasstes Kräuterbuch.* Germantown, Penn., Christoph Sauer, 1762–1778. Published in yearly installments.

Schellhammer, Maria Sophia. *Das brandenburgische Koch-Buch.* Berlin and Potsdam: bey Johann Andreas Rüdiger, 1732.

Schwinn, Karl. *Speis und Trank im Odenwald.* Mörlenbach: Verlag Marga Hosemann, 1984.

Stopp, Hugo. *Das Kochbuch der Sabina Welserin.* Heidelberg: Carl Winter/Universitätsverlag, 1980.

Stoudt, John Baer. *The Folklore of the Pennsylvania Germans.* Philadelphia: William J. Campbell, 1916.

Stoudt, John Joseph. *Consider the Lilies How They Grow.* Allentown, Penn.: Schlechters, 1937.

Thomas, Edith Bertels. *Mary at the Farm and Book of Recipes.* Norristown, Penn.: John Hartenstine, 1915.

Troll, Thaddäus. *Kochen wie die Schwaben.* Munich: Mosaik Verlag, 1977.

Turner, Robert, ed. *Lewis Miller: Sketches and Chronicles.* York, Penn.: The York County Historical Society, 1966.

Vollmer, William. *Vollständiges deutsches Vereinigten Staaten Kochbuch.* Philadelphia: Verlag von John Weik, 1856.

Vollmer, William. *The United States Cook Book.* Philadelphia: John Weik & Company, 1856.

Vollständiges Nürnbergisches Koch-Buch. Nuremberg: Wolfgang Moritz Endters, 1691.

von Gropper, Wolfgang. *Kulinarische Streifzüge durch die Pfalz.* Künzelsau: Sigloch Edition, 1983.

Weaver, William Woys, *The Christmas Cook.* New York: Harper/Collins, 1990.

———. "Early Printed Cookbooks of the Pennsylvania Germans: Their Sources and Their Legacy." In Karl Scherer, ed. *Pfälzer-Palatines.* Kaiserslautern: Selbstverlag der Heimatstelle Pfalz, 1981.

———. *Sauerkraut Yankees: Pennsylvania German Foods and Foodways.* Philadelphia: University of Pennsylvania Press, 1983.

———. "Viticulture Among the Pennsylvania Germans." *The Journal of Gastronomy* VI:3 (Winter 1990/1991), pp. 113–129.

Wilhelm, Johann. *Architectura civilis.* Nuremberg: Paul Fürsten seel, Wittib und Erben, 1668.

Wiswe, Hans. *Kulturgeschichte der Kochkunst.* Munich: Heinz Moos Verlag, 1970.

Wollenweber, Ludwig. *Gemälde aus dem Pennsylvanischen Volksleben.* Philadelphia and Leipzig: Schäfer und Koradi, 1869.

Wurmbach, Annemarie. "Kuchen-Fladen-Torte. Eine wort-und sachkundliche Untersuchung." *Zeitschrift für Volkskunde* LVI (1960), pp. 20–40.

ACKNOWLEDGMENTS

Since work on this project began nearly twenty-five years ago, the list of people and institutions that helped me over that time is enormous. Several elderly informants are now deceased, so I will never have the pleasure of returning their kindnesses with a gift of this book. The names of their families or of particular individuals are scattered throughout the preceding pages in a respectful nod to their memory.

Ivan Glick, to whom I dedicate this project, works the north sixty acres of my family's ancestral farm in Lancaster County. The Glicks have owned that property for more than fifty years. It is the epicenter from which the rediscovery of my family roots began. Ivan has a keen mind and a German library. He is among that old breed of bookish farmers so peculiar to the Pennsylvania Dutch. Because of men like Ivan, rural philosophers are still part of our culture and are one persistent reason why the sway of ideas exerts such a pervasive influence on our culinary history.

The intellectual study of the Pennsylvania German people is promoted foremost by the Pennsylvania German Society. I would like to thank the society for its material support in the form of a grant that helped pay for part of the photography in this book. In particular, I would like to mention Richard Druckenbrod, the society's president, for enthusiastically taking up my cause, as well as the society's Publication Committee, which has stood by my project consistently.

Several personal friends have contributed to this book directly. Alton Long, a Pennsylvania wine specialist, lent me several bottles of scarce wines from his cellar for use in the photography. Likewise, Eric Miller, vintner of Chaddsford Winery, provided me with several of his finest chardonnays and much advice and direction on the state of viticulture in Pennsylvania today.

Fritz Blank, chef and owner of Deux Cheminées in Philadelphia, cooks French professionally and Pennsylvania Dutch at home. His mother was a Groff, so he has "Dutchness" in his blood. If I could ever induce him to go public with those talents, he would make waves in the world of food. But then, he already has. A true soulmate when it comes to the scholarly aspects of cookery, Fritz was the astute reader of most of the recipes in this book, and his technical, sometimes feisty, advice was manna.

Other guardian angels in my culinary circle include my friend Ellen Slack, who, at a moment's notice, brought me purslane from her Bucks County garden to photograph after mine was hit by frost. Steve Miller at the Landis Valley Museum not only lent me heirloom beans, rare tomatoes, and melons but gave me a full day of his valuable time during photographic sessions at the museum. So, too, did Martin Franke, director of the Hans Herr House, where some of the most extraordinary pictures in this book were taken.

Harold Dabbs Woodfin of the Nathaniel Newlin Grist Mill threw open his historic site not once but twice to waves of equipment and food that my team hauled to that picturesque location. Our work was cold and wet, and our only light source came from eighteenth-century lanterns, but the results of those sessions are truly memorable. Susan Lucas, hearth demonstrator at the mill, was especially helpful in making arrangements and just being there to lend a hand.

Special thanks must be given to Verna Dietrich of Dietrich's Meats in Krumsville for allowing me to bring my photo crew on site when the shop was jam-packed with hunters hauling in their take of deer for the season. The Dietriches good-naturedly put up with the interruptions we caused to that madhouse scene.

I also want to mention Roland Paul of Kaiserslautern, Germany—a distant cousin of mine through his mother—for arranging contacts with many country cooks and butchers in the Pfalz over the years. Raymond W. Shepherd of Old Economy Village at Ambridge, Pennsylvania, must be thanked for the generous use of a picture of the Virgin Sophia. So, too, must I thank the following: Leon Hoernchemeyer of Norwalk, Ohio, for the spelt he sent directly from his fields; Avice Hepler Morgan of Pitman,

Pennsylvania, for hosting my photo crew while we made photographs in the Mahantongo Valley; Don Davis of Zions Grove, Pennsylvania, for finding many rare cooking implements now in my collection and illustrated in this book; Malinda Z. Stoltzfus and Miriam Beiler for their cheerful cooperation in filming the noodle-making scene; the Troutman clan—Steve Troutman in particular—for the tour of their Klingerstown meat plant and for permission to photograph the bakehouse on their property. Also, I want to express my gratitude for the photographs provided by the Schweizerisches Landesmuseum in Zurich and the Kölnisches Stadtmuseum in Cologne.

None of the food would have achieved such a distinctive "look" in this book had it not been for the genius of my photographer, Jerry Orabona. He is a consummate artist, an inspiration to work with, and he assembled a work crew that included Andrew Ety (also an accomplished photographer), Jerry's own affable wife, and his partner, Steven Lopez. Steve's sense of humor carried the day when disasters struck—and there were some.

Two people must be thanked for their extraordinary patience and their belief in my work. One is my agent, Blanche Schlessinger, who has stood by me through thick and thin. The other is my editor at Abbeville Press, Sarah Key, who quietly but persistently mid-wifed my manuscript into a book. Just when I thought the emotional drain of writing was about to do me in, Blanche and Sarah would recharge me with encouragement.

Danny Smartt figured out how to feed my thoughts into my ancient, creaking com-puter, and with an editor's eye for detail, he caught little things I missed. Computer whiz, art historian, linguist, and fellow runner, Danny kept me on course and on schedule when I needed it most.

After toiling over recipes for almost four years and after styling all the food myself for Jerry Orabona's masterful camera, the time came to let go and turn the creation over to yet one more magician: Patricia Fabricant. She has taken all the pieces I assembled and designed a book that is truly beautiful.

RECIPES ARRANGED BY CATEGORY

➤•◄

INDEX

PHOTOGRAPHY CREDITS

All photographs by Jerry Orabona except as noted below.
Photograph on page 123 by Jerry Orabona, apples courtesy of
Dr. & Mrs. Richard Levin.

William Woys Weaver: 1, 27, 106, 170; Slide Collection, Old
Economy Village, Ambridge, Pennsylvania: 11; Roughwood
Collection: 40, 43, 46, 59, 74 (left), 76, 133, 152 (left), 153 (right);
Dietrich's Meats: 136 (left); Rheinisches Bildarchiv, City Museum
of Cologne: 144.